THE CASTRATI
IN OPERA

Da Capo Press Music Reprint Series

GENERAL EDITOR
ROLAND JACKSON
UNIVERSITY OF SOUTHERN CALIFORNIA

THE CASTRATI
IN OPERA

by
Angus Heriot

DA CAPO PRESS · NEW YORK · 1974

Library of Congress Cataloging in Publication Data

Heriot, Angus, 1927-
  The castrati in opera.

  (Da Capo Press music reprint series)
  Reprint of the 1956 ed. published by Secker & Warburg,
London.
  Bibliography: p.
  1. Singers—Biography. 2. Castrati—Biography.
3. Opera—History and criticism. I. Title.
[ML400.H47 1974]   782.1'09'033   74-1332
ISBN 0-306-70650-4

782.109

H42c

93575

June 1975

This Da Capo Press edition of *The Castrati in Opera* is an unabridged republication
of the first edition published in London in 1956.

This reprint is published by exclusive agreement with Martin Secker & Warburg
Limited.

Published by Da Capo Press, Inc.
A Subsidiary of Plenum Publishing Corporation
227 West 17th Street, New York, N.Y. 10011

THE CASTRATI IN OPERA

FARINELLI
from the painting by Amiconi

Angus Heriot

THE CASTRATI
IN OPERA

London : SECKER & WARBURG : *1956*

Made and printed in Great Britain by
William Clowes and Sons Ltd, London and Beccles
and
first published 1956
by
Martin Secker and Warburg Ltd
7 John Street, London
W.C.1

CONTENTS

I RISE AND FALL OF THE CASTRATI   9

II CAUSES OF THE CASTRATI'S SUPREMACY   23

III LIFE AND TIMES OF THE CASTRATI   38

IV THEATRICAL CONDITIONS   64

V CAREERS OF SOME WELL-KNOWN CASTRATI   84

VI THE STORY OF ONE CASTRATO   200

APPENDIX : A Castrato Voice on the Gramophone, by Desmond Shawe-Taylor   225

BIBLIOGRAPHY   229

INDEX   233

List of Illustrations

Farinelli *Frontispiece*

1 The castrato Menicuccio *facing p.* 32

2 The castrato Porporino 32

3 Famous singers of the XVIII and early XIX centuries 64

4 Domenico Annibal 96

5 Giovanni Carestini 128

6 Luigi Marchesi 160

7 Giovanni Manzuoli 160

8 Angelo Maria Monticelli 192

9 A musical party at Ismaning 224

10 Filippo Balatri 224

I

RISE AND FALL OF THE CASTRATI

THE origin of the castrati is shrouded in mystery. Eunuchs, we know, have existed almost since the dawn of civilisation, both for the service of harems and similar purposes, and for the worship of certain deities, and many of them must have been singers: but at what point children began to be castrated *specifically* for the sake of their voices seems almost impossible to determine. There is a solitary and rather obscure reference by Dio Cassius to such a practice in the reign of the emperor Septimius Severus: but it was the coming of Christianity that first provided a genuine musical reason for their existence.

Women were held expressly to have been forbidden to sing in church by St Paul, in the words "mulier taceat in ecclesia"—an interdiction that lasted everywhere until the seventeenth century, and in some places much later—so that when high voices were required, either boys, falsettists, or eunuchs would have to be employed. As late as 1772 Burney, on a visit to Brussels, thought it worth while to note that "I was glad to find (at Ste Gudule) among the voices two or three women who . . . proved that female voices might have admission in the church without giving offence or scandal to piety, or even bigotry. If the practice were to become general, it would, in Italy, be a service to mankind, and in the rest of Europe render church-music infinitely more pleasing and perfect."

The disadvantages of boys are obvious—they are mischievous and troublesome, and by the time they have really learnt their job their voices are usually on the point of breaking: falsettists do not share these drawbacks, but their voices are of a peculiar and unpleasant quality, and as a rule cannot attain as high as the soprano range. It would thus not be surprising if eunuchs had been in use in Rome as early as the fourth century, though there is simply no evidence either for or against such a theory: and, even if they had existed, they might well have masqueraded as falsettists, as at various times they unquestionably have.

At Constantinople, however, it appears that eunuchs were constantly in use. Theodore Balsamone, tutor to the Emperor Constantine Porphyrogenitus and possibly himself a eunuch, wrote a treatise in defence of the species, in which he speaks of them as being habitually employed as singers; whilst a eunuch called Manuel is recorded to have arrived at Smolensk in 1137, and to have sung there. Vocal 'abuses' of one kind and another were early in evidence in the churches of Constantinople, and soloists were censured for interpolating passages of coloratura into their music; all of which sounds remarkably like the accusations later to be levelled against the castrati. The Byzantine Exarchate in Italy, with its capital at Ravenna, kept that country well up in the latest fashions from Constantinople, and such vocal effusions may well have been among them.

This is, however, pure supposition, and there occurs no definite mention of eunuch singers in Italy for many centuries: and how they finally came to the fore is again a matter of considerable doubt. The elaborate *a cappella* style, which began to flourish about the middle of the fifteenth century, necessitated a much wider range of voices and a higher degree of virtuosity than anything that had gone before, and the existing choirboys and falsettists became obviously inadequate. Something new had to be found, and it first appeared in the shape of Spanish falsettists of a special kind. Ordinarily, as has been said, a normal man singing falsetto is not able to exceed the alto range; but the Spaniards had evidently found some way of developing the voice even higher, by an unknown method that did not involve castration, to produce a male falsetto soprano. Spanish singers of this kind became much in demand, and were to be found in cathedrals and chapels all over Europe.

Some Italian writers, among them Fantoni and Monaldi, have argued that these falsettists actually *were* castrati, presumably in an attempt to blame the introduction of castration onto the Spaniards: that as a rule they were not seems apparent from Della Valle's famous Discourse, in which he remarks: "You are pleased to compare the *falsetti* of former times with the *soprani* which at present are so common? But who ever sung then like a Guidobaldo, a Cavalier Loreto, a Gregorio, an Angeluccio, a Marcantonio, and many more that might be named?" . . . and so on. Yet the position is not so simple as it appears; for there is no doubt that some castrati pretended to be falsettists for the benefit of public opinion, and it seems likely that the appearance of castrati in considerable numbers around 1600 was to some extent an admission of their existence rather than a completely new introduction. Orlandus Lassus, when kapellmeister at Munich in the 1560's and 1570's, already had six castrati among his singers, whilst there is a reference to their use in Portugal, during the reign of Don Sebastian (1557–78). These Portuguese eunuchs had apparently been imported from Spain, which makes one wonder whether all the Spanish 'falsettists' were what they claimed to be: and it may be that the Spanish falsetto method was supplemented by clandestine castration. Moorish influence would seem to make it not unlikely; yet the practice, if it ever did exist, must have died out in Spain very rapidly. There is a solitary reference to a Spanish eunuch singer in Saragossa Cathedral in the eighteenth century, but he, on his own account, had been mutilated in a childhood accident, and the excuse seems for once to have been genuine: for the rest, all the castrati who performed in Spain had to be imported from Italy.

One Spanish singer in the papal chapel, Padre Soto, first heard of in 1562, is referred to by Della Valle as one of the earliest of the castrati, but appears in the Vatican records as a falsettist, and another singer, Giacomo Spagnoletto (engaged in 1588), is in a similar position: but the first admitted castrati at Rome were Pietro Paolo Folignato and Girolamo Rossini, who appear in the books for 1599 (not 1601 as Burney has it). Pope Clement VIII was much impressed with the sweetness and flexibility of their voices, and compared them very favourably with the shrill and acidulous tones of the soprano falsettists, who laboured under an additional disadvantage: their forced and unnatural manner of singing tended to wear out the vocal chords at an early age. The castrati, once sanctioned by the highest authority in Christendom, rapidly became more numerous.

The last of the Spanish soprano falsettists at Rome, Giovanni de Sanctos, died in 1625, and by this time the castrati reigned supreme as soprani in the Vatican chapel and elsewhere. Contralto voices were still, however, provided by falsettists for some time, and it was not until 1687 that the authorities, finding difficulty in obtaining enough of these singers, ordered one of the castrati, Raffaelle Raffaelli, to sing thenceforth as a contralto. After this, as the surviving falsettists one by one died out, they were replaced by castrati, and the eunuchs' triumph was complete.

Meanwhile, however, there had arisen a new art-form—opera —which was to form, perhaps, the principal activity of the Italian nation during the next two hundred years, and which gave the castrati their greatest fame and their most glittering triumphs. It is unnecessary once more to retrace the history of opera in its various forms—the early highbrow experiments in Florence and Rome, the popular works of the Venetian period with their elaborate machinery and transformation scenes and contorted plots, the high summer of Metastasian *opera seria* with its symmetrical pairs of heroic lovers, elegant poetry and scientifically-classified arias, the *comédies larmoyantes* and melodramas of last-minute rescue that came into fashion towards the end of the eighteenth century—and we need merely to recall certain aspects of it that have a bearing on the castrati themselves, and in particular on their gradual fall from grace.

Opera was above all unlike the 'legitimate' theatre in that, like certain wines, it 'travelled' well: it was the first form of entertainment that was both popular and to a certain degree international. Not many people spoke Italian, but, whatever the purists might say, it did not really matter whether one understood the words or not so long as the music were enjoyable—and in any case, during the Metastasian period, the practice of using the same libretti over and over again made the words seem more and more a mere excuse for singing. Thus, for the first time in history, a kind of international star-system could arise—the first remote foreshadowing of modern Hollywood's ubiquitous deities. The great singers of the eighteenth century were in a sense the precursors of Clark Gable and Marilyn Monroe, and—though of course their fame was not one-hundredth as universal as the latter's—they were discussed, compared, and criticised in fashionable drawing-rooms, at any rate, from Russia to Portugal and from Ireland to the borders of the Ottoman Empire. There were many singers who attained such celebrity, and most of them were castrati: there were, too, well-known women singers, but it is doubtful whether any of them could equal the fame of, say, Farinelli, whilst normal men's voices were at a discount and reserved for subordinate parts.

The reasons for this strange situation will be discussed in a later chapter: the important part, however, is that Italian opera was, till the late eighteenth century, almost synonymous with the castrati, and that Italian opera was the opera that really mattered. Most nations had, in addition, some form of native opera of their own: but in general this ranked lower, so to speak, in the social scale, and was but indifferently sung, whilst its Italian competitor enjoyed the highest standard of singing that had ever been known, and one that, in all probability, will never more be attained.

Thus by the 1720's, Europe, musically speaking, had come to form one single country, with the exception of France, which still stubbornly clung to its ancient traditions, to its refusal to admit Italian singers, and its virtual ban upon the castrati. But then, foreign visitors to Paris in the eighteenth century were unanimous in declaring that French vocal music was no music at all, and that the noise made by French singers was intolerable to the ears of all but their compatriots: "French music", says Mann, "resembles gooseberry tart as much as it does harmony." It is, incidentally, curious that, while the French in their own country turned up their noses at Italian opera, French travellers to Italy were the most uncritically full of admiration for everything pertaining to the Italian opera; one has only to contrast Burney with La Lande. In fact, their attitude was basically political, and not musical at all, as can be seen from any account of the 'Guerre des Bouffons' or the war between Gluckists and the Piccinnists. By all accounts, a Frenchman of the early eighteenth century who had never travelled could never have heard anything worthy of the name of singing: when he did hear it, he was at first uncertain as to how to take it. De Brosses, more impartial than most, is at first rather hostile to the castrati: "As for castrati, this sort of voice does not please me at all; except for one or two, all I have heard have seemed to me miserable. It is not worth while forfeiting one's effects for the right to chirp like that."

Later, he becomes reconciled to them, and remarks: "One must be accustomed to the voices of castrati in order to enjoy them. Their timbre is as clear and piercing as that of choirboys and much more powerful; they appear to sing an octave above the natural voice of women. Their voices have always something dry and harsh, quite different from the youthful softness of women; but they are brilliant, light, full of sparkle, very loud, and with a very wide range." It must be confessed that 'soft' is hardly the word that springs to the mind in describing the average Frenchwoman's voice even today; and in those days, by all accounts, they were even worse.

Elsewhere, the ingratiating Neapolitan style monopolised the serious operatic stage; and even the ballad operas and other lighter and more localised genres did not hold out so successfully against it as is often supposed. The singers were everywhere Italians, with a few foreigners trained in the Italian style; while composers were everywhere forced to adapt themselves to the prevailing taste. Perhaps the most illustrious and typical of the composers of Metastasian opera was the German Hasse—who only wrote one or two works in his own language in his life. There were other Germans—Gluck, who started as a thorough-going Metastasian, Graun, Naumann, and Bach's son Johann Christian; the Spaniards Terradellas and Perez; the Englishman Arne (not a very successful Italianiser); the Bohemian Mysliwe-czek; and even a couple of Russians, Berezovsky and Bortnyansky. In every opera-house from Lisbon to St Petersburg and from London to Odessa could be seen and heard the same limpid and elegant, but rather vapid, music, the same strutting songbirds in their fantastic costumes *à la romaine* bedizened with feathers and gold lace, the same Baroque palaces of impracticable splendour and elaboration painted by one of the innumerable Bibiena family or their peers on impermanent canvas. Nightly, the heroes of antiquity majestically postured and pathetically expired amidst a glory of roulades and the hushed attention of their admirers, who took so little notice of the rest of the opera, and between the big arias turned with a sigh of relief to cards and refreshments and love-making in their luxurious boxes. . . .

Such was the state of opera in the middle of the eighteenth century, in the heyday of the singers' omnipotence. But it is not in the nature of art to stand still, and before long influences were at work that were to bring down the whole of this pleasant structure, as, almost simultaneously, the ancient regime itself was to totter and fall: artistic revolutions almost always herald a political upheaval. The reforms of Gluck and certain like-minded composers represented a reaction towards purity, simplicity, and naturalness that was paralleled, in other spheres of art, by the vogue for 'sensibility' in the manner of Richardson, the change-over from rococo to the Louis XVI and Adam styles, and the more scientific attitude towards classical antiquity whose prophet was Winckelmann. It was not surprising that singers and their ever-frothier *raffiorimenti* should have come in for renewed attack, not only from pedants and purists, but from all the fashionable avant-garde: and these developments, in fact, may be said to have heralded the end of the castrati's supremacy.

There was as yet no explicit opposition to them, and Gluck in his 'reformed' Vienna operas wrote for the celebrated male contralto Gaetano Guadagni (who, unlike most of his tribe, excelled rather at dramatic expression than in passages of brilliant execution) and the soprano Millico, but his style was by no means ideal as the vehicle for the average castrato. He gave no scope for extempore *fioriture*, which were their especial delight and their greatest glory, and seldom made up for it by writing a bravura aria; other reforming composers such as Jommelli and Traetta were not so strict, but even so their operas were much less of a field-day for the singers than those of the ordinary Neapolitan school. Yet in the long run, perhaps, the effect of these reforms, on the average composer of the 1770's and 1780's, has been exaggerated. The public still longed to be dazzled, whatever the pundits said, and coloratura continued to proliferate as ever, like frog-spawn in a pond.

The other, and even more powerful, influence on the *opera seria*, that to some extent undid the work of these reforms, was that of the comic opera. It had been invented at Rome quite early on, but for some time did not really prosper; and it was not until Naples came into the picture as an operatic centre that progress began to be made. The Neapolitan *opera buffa* arose in the early 1700's and quickly became very popular; the great Alessandro Scarlatti did not disdain it—his comic masterpiece 'Il Trionfo dell'Onore' had recently been revived—and, after him, the majority of composers were as active in the comic as in the serious field (though of course some were more successful in one, and some in the other). In a few years no major Italian town was without its comic opera, and there were numerous touring companies as well.

The *opera buffa* was everything that the serious opera was not. It was natural, lively, based on everyday life, and often in the local dialect.[1] It was also cheap to put on; it was given generally

[1] A curious custom was prevalent as also in the Commedia dell'arte, whereby

in unpretentious little playhouses known as *Teatrini*,[1] and did not require superb singers, but rather good all-round artists with a comic flair and ability to look either good or really ridiculous on the stage.[2] It even acquired, a little later on, a really distinguished librettist, Goldoni, who was to comic opera almost what Metastasio had been to the serious.

It is an exaggeration to say, as do certain authors, that the castrati "had no place in comic opera". At Rome, for instance, where women were banned from the stage throughout the eighteenth century, the female parts had to be taken by male sopranos, in comic as in serious operas[3]; elsewhere, the male part of the 'primo amoroso' was frequently allotted to a soprano or contralto voice, to be sung either by a castrato or by a woman *en travesti*,[4] and Guadagni for one began his career in just such roles. But it is certainly true to say that the comic opera did not *depend* on castrati, and as often as not did without them altogether.

the pair of 'serious lovers' sang in orthodox Italian, while the comic characters used Neapolitan, Venetian, or whatever it might be. Wolf-Ferrari revived this usage in one or two of his works.

[1] The San Carlo gave a comic opera—Auletta's 'La Locandiera'—in 1737, but did not repeat the experiment; others of the larger opera houses occasionally followed suit. But a more intimate atmosphere really suited the *opera buffa* better.

[2] Performers were commonly engaged to play one particular type of role—serious lover, soubrette, ridiculous old man, etc.

[3] There were even castrati who specialised in this kind of thing. The following poem was composed in honour of one of them, Andrea Martini (q.v.), when he sang in Cimarosa's 'I due baroni di Rocca Azzurra' in 1783 :

La tua voce soave, allor che canti,
Passa veloce dall'orecchio al core
Ivi desta il piacer, desta l'amore
E i più tristi pensier fuggono erranti.

Many years earlier the soprano Guiseppe Acquini, according to Quadrio, "was excellent in burlesque singing. He obtained incredible applause in the part of an old woman in 'Il Palazzo del Segreto', Milan, 1683."

[4] In 1744, the Teatro della Pace, one of the Naples *Teatrini*, engaged a certain Antonia Cavalluccio as first man; in 1747 there were two—Angela d'Alessandro and Berenice Penna. In 1772, at the Elector Palatine's summer theatre at Schwetzingen, Burney saw the comic opera 'La Contadina in Corte'

Comic opera soon spread to other countries, and, making use
as it did of native singers, developed many more local variants:
the English ballad opera, the German *Singspiel*, the Spanish
zarzuela. But for long the most interesting and musically important offshoot was the French, originally inspired by the epoch-
making visit of 'La Serva Padrona', which in turn had a
considerable retroactive influence on the Italian school. The
French composers early showed a tendency away from purely
comic subjects, experimenting with 'sensibility' after Richardson,
Gothick horrors in the manner of 'Monk' Lewis, medieval history, fairytales, and so on, till by the end of the century the
term *Opéra comique* had come to mean any work, however
serious its subject, which had some spoken dialogue (a good
instance is Cherubini's 'Medea'). Today, of course, the theatre
called the Opéra-Comique in Paris gives many through-composed
works as well, and the name has no real meaning at all.

The same tendency was evident in Italy. Piccini's 'Cecchina,
o La Buona Figliuola' (Rome, 1760), one of the most famous of
Italian comic operas, is based rather distantly on Richardson's
'Pamela'; whilst Paesiello's 'Nina' (1789), on an originally
French libretto already set by Dalayrac, is a most affecting piece
that cannot really be called 'comic' at all. It is, in fact, a sort of
operatic equivalent of 'Paul et Virginie', which was making such
inroads on susceptible hearts at the time. Cimarosa's 'L'Infedeltà
Fedele' (1779) was deliberately designed as a cross between
serious and comic opera, and in due course the term *opera semi-
seria* was coined to describe such hybrids. Sometimes they made
use of castrati—as did for instance Bianchi's 'Disertore Francese',
in which Pacchieretti made such a sensation—and sometimes not.[1]

by Sacchini, with the castrato Giorgetto as first man; while Lord Mount
Edgcumbe, after enumerating the various sorts of buffo singer in a company
adds: "There were also the *uomo serio*, the *donna seria*, generally the second man
and woman of the serious opera." He had previously specified the 'second man'
to have been a soprano.

[1] It is curious, incidentally, that when Grétry's 'Zemire et Azor' was first
given in London, in an Italian adaptation, the principal male role was transposed upwards for the castrato Angelo Monanni, known as Manzoletto.

The castrati for their part, and Marchesi in particular, seem to have welcomed the chance to play characters nearer to everyday life than Alexander the Great and Orpheus, and even encouraged the trend; though had they thought more deeply, they might rather have opposed it. Where realism is beginning to be prized, a tenor or baritone hero is obviously more suitable than one with a soprano voice.

Operas on the old Metastasian type of subject continued to be written, but they too showed an increasing tendency to approach the comic in style, as the comic had already evolved towards the serious. It is often stated that the comic opera had "driven opera seria from the stage" by 1790 or 1800 at the latest; but this is very misleading. A glance at a list of their works will show that Paesiello, Sarti, and Cimarosa wrote many serious operas, and, for instance, the 'Giulio Sabino' and 'Gli Orazii ed i Curiazii' of the two latter composers were respectively as famous in their day as their 'Litiganti' and 'Secret Marriage'. The eighteenth-century serious opera, in fact, merges imperceptibly into that of the nineteenth century, and as late a work as 'Norma' is still very much in the tradition of, say, the 'Orazii'.

It is a fact, however, that the musical climate of Italy in the 1790's was distinctly frivolous. We read, for instance, that Mattei, a famous musical pundit of the day, visiting the Neapolitan conservatorios in 1795 was surprised to see that "even the most recent scores of Leo and Durante[1] were missing from the shelves. The Conservatorios had nothing but a few rondos and pieces of buffo music; and the youngsters, supposing that no other kind of music existed, composed arias of this kind not only for the tragedy, but also for litanies and the Salve Regina. The distinctions between chamber music, church music, and serious and comic theatrical music were quite obliterated. The sublime arias of Titus, Themistocles and Achilles were heard set to the same musical phrases as those of Pantalone and Harlequin. . . ." The Neapolitan equivalent of a Royal Commission was appointed to look into this

[1] Considering these composers had died respectively in 1744 and 1755, it is hard to see how any of their scores could have been particularly recent.

unfortunate situation, but, before much could be achieved, the French invaded Italy, and people had other things to think about than music. . . .

The Napoleonic period was not one of the most distinguished in Italy's musical history, and the principal composers—the Italianised German Simon Mayr, Paer (who was an Italian despite his name), and Zingarelli—scarcely surpassed the level of competence. Yet important changes were introduced on the dramatic side of opera: the French revolutionary 'rescue opera' spread to Italy (both Mayr and Paer setting an Italian version of the libretto of 'Fidelio'), and the type of romantic subject later popularised by Donizetti and Verdi began to appear, alongside the old-fashioned Metastasian libretti.[1] With Mayr, too, a heavier type of orchestration, hitherto confined to Germany and France, was introduced to the Italian stage and generally accepted—partly, perhaps, because the singers were no longer good enough not to need some camouflaging. In the confused political situation, the conservatorios fell into neglect, and first-class singers were for a time increasingly hard to come by.[2]

The new tendencies in music, towards an increase in energy and fire even at the price of a certain vulgarity, were summed up in the work of a great natural genius, Rossini, whose first success, 'Tancredi', came out in 1813. Rossini may be said to have sung the burial service over the castrati in opera; for when in 1814 he composed 'Aureliano in Palmira' for Velluti, the last great male soprano, he was so enraged at the virtuoso's lavish embroidery of

---

[1] A very popular opera of the day, showing a strange mixture of old and new tendencies, was Zingarelli's 'Giulietta e Romeo' (1796), in which the hero's role was sung by a castrato. Tradition dies hard, and in Bellini's version of the Shakespearean tragedy ('I Capuleti ed i Montecchi', 1830) the part was taken by a woman.

[2] It is noteworthy that, at the première of Cimarosa's last opera, 'Artemisia', at Venice in 1801, the principal roles were sung by English singers—Braham and Mrs Billington. Kotzebue, visiting Rome in 1804, found the principal role in Guglielmi's 'Ines de Castro' being sung by a seventeen-year-old castrato, Domenico Sgatelli, who was miserably inadequate: but evidently the management had had to make do with what they could get.

his already florid music that he vowed never again to let his singers depart from the written notes. And, being a person of much character, he was generally successful in seeing that his wishes were respected. Velluti in his turn was shocked by such presumption, and swore never to sing Rossini's music again (though in fact he did occasionally do so in later years).

Thus it was not Rossini but Meyerbeer who gained the strange distinction of being the last operatic composer of importance to write for the male soprano voice; his 'Il Crociato in Egitto', produced at Venice in 1824, was designed specially for Velluti, and it was in this work that this singer appeared in London on several occasions, the last in 1829. He was almost the last of his kind, and certainly the last of any importance, and after that date he rarely sang again. Another castrato, Pergetti, was heard in London as late as 1844—at a time when Wagner and Verdi were already becoming famous—but by then he must have been almost a freak, a kind of abominable snowman or woolly mammoth.

So, after two hundred years of splendour, and a long and gradual sunset, the story of these strange creatures mutilated in the name of art, but sometimes reaping rewards more glittering than those any other singers have achieved, had almost ended; and succeeding generations regarded their memory with derision and disgust, congratulating themselves on living in an era where such barbarities were no longer possible. Actually, they were possible, for in the Vatican chapel and some other Roman churches the castrati lingered for many years, and boys were mutilated for their voices almost up to the time when Garibaldi entered Rome.[1] A celebrated male soprano of this era was Domenico Mustafà (1829–1912), who was director of the Papal music until his retirement in 1895, when he was succeeded by

[1] It seems no longer to have been fashionable, by this time, to claim that the operation had been necessitated by some malady: the child in question was instead alleged to have been attacked by a pig. Wagner heard some of these last castrati, and was much taken with them: he is even said to have contemplated enticing one away from Rome to play the part of Klingsor, transposing the latter accordingly, but abandoned the idea.

Perosi[1]; the last of all seems to have been Alessandro Moreschi[2] (1858–1922), noted for his singing of the Seraph in Beethoven's oratorio 'Christus am Ölberge', who performed at the funerals of two kings of Italy—Victor Emmanuel II and Umberto I. He retired in 1913.

In the late nineteenth century, propriety was so outraged by the persistence of these curious survivals that various absurd attempts were made to deny it or hush it up: the castrati were alleged to be merely falsettists, were given permission to marry and even encouraged to do so, or were provided with medical certificates of the condition known as cryptorchidism. As late as 1899, 'Germania', a German Catholic publication, solemnly stated, with appropriate fulminations, that castration was still then being carried on: but there seems to be no evidence in support of such an assertion.

In opera, the last faint remembrance of the castrati was in the series of 'breeches' parts that composers continued to write, and sopranos vain of their figures continued to sing—from Orsini in 'Lucrezia Borgia' through Siebel to Strauss's Octavian. There was even an opera by Balfe in which the role of Falstaff was taken by the famous contralto Maria Malibran, with great success. Perhaps, too, it may not be too fanciful to think of the 'principal boys' of English pantomime as remote descendants of Farinelli and Pacchierotti. And now it looks as if 'principal boys' in their turn have had their palmiest days and may before long be extinct. . . .

---

[1] Emma Calvé heard Mustafà when in Rome for the première of 'L'Amico Fritz' and was particularly impressed by "certain curious notes he called his fourth voice—strange, sexless, superhuman, uncanny." She took lessons from him, and learnt the secret of these tones. "They are," says Mr. Desmond Shawe-Taylor, "presumably the very high floating notes which Calvé could suddenly produce, as though from nowhere, and sustain for an extraordinary duration."

[2] See Appendix.

II

CAUSES OF THE CASTRATI'S SUPREMACY

AS was shown in the last chapter, the castrati were very important figures in opera almost from its inception until 1800 and even a little later, and were absolutely pre-eminent during a large part of that time; yet the causes of their popularity have never, perhaps, been quite satisfactorily explained. Why was so strange and cruel a practice thought worth while, and why should audiences of succeeding generations have preferred these half-men with voices as high as women's, both to women themselves and to natural men? Since we have never heard their voices, it is impossible for us to judge of their beauty, which in itself no doubt made up for many other things: but there are other reasons which may still be investigated.

Castrati, as was mentioned earlier, were made use of in churches because women were not allowed to sing there; and the introduction of castrati on to the stage undoubtedly arose from a similar reason. The disapproval of female theatrical performers and the coupling of their name with that of prostitution and licentiousness was an ancient tradition, going back to the days of St Augustine and even earlier[1]—and it seems, both then and later, to have had

---

[1] Tertullian, who attacked the theatre in general, reserved his particular opprobrium for the practice of making prostitutes cry their wares publicly from the stage during the festival of Floralia. This strange custom is described in greater detail by Valerius Maximus; but it seems to have been Tertullian's

considerable foundation in fact. So strong was the prejudice, that when in one country of Europe after another the drama began to flourish again, it was taken as axiomatic that women should be kept off the stage. As far as straight plays were concerned, this presented no very serious difficulties, and we find Shakespeare and his contemporaries quite happily accepting the situation as they found it: the Japanese 'No' drama is an instance where the prejudice against actresses has survived to the present day.

When it came to opera, however, the situation was very different. It would have been absurd to have a tenor or bass singing a feminine part; whilst boys soon proved as unsatisfactory as stage singers as they already had in church choirs. In some cases, tradition was boldly disregarded and women were admitted on to the stage (as at Mantua in 1608); where they were not, the only course left open was to make use of castrati. On the whole, women were slow in making headway in opera. The early seventeenth century was in fact an age of celebrated women singers: but it is probable that they themselves, or most of them, as respected and lionised members of society, would not have been willing to lose caste by appearing on the stage in public. Besides, they were essentially singers *da camera*, with a style no doubt akin to that of a present-day *lieder* singer, and their delicate and intimate art would have been dissipated in the yawning spaces of the theatre.[1]

The Church was placed in a curious quandary: for, in discouraging women from the lyric stage, with the estimable aim of safeguarding public morals, it implicitly necessitated the practice of castration, which in theory it should have opposed with all its might—quite apart from encouraging the more abstruse forms of sin that were in any case prevalent. Successive Popes vacillated

condemnation of it, interpreted as applying to *all* actresses, that formed one of the principal texts concerned.

[1] Though it was said of the famous Leonora Baroni (with whom Milton was so taken on his visit to Rome) that "she would have seemed more at home on the stage than in a drawing-room". Perhaps, however, this was intended to be spiteful.

one way and the other, some half-heartedly allowing women on the stage, and others reimposing the ban. Some—notably Clement XIV—fulminated against the *musici*,[1] but they did not dare to forbid their use; the famous 'Papa Minga',[2] Innocent XI, went to the length of shutting down the theatres, but his severities were detested by the frivolous population of Rome—in particular by the exiled Queen Christina of Sweden, who made a thorough fool of the pure-minded pontiff—and in the end the wretched man gave up in despair. The theatres soon re-opened. Innocent XII, however, actually caused the Tor di Nona opera house to be pulled down, but before long it was re-erected.

The attitude of the Church towards the practice of castration continued to be absurdly inconsistent and unreasonable throughout the eighteenth century: anyone known to have been connected with such an operation was punishable with excommunication, yet no attempt was made to discourage the use of *evirati*. Every church in Italy, including the Pope's own private chapel, had castrati on its staff—in the 1780's, there were reckoned to be over two hundred of them in churches in the city of Rome alone —and it did not seem to occur to anyone that the operation would continue to be performed so long as the financial rewards continued to be earned.

Papa Minga had again confirmed the ban on actresses, as far as his temporal dominions were concerned, in 1676,[3] and, with a

---

[1] The word 'musico' came to be used very nearly exclusively as a synonym for 'castrato', though originally it had no such connotation. 'Evirato' is another commonly-used term.

[2] So called because 'minga' in the Milanese dialect means 'no' and this Pope, a Milanese, said no to everything.

[3] The ban held good over most, though not all, of the States of the Church; at Bologna (a city which retained a considerable degree of independence) and in the legations of Ferrara and the Romagna, women were allowed on the stage as elsewhere. An English authority of 1704 remarks: "No women are suffered to sing on the theatres at Rome or Düsseldorf; nor were they allowed at Vienna in the late Emperor's time." Frederick the Great, as late as 1768, attempted an all-male revival of Graun's 'Ifigenia in Aulide' in Berlin, but this was much ridiculed.

few backslidings early on, it continued in force until 1798.[1] In
that year the ephemeral Roman Republic was set up, and, filled
with liberal and progressive ideas, went to the opposite extreme
and banned the *musici*.[2] This interdict in turn was lifted in the
following year, when Rome was occupied by the King of Naples;
but women were not again forbidden the boards. Thus la Tosca,
had she existed, could not have sung publicly in Rome until
1798—a fact which Sardou either did not know or chose to ignore.

Many visitors have recorded their impressions of the Roman
opera during the years when it was deprived of women, some
being hostile but the majority much impressed—though the effect
of an opera in which almost all the voices were of the same kind
must have been decidedly monotonous.

Goethe, of all unexpected people, was so enthusiastic about the
travestied castrati that he went so far as to advocate their super-
seding of actresses in every type of theatrical production (!).
Analysing his reactions, he writes: "I reflected on the reasons why
these singers pleased me so greatly, and I think I have found it.
In these representations, the concept of imitation and of art was
invariably more strongly felt, and through their able performance
a sort of conscious illusion was produced. Thus a double pleasure
is given, in that these persons are not women, but only represent
women. The young men have studied the properties of the female
sex in its being and behaviour; they know them thoroughly and
reproduce them like an artist; they represent, not themselves, but
a nature absolutely foreign to them." All of which is a rather
confused way of saying that the more artifice there is in art, the
better.

Among those repelled by these much-bedizened gentlemen was

[1] The first opera at Rome in which women took part was F. Federici's
'Virginia', and not, as sometimes stated, Niccolini's 'La Selvaggia nel Messico',
which did not come out until 1803.

[2] The Cisalpine Republic in Northern Italy had, too, banned castrati from
the stage; but under Napoleon's reconquest of Italy they were once more
admitted. Women were not, as sometimes stated, banned again under Leo XII
(1823–9).

Pöllnitz, who remarked: "the women are travestied men . . . which makes the Rome opera always inferior to the others in Italy" (the Romans were of quite the opposite opinion)[1]; whilst de Brosses, though praising Porporino as being "as graceful as the most graceful young lady", was amused by Marianino, "who, at six foot, was the tallest princess anyone had ever seen". Six foot was then, of course, considered a much more exceptional height than it is today. Others, again, refused to believe that the travestied castrati were not in reality women, and among many anecdotes is that of the French sculptor Sarassin, who pursued the castrato Zambinella with his attentions in the conviction that he was a woman, until the singer's protector, Cardinal Cicognara, had the importunate Frenchman assassinated; this story was afterwards written up by Balzac. Consolino, another castrato, was able to carry on an affair with a society woman under her husband's nose, by the simple expedient of arriving in one of his stage costumes; and it was not uncommon for castrati to go about in women's clothes all the time.

Occasionally, it seems, women did appear on the Roman stage, pretending to be castrati pretending to be women—a singular state of affairs which was of course quite illegal. One of Casanova's lady friends made a point of this, for reasons related elsewhere,[2] and was able to pass the examination (carried out as a rule by some elderly and gullible priest) with the aid of an instrument which she taped to her body in the appropriate position.

When it came to the 'straight' theatre in Rome, even more curious results were observed. According to Archenholz, who was fairly enthusiastic about the travestied castrati: "The scale turns with regard to the other theatres, where pitiful jack-puddings are acting comedies. When these are disguised, and pretend to

---

[1] To argue the superiority of their musical taste and discrimination, they pointed out that, whereas every opera applauded in Rome that had afterwards been given at Naples had succeeded in that city, several operas received with ecstasy at Naples had flopped when put on in Rome.

[2] See p. 182.

imitate the soft gestures of the fair, with their beards and rough
voices, nothing can be imagined more ridiculous. I saw acted by
them Voltaire's 'Zaire'. A rude fellow, a butcher by trade, who
had been engaged as a performer for that carnival, performed the
part of Zaire, and put forth with all his might his knotty fists for
the tender Orosman to kiss them. In another show, one of the
merry jacks came upon the stage, and made an apology to the
spectators for the delay in beginning the performance, as 'Zaire
was gone to be shaved'." Beckford, visiting Portugal at a time
(1787) when similar regulations were in force, has the same kind
of observations: ". . . the actors, for there are no actresses [are]
below criticism. Her Majesty, who to be sure is all prudence and
piety, has swept females off the stage and commanded their places
to be supplied by calvish young fellows. Judge what a pleasing
effect this metamorphosis must produce in the dances, where one
sees a stout shepherdess in virgin white with a soft blue beard and
a prominent collar bone . . . clenching a nosegay in a fist that
would almost have knocked down Goliath, and a train of milk-
maids attending her enormous footsteps. . . ." Sometimes a castrato whose singing voice had been impaired by some accident
turned to the straight theatre as a *pis aller*, and no doubt would
have given a better account of himself than the usual run of
performers.

In other parts of Italy, particularly at Venice, women were
very soon taking the stage: at the first public performance of an
opera (Manelli's 'Andromeda' in 1637) one woman—the composer's sister—took part, though other feminine roles, including
Venus (!) were sung by men. Altogether, until 1700 and even a
little later, there seem to have been curiously few female opera-
singers of any renown. Those that did exist led the most dissipated
and notorious lives: there was, for instance, Giulia di Caro at
Naples, who spent most of her time in amorous dalliance, or
riding about the town in an open carriage, dressed to the nines
and surrounded by numerous admirers; her approach could be
detected a mile off by her vociferous laughter and shrieks, and
the ironic plaudits of the bystanders. She earned the title of

'Madonna del Bordello', and the love of the Spanish Viceroy; but such an existence can scarcely have been conducive to the practice and study which are essential to a singer. In fact her performance suffered, not only from her innumerable caprices and fits of the sulks, but also from her mode of life; a naturally brilliant singer, she early lost her voice, and not long afterwards her looks as well, and in 1696 she died, in poverty and disgrace.

Female singers, in fact, as often as not owed their position to factors independent of any vocal accomplishments they might have had. There was, for instance, the lady known as La Giorgina,[1] who started her career, in Rome, as a protégée of Queen Christina, and after that monarch's death (of which she was perhaps the involuntary cause), succeeded in captivating the Duke of Medinaceli, the last but one Spanish Viceroy of Naples. She became the Duchess's lady-in-waiting and amassed a considerable fortune, though her singing was erratic, to say the least; while her sister was married to a nobleman, Don Bartolommeo di Specchio, the governor of Orbetello,[2] with a dowry of 30,000 ducats presented by the Viceroy.[3]

The status of female singers gradually improved during the eighteenth century (although, according to Benedetto Croce, "in the *teatrini*, 'virtuosa' and 'prostitute' were still absolute synonyms"), and such singers of serious opera as Vittoria Tesi, Faustina Bordoni[4] (who married the composer Hasse), and Cuzzoni were respected and admired; yet for other reasons the castrati continued to hold their own, and on the whole to surpass their female colleagues in celebrity.

[1] Her real name was Angela Voglia.

[2] Orbetello was a fortified Spanish enclave on the coast of Tuscany.

[3] Yet when in 1699 a Modenese nobleman, Count Nicola Fava, married the *virtuosa* Marchesini, a most terrible furore ensued. The government went so far as to issue an order to the effect that "non si avessero da ammettere nei magistrati quei tali, che avessero sposate o sposavano *simili* donne".

[4] A scandal was, however, aroused by Faustina, when in 1723 a medal was struck in her honour at Florence. Many voices were heard to complain that she was unworthy of so signal an honour, which had hitherto been reserved for 'great artists'.

In an age when improvisation played so great a part in vocal music,[1] other qualities looked for in a singer, beyond agility and beauty of voice, were the taste and knowledge which he exhibited in introducing his ornaments. It was important that the *fioriture* should be appropriate to the aria concerned; so that, for instance, brilliant and cheerful roulades should not intrude upon pathos and lamentation, or sobbing appoggiaturas turn a song of joy into a dirge. Again, with the common practice of doubling the written voice part with a solo instrument while the singer embroidered upon it, it was fatally easy for an inexpert performer to wander off into a dissonant key, with horrid results.

It was in these particulars especially that the castrati were considered superior to women: their training was in general much more rigorous and sound, and they possessed more application and perseverance. Tosi, in his renowned 'Observation on the Florid Song', remarks: "If, out of a particular Indulgence to the Sex, so many female Singers have the Graces set down in writing, one that studies to become a good Singer should not follow the Example; whosoever accustoms himself to have Things put in his Mouth, will have no Invention, and becomes a Slave to his Memory." A little later, he adds: "The Presumption of some Singers is not to be borne with, who expect that a whole *Orchestra* should stop in the midst of a well-regulated Movement, to wait for their ill-grounded Caprices, learned by Heart, carried from one Theatre to another, and perhaps stolen from some applauded female Singer, who had better Luck than Skill, and whose Errors were excused in regard to her Sex. . . ." From which it seems that the best women singers were only equal to the less competent castrati.

---

[1] Not, however, at Berlin; where, if any Italian singer ventured to add a single note to the written music, he was severely taken to task by Frederick the Great in person. Tosi, on the other hand, complains bitterly of the impudence of composers who dare to write in appoggiaturas, etc., in their scores. Do they, he asks, claim to know the singer's business better than he does himself? "If I mistake not," he adds, "one [singer] that abounds in Invention, though a moderate Singer, deserves much more Esteem than a better who is barren of it."

Marcello, in the 'Teatro alla Moda', by far the most famous satire on opera, gives the female singers an even more severe pasting: "If (a singer) have a role in a new opera, she will at the first possible moment take all her arias (which in order to save time she has had copied without the bass part) to her Maestro *Crica* so that he may write in the passages, the variations, the beautiful ornaments, etc.,—and Maestro Crica, without knowing the first thing about the intentions of the composer either with regard to the tempo of the arias, or the bass, or the instrumentation, will write below them in the empty spaces of the bass staff everything he can think of, and in very great quantity, so that the *Virtuosa* may be able to sing her song in a different way at every performance . . . and if her variations have nothing in common with the bass, with the violins which are to play in unison with her, or with the concertising instruments, even if they are not in the same key, that will be of no consequence, since it is understood that the modern opera director is both deaf and dumb." There were, of course, many castrati to whom this would equally have applied; yet it is significant that this particular squib should have been aimed at female singers. The castrati were, on the whole, a good deal more musicianly, though they had plenty of eccentricities of their own—which will be dealt with in due course.

So much for the rivalry between the castrati and female singers: but what remains to be examined is the singular neglect of natural male voices throughout the period in question. It has been computed that, in the eighteenth century, seventy per cent of all male opera-singers were castrati; whilst, until its last decade or two, the only male singers who were not castrati, yet attained a degree of fame at all comparable to theirs, were the tenors Raaff[1] and Annibale Pio Fabri.

One reason was undoubtedly a purely physical one; for a man's vocal chords inevitably thicken at puberty, and in doing so lose a good deal of their agility. No natural man's voice could have encompassed the fantastic bravura passages that were then so much

[1] For whom, when he (Raaff) was sixty-seven years old, Mozart wrote the title role in 'Idomeneo'.

admired, and considered indispensable for the principal characters in an opera. There seems, too, in the seventeenth and early eighteenth centuries to have been a kind of prejudice against the sound of the tenor and bass voices, which were accused of being intolerably rough and coarse; and it is very possible that the training methods then in favour, though so brilliantly successful with sopranos and contraltos, were not so well adapted to the lower registers. Tenors were generally relegated to the roles of old men—the roles assigned to basses in later operas—while the basses were often reserved for special effects such as the pronouncements of Neptune's oracle in 'Idomeneo': though the practice varied in individual cases, composers being governed by the voices that happened to be available. It is noticeable, however, that on one occasion Handel excused himself for engaging a German bass, on the grounds that "there were none worth having in Italy".

The percentage of castrato parts in individual operas was at its highest during the early Roman and Venetian periods, where frequently all the male characters were assigned to sopranos and contraltos, and female characters were proportionately few—as they are, generally speaking, in Shakespearean drama. Later on, in the Metastasian era, owing to the symmetrical structure of interlocking love-affairs which that dramatist favoured, there had to be nearly as many female as male characters—though, of course, whether they were played by female singers was a matter of taste or convenience. Towards the end of the eighteenth century, in the serious opera, there was a tendency to employ tenors more and more in the parts that would have been taken by a 'second' castrato, and there was often not more than one castrato part in an opera: not so much because the castrati were going out of favour, as for the sake of variety—for the very popular comic opera had by then reconciled audiences to a larger dose of tenor and bass voices.

As an example of the distribution of parts, in the days before Metastasio, may be quoted the following—that of Alessandro Scarlatti's 'Pompeo', given at Naples in 1684:

2. THE CASTRATO PORPORINO
by a Roman caricaturist

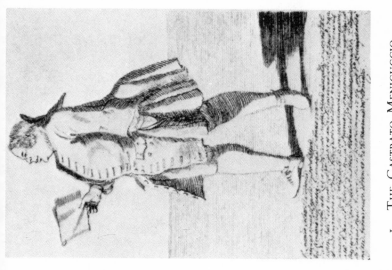

1. THE CASTRATO MENICUCCIO
by a Roman caricaturist

Pompeo	.	.	Michele Fregiotti, *musico*
Cesare	.	.	Giovanni Hercole
Sesto	.	.	Giuseppe Costantini
Giulia	.	.	Teresa Laora Rossi
Claudio	.	.	Maria Rosa Borrini
Scipione	.	.	Paolo Pompeo Besci, *musico*
Mitridate	.	.	Giovanni Francesco Grossi, *musico*
Issicrate	.	.	Giulia Zuffi
Farnace	.	.	Giulio Cavalletti
Harpalia	.	.	Domenico Gennaro, *musico*
Il Capitano Generale	.	Ortensia Paladini

Thus, out of eleven characters, four were sung by castrati, three by natural male voices, and four by women. Of the women, however, three were singing male roles, which in another performance might equally have been sung by castrati.

It is often difficult to distinguish cause from effect; and whether it was the presence of castrati that gave the Italians of that period their taste for peculiar sexual and vocal reversals on the stage, or vice versa, is a doubtful question. In any event, not only was *travesti* as common a feature of seventeenth-century plots as it was in the Elizabethan and Jacobean drama, but further oddities were gratuitously introduced in the writing for the voice and in the casting. A few examples will show what is meant.

In Monteverdi's 'L'Incoronazione di Poppea', the parts of Nero and Ottone are for soprano, while Ottavia and Poppea were sung by (female) contraltos: thus, the male characters actually sang in a higher voice than the female, though these were played by women. Later, the female contralto seems to have gone very much out of favour, and such women singers as there were with this type of voice almost invariably sang a man's part—sometimes opposite a castrato in a female part. Even more eccentric, Cavalli's 'Eliogabalo' has the parts of Eliogabalo, Alessandro, and Cesare for sopranos, and Zenia (a woman) for the tenor voice. In Vinci's 'Catone in Utica' at Naples in 1732, the soprano role of Julius Caesar was sung by a woman, Lucia Facchinelli (!), and another woman, some years later, sang Hercules in Gluck's 'Le Nozze

2

d'Ercole e d'Ebe'. For the opening of the San Carlo in 1737, the work chosen was Metastasio's 'Achille in Sciro', with music by Sarro. In this drama, Achilles is supposed to be disguised as a woman during most of the evening, but to throw off his feminine trappings at the end and reveal his real sex. Unfortunately, the singer chosen for the title role was a woman, the famous Vittoria Tesi,[1] which made the whole thing rather absurd.[2] In comic opera, too, the same sort of thing went on, and we find tenors taking the parts of decrepit old women, etc., etc.

It is difficult to believe that these practices arose altogether from necessity, and one can only conclude that such ambiguities were valued for lending a spice of double-entendre, even to the most tragic situations: thus Shakespeare's passage, in which Cleopatra fears to see "some squeaking Cleopatra boy my greatness i' the posture of a whore", can never have failed to raise a horse-laugh among his audience, considering that just such a squeaking boy was speaking the lines. Tastes change, and today this may seem tediously silly and out of keeping with the dignity of serious art; but it must be remembered that an opera of Scarlatti or Hasse fulfilled the functions, not only of 'Tristan' or 'Aïda' today, but also those of 'Oklahoma' and 'The Merry Widow', and there was no distinction between brows of varying heights.

Some indication was given in the preceding chapter of the commonly accepted reasons for the decline of the castrati—the reforms of Gluck, the popularity of comic opera, and so on—yet they are not entirely satisfactory. The reforms of Gluck had little

[1] La Tesi objected to singing a man's part, on the grounds that it was 'harmful to her health' (why?). She wanted to switch parts with Anna Peruzzi, known as La Parrucchierina, who was singing Deidamia; but this was not allowed as Tesi was much the taller and more strapping of the two. In fact the Tesi was well known as a singer who 'recitò da uomo', as it was called; whilst a certain Maria Cerè was considered so ugly that she was never allowed to take female parts at all. Pisaroni, for whom Rossini wrote the part of Arbace in his 'Semiramide', was a later performer whose appearance induced her to specialise in 'breeches' parts.

[2] In recent revivals of Handel's 'Deidamia', which is on the same subject, a similar course had perforce to be followed.

enough effect on the average Italian opera of the late eighteenth century, and, as was shown, comic opera was by no means devoid of castrati itself. Yet Velluti, in the best years of his career, in the decade immediately following the fall of Napoleon, was almost without competition on the operatic stage. What had happened to those who should have been his rivals?

It seems, in fact, as if their extinction came about more from accident than design. Velluti was born in 1781, and thus would have been about fifteen when the French invaded Italy; his training would have been nearly complete, and his technique well on the way to being established. But this could not have been the case with anyone born much later; for, in the confused political situation that marked the opening of the nineteenth century, the conservatorios fell into serious neglect, and there was a shortage of young singers of all kinds. In 1799, the Pietà dei Turchini conservatorio in Naples still had eight young castrati among its pupils; but many pupils of all kinds, chafing at the severe discipline and filled with vague revolutionary ideas, had deserted on the proclamation of the Republic earlier that year. Again, the various Napoleonic governments of Italy took measures to oppose the practice of castration, which were much more energetic and effective than those of their predecessors—to the horror of many music-loving Italians, who cried, "Evviva il coltello! Il benedetto coltello!" and protested that without castrati Italy would be lost irretrievably.

Stendhal, a convinced Bonapartist, does not scruple to blame Napoleon[1] indirectly for the decline in the standard of Italian singing, about which everyone complained in the 1810's and 1820's; and one aspect of that decline was a dearth of new castrati. Composers soon made a virtue of necessity, and wrote in a new

[1] It is sometimes stated that Napoleon disapproved of the castrati and sought to ban them: but this is clearly untrue. On first hearing Velluti, he exclaimed, "One must be only half a man to sing like that!" And he so admired Crescentini that he persuaded him to come to Paris, where the singer remained six years; thus it was only at the very end of their history that the castrati really added France to their conquests.

way designed to make the best of what singers they had; which way in turn would not have suited the castrati, had any remained. And thus their fall from glory was as rapid and complete as their enjoyment of it had been long and uncontested. In looking through extant cast-lists of the period, one finds evidence that the supply of castrati began to dry up, quite suddenly, in about 1807–8. Marchesi had retired in 1806, Crescentini was in Paris, and Velluti alone remained among singers of the top rank. The first man's part had increasingly often to be given to a woman, as at Florence in 1809 and at Naples in 1809–10 (they were described on playbills as 'primo uomo') or else the part was transposed for tenor, as when Camporese sang Sesto in Mozart's 'La Clemenza di Tito' in London. Composers then began to write the first man's part for the tenor voice, as well as the 'old man' and 'king' parts (there being as yet few basses trained to the style of serious opera); and for a few years there are operas with four or five tenor parts— e.g. Rossini's works designed for Naples, such as 'Elisabetta, Regina d'Inghilterra' and 'Armida'. The 1820's saw the emergence of the regular pattern that has survived to the present day, with tenor, baritone, and bass, the baritone being for the first time recognised as a special category, and not merely a rather high bass, or a low tenor. In a revival of 'Arminio' at Bologna in 1821 Carolina Bassi was described as 'primo musico': and as late as 1858, in Rossini's 'Semiramide', Antonietta Fricci is distinguished from the mere 'Prima Donna' as 'Prima Donna Soprano assoluto': though, oddly enough, in the male contralto part of Arbace.

As a final tribute to the art of the castrati may be quoted the opinion of the musical historian Enrico Panzacchi (1840–1904), who, quite late on in the nineteenth century, heard with rapture one of the surviving castrati in the Vatican chapel: "What singing! Imagine a voice that combines the sweetness of the flute, and the animated suavity of the human larynx—a voice which leaps and leaps, lightly and spontaneously, like a lark that flies through the air and is intoxicated with its own flight; and when it seems that the voice has reached the loftiest peaks of altitude, it starts off again, leaping and leaping still with equal lightness and equal spontaneity, without the slightest sign of forcing or the faintest indication of artifice or effort; in a word, a voice that gives the immediate idea of sentiment transmuted into sound, and of the ascension of a soul into the infinite on the wings of that sentiment. What more can I say? I have heard Frezzolini and Barbi *in camera*, and Patti in the theatre; I have admired Masini, Vogel, and Cotogni; but in the midst of my admiration there remained always something unappeased in the depths of my desire; there remained a certain disparity between the artist's intention, however lofty it might be, and her artistic means. . . . Here, however, all my being was marvellously satisfied. Not the least mark of the passage from one register of the voice to the other, no inequality of timbre between one note and another; but a calm, sweet, solemn and sonorous musical language that left me dumbstruck, and captivated me with the power of a most gracious sensation never before experienced. . . ." The writer's style is somewhat perfervid—as Italian so often is—but he does convey some idea of the reasons why the castrati once reigned supreme. One cannot but be thankful for the passing of the custom; yet how much may have been lost by that passing we can only guess.

III

LIFE AND TIMES OF THE CASTRATI

T HE castrati were born, as a general rule, of humble parents[1];
for only those in fairly pressing need of money would have
consented to the mutilation of their children. Among these un-
fortunates, however, it was the accepted thing to sell any male
child who showed the slightest aptitude for music, or signs of a
potentially fine voice, into such musical slavery, much as the poor
of industrial England sold their children to be sent down the mines,
or to become chimney-sweeps.

The practice did, however, vary in individual cases; the parents
sometimes sold their children outright to some teacher or musical
institution, but sometimes, too, themselves scraped together
enough money to start their son off on a course of training with
some reputable singing-master. They looked on this as a fairly
safe investment, being convinced that *their* child was bound to
become the most famous and affluent singer of his age, who would
provide lavishly for them in their old age—though why they

[1] But they were not keen on admitting the fact. "When a *virtuoso* is a *contraltist*
or *sopranist*," says Marcello, "he will have an intimate friend who will speak
of him in the *Conversazioni*, declaiming (out of a pure love of truth) 'that he
comes from an honourable family; that because of a serious accident he had
to submit to his *execution*; that he has one brother who is a professor of
philosophy, and another a doctor, a sister who is a nun, another married to a
prosperous bourgeois, etc., etc.'" There were, however, castrati, who came of
quite good families—among them Farinelli.

should have expected him to be so full of gratitude it is difficult to imagine.[1]

It is to the singing-masters of that age—Pistocchi, Bernacchi, Porpora,[2] and others—that the perfection of the art must unquestionably be attributed. The list of those who, at some time, studied with any one of them is a string of one illustrious name after another; and no one has since rivalled them in perseverance and thoroughness, and in their perfect knowledge of the capabilities and shortcomings of the human vocal organs. They sometimes had their own singing-schools—and those of Bologna were famous—but more often they worked in one of the remarkable institutions known as the conservatorios, although they might take private pupils 'on the side' as well (as Porpora, for instance, did).[3]

There were conservatorios in various Italian cities—those of

[1] "The evirati did not always know who their fathers were; and when the latter did make themselves known, they often gained little advantage from such courage. When the *musico* Vitorio Loreto [Loreto Vittori] was at the height of his fame, one day, a man came to him, in fear and trembling, claiming to be his father. He was able to prove it, and on the strength of this begged for money. 'Willingly,' answered the singer, 'but I must pay you in your own coin.' So saying he drew an empty purse from his pocket, and gave it to him." (Parolari)

[2] For Pistocchi and Bernacchi, see Chapter V. Nicola Porpora (1686–1766) was, in his day, equally famous as a composer and as a singing-master numbered among his pupils Porporino (who, following a common custom, took his stage name from his master), Farinelli, Caffarelli, and Salimbeni.

[3] Tosi somewhat tartly observes: "Let him the master hear with a disinterested Ear, whether the Person desirous to learn hath a Voice, and a Disposition; that he may not be obliged to give a strict account to God of the Parents' Money ill spent, and the Injury done to the Child, by the irreparable Loss of Time, which might have been more profitably employed in some other profession. I do not speak at random. The ancient Masters made a Distinction between the Rich, that learn'd Musick as an Accomplishment, and the Poor, who studied it for a Livelihood. The first they instructed out of Interest, and the latter out of Charity, if they discovered a singular Talent. Very few modern Masters refuse scholars, and, provided they are paid, little do they care if their Greediness ruins the Profession."

Says Marcello: "Out of the goodness of his heart [the singing-master] will

Venice were renowned for the training of female singers—but for castrati the main centre was Naples. Naples had four conservatorios—Sant' Onofrio, Pietà dei Turchini, Santa Maria di Loreto, and Poveri di Gesù Cristo[1]—which had originally been founded at various dates in the sixteenth century as purely charitable institutions for the upbringing and general education of poor children. But by the middle of the seventeenth century they had dropped all courses of instruction save that of music[2]; though this subject was itself subdivided into a number of separate courses, for composition, for the various instruments, and for the soprano, contralto, tenor, and bass voice. Meanwhile, with the constantly rising cost of living, the original foundations were proving insufficient, and the conservatorios took to hiring out their students for various musical purposes, both private and public (receiving for the latter a yearly fee from the municipality of Naples and other nearby towns). According to Florimo, "The work of these pupils was turned to profit. The smallest were sent to serve the Masses in various churches . . . others acted as 'angioletti' attending the dead bodies of children. . . ." The larger pupils acted as pall-bearers in funerals, carried images through the streets in religious processions, etc., etc. Later, says Florimo, "to increase the profits still further, they had the idea of reinforcing the musical executants, by admitting to the Conservatorios young men who were already well versed in music, who were promised an annual payment, with the obligation to

give lessons gratis to poor young people of either sex, contenting himself merely with drawing up an engagement whereby they undertake to make over to him two-thirds of their salary for the first twenty-four performances, half for the next twenty-four, and one-third for the rest of their life."

[1] The Poveri di Gesù Cristo was counted as an archiepiscopal conservatorio, founded in 1589, and closed down in 1743. The others were all royal. S. Maria di Loreto was founded in 1543, S. Onofrio in 1578, and the Pietà dei Turchini in 1583. All these survivors were amalgamated in 1807, by order of Joseph Bonaparte, during his brief reign as King of Naples, to become the Real Collegio di S. Pietro Majella, still in existence.

[2] Though to the musical curriculum was added a certain amount of instruction in the usual 'three R's'.

remain for a number of years." At the same time the institutions ceased to be purely charitable, and began to take in paying pupils, who lived the same life as those other boys, though they were exempt from some of their duties. It is not clear what proportion of the students were taught wholly or partly at their parents' expense, as against those supported entirely out of the conservatorios' funds, and in some cases a pupil might change from one to the other. We find, for instance, Porpora himself as a youth entered in the books of the Poveri di Gesù Cristo conservatorio paying "18 ducats a year, commencing September 29th, 1696", whilst a later entry (in 1699) mentions that "he no longer pays", though he apparently remained there some time longer. Evidently, he was an unusually promising pupil, and, when his father either died or found himself unable to keep up the payments, the conservatorio decided to keep him on for nothing.[1]

There are extant various interesting records of transactions concerning young castrati, among the documents of these institutions. Among the accounts of the Sant' Onofrio conservatorio for 1673, for instance, there is an item: "a suit of clothes for one Sebastiano, eunuch of Andria [a town in Apulia], together with shoes, hat, and stockings, costing in all 16 ducats and 2 carlini: the clothes are of black material, since the eunuchs are always dressed in black".[2] Two years later, there is the following: "On the 26th January 1675, I sent to Rome 12 scudi in Roman currency . . . for the boat-fare, and food during the journey, for two soprano children [figlioli, the term always used to describe the students], who are coming to Naples from Rome to serve our Conservatorio. On the 14th February, one of the aforementioned sopranos arrived: his name is Niccolò Fortuna, eunuch, and he is a sound singer. As our Conservatorio needs him for the music, he has been promised 15 ducats in Roman currency . . . with the

---

[1] He was, of course, principally learning composition. Not himself a castrato, he no doubt also learnt to sing in the tenor or bass voice.

[2] The young castrati were always dressed in distinctive costumes. At the Pietà dei Turchini they were to be known by their red belts and 'Turkish berets', whatever these may have been.

obligation to serve our Conservatorio for seven years." This person, evidently, came 'already well versed' as a performer for the chapel, rather than as a student. In 1676, two eunuchs were sent for from Foggia; and there are numerous similar entries. Conversely, in 1739, Nicola Reginella[1] entered the Pietà dei Turchini, "paying 24 ducats yearly", apparently at the expense of a certain Duke of Monteleone.

Since anyone known to have been concerned with castration was punishable with excommunication, as well as liable to civil penalties imposed by the various governments, the business had to be carried out more or less clandestinely; and there has been a good deal of discussion as to where it actually took place. Burney's remarks may be quoted in full: "I enquired throughout Italy at what place boys were chiefly qualified for singing by castration, but could get no certain intelligence. I was told at Milan that it was at Venice; at Venice that it was at Bologna; but at Bologna the fact was denied, and I was referred to Florence; from Florence to Rome, and from Rome I was sent to Naples. The operation most certainly is against law in all these places, as well as against nature; and all the Italians are so much ashamed of it, that in every province they transfer it to some other. However, with respect to the Conservatorios at Naples, Mr. Jemineau, the British consul, who has so long resided there, and who has made very particular enquiries, assured me, and this account was confirmed by Dr. Cirillo, an eminent and learned Neapolitan physician, that this practice is absolutely forbidden in the Conservatorios, and that the young Castrati come from Leccia in Puglia; but, before the operation is performed, they are brought to a Conservatorio to be tried as to the probability of voice, and then are taken home

[1] It is difficult to understand this entry, unless there were two castrati of the name of Nicola Reginella, or Reginelli, perhaps uncle and nephew; a singer of this name was evidently quite well known in the previous year, when he had a fight with Caffarelli (see p. 144). He came to London in 1746, and Burney writes of him: "Reginelli, an old but great singer, whose voice, as well as his person, was in ruin, first appeared on our stage in a *pasticcio* called 'Annibale in Capua'. This person was now turned of fifty; his voice was a soprano but cracked, and in total decay."

by their parents for this barbarous purpose. It is said, however, to be death by the laws to all those who perform the operation, and excommunication to every one concerned in it, unless it is done, as is often presented, upon account of some disorders which may be supposed to require it, and with the consent of the boy.[1] And there are instances of its being done even at the request of the boy himself, as was the case of the Grassetto at Rome."[2] Later the Englishman adds: "M. de la Lande was more fortunate [than myself], having ascertained that there are shops in Naples with this inscription: 'Qui si castrono ragazzi'; but I was utterly unable to see or hear of any such shops during my residence in that city."

It is certainly not true that all, or even most, of the castrati came from Apulia; a glance at the biographies of the most famous ones will show them to have been natives of every part of Italy. But, for the rest, the story seems likely enough. Another place that was notorious for the practice, however, was Norcia,[3] a small town in the Papal States, about twenty miles east of Spoleto on the borders of Umbria and the Marches; and it seems probable, in fact, that operations were performed anywhere that was sufficiently remote, and as immune as possible from governmental interference—which was dilatory enough in any case. According to La Lande, again, the soprano Angelo Monanni, called Manzoletto, was operated on in Florence, and this in turn caused a scandal; but he implies that this was an exceptional case.

---

[1] It is perhaps in connection with boys that expressed such an intention that Tosi makes the somewhat mysterious remark: "The Master must want Humanity, if he advises a Scholar to do anything to the Prejudice of the Soul."

[2] In Rome, Burney had heard "il Grassetto, a boy who submitted to mutilation by his own choice, and against the advice of his friends, for the preservation of his voice, which is indeed a very good one . . .".

[3] Salvator Rosa, Satire. La Musica:

> Bella legge Cornelia ove n'andasti
> In questa età, che per castrare i putti
> Tutta Norcia per Dio non par, che basti?

See also page 209, footnote.

The doctors most esteemed for the operation (as, indeed, for all forms of surgery in Italy at the time) were those of Bologna: they were in demand not only in Italy, and were exported abroad for the express purpose of castrating boys, rather like the expert horse-gelders of today.[1] In 1752, for instance, the Duke of Württemberg—a prince so fanatically addicted to opera that he almost ruined his subjects to pay for it—had two Bolognese surgeons called to his court; and these gentlemen, or their successors, were still in office in 1772, when Burney visited Ludwigsburg, the local Versailles. The castrati at that time in the Duke's service numbered fifteen, and it is probable that a large proportion of them were of German nationality. Other German courts formed similar offshoots of the Italian tradition; yet only one German castrato ever seems to have attained any degree of fame—Berenstadt, described as "virtuoso of the Elector of Saxony", who sang in some of Handel's operas in London, and in various leading theatres abroad. Dreyer and Porporino were also of German parentage, but were born and brought up in Italy; and the only other non-Italian on record who may have been a castrato is the well-known English singer John Abell (c. 1660–1736), who was sent to Italy by Charles II to be trained, and also, allegedly, "to show the Italians that other nations had good voices, too". He is often said to have been a falsettist, yet Evelyn, who must have been familiar with the ordinary English altos of the day, noticed Abell's voice as something quite different, and "as high as any woman's". Abell may,

---

1 The operation, as described by d'Ancillon, in the 'Traité des Eunuques', was usually performed as follows: the child, often drugged with opium or some other narcotic, was placed in a very hot bath for some time, until it was in a state of virtual insensibility. Then the ducts leading to the testicles were severed, so that the latter in course of time shrivelled and disappeared. Eunuchs of this type were known in ancient times as 'Thlibiae' or 'Thlasiae', in contradistinction to eunuchs proper who had been subject to full castration. The latter operation does not seem ever to have been practised in the case of the castrato singers. It was often supposed that, the later a child was castrated, the lower its voice would be: others however, and more convincingly, have supposed that those who would naturally have been tenors became sopranos, and those who would have been baritones or basses became contraltos.

of course, have rediscovered the secret of the Spanish soprano falsettists; but it seems more probable that he really was a castrato, but chose to conceal the fact.

Discipline in the conservatorios was strict, and the curriculum strenuous, and the students were even liable to be put in prison they proved too disobedient. The castrati enjoyed certain advantages as compared with the rest of the *figlioli,* who for instance had to practise together in one room, in the midst of the most infernal racket; they were considered delicate, given better food than the others (though this was not saying very much), and their health carefully attended to.[1] "There are in this college", says Burney of Sant' Onofrio ,"sixteen young castrati, and these lye up stairs, by themselves, in warmer apartments than the other boys, for fear of colds, which might not only render their delicate voices unfit for exercise at present, but hazard the entire loss of them for ever."

Despite such coddling, the castrati do not seem to have enjoyed their years of training very much, and not only because they had to work hard. The rough-and-ready methods of those days took little account of the psychological difficulties that must have beset such beings marked out from the ordinary of society, and they no doubt underwent merciless 'ragging' at the hands of the other students whenever the masters' backs were turned. Over and over again, in reading the lists of pupils of the Neapolitan conservatorios, one comes across an entry: "So and so, *eunuco,* entered... *se n'è fuggito*"—"he ran away". The other students were quite often dismissed for idleness or want of capacity, but they seldom ran away; and the fact speaks for itself.

There were many, too, whose voices failed, or did not prove up to expectations. Burney, for instance, remarks: ". . . as to the previous trials of the voice, it is my opinion that the cruel operation is but too frequently performed without trial, or at least without sufficient proofs of an improvable voice; otherwise such

[1] In 1699, at S.M. di Loreto, we read that "owing to the dampness of the situation, the Eunuch *figlioli* are suffering from a certain raucousness of voice. From now on, in the winter, they will be given petticoats [*giupponi*] of flannel . . .".

numbers could never be found in every great town throughout Italy, without any voice at all, or at least without one sufficient to compensate such a loss. Indeed, all the *musici* . . . in the churches at present are made up of the refuse of the opera houses, and it is very rare to meet with a tolerable voice upon the establishment in any church throughout Italy. The virtuosi who sing there occasionally, upon great festivals only, are usually strangers, and paid by the time."[1] As a confirmation of this opinion may be cited an anecdote related by that curious figure the Marchioness Solari: "Paisiello having completed a new oratorio, at the first representation at which the king and queen and all the court were present, the composer came to conduct Lady Hamilton and myself to the church, which was very much crowded. As *dilettanti*, we were placed by the composer in a situation the best calculated for us to appreciate its merits. It was really a good composition . . . on this occasion, there happened to be no fewer than a hundred of those 'noun adjectives of the neuter gender' . . . employed in the chorusses; and so abominably did they sing out of tune, that poor Paisiello, forgetting where he was, jumped from his seat in a passion, and exclaimed, "Ah! managgio dei morti, siete stati tutti castrati in cattivo tempo!" alluding to the fact that these degraded beings never sing in tune, when the maiming operation has taken place in bad weather: the church resounded with the laughter of the whole congregation; and thus ended the 'enraged musician's' oratorio!"

Archenholz has the following summing-up of the matter: "Here in Naples alone these horrible mutilations are performed, which have been thought so necessary to our operas. They are generally people of the meanest description who give their children for such operations, in hope, that they may be able one day to support their parents. But this hope is frequently disappointed in many different respects; sometimes the voice does not display itself, or the child has no natural parts for music. Such a boy [i.e. presumably, those that do *not* fall by the wayside] is very

---

[1] But, on his own account, this was not the case at Padua, where the great Gaetano Guadagni was on the establishment of the church of San Antonio.

soon put out as an apprentice, and an agreement made with the master to whose care he is committed, that as soon as his pupil can appear in public, he is to receive his pay for a certain number of years. This is the reward for his instructions, which are never graften in but with the whip. It may be said that the poor child is inoculated by dint of lashes for the acquisition of this fine art, the delight of the courts of Europe.

"The number of these victims is so great, that they surpass the want of singers of all kings and princes; for which reason, they have been allowed to take orders; but they can only be secular priests, and are permitted to say mass. But as the ecclesiastic laws of the church of Rome require, for this purpose, a person that has not been mutilated, the sophists of that persuasion have thought it sufficient for such a priest to have his amputated genitals in his pocket, when he approaches the altar." One suspects that the last strange particular was a tale *pour les touristes,* swallowed wholesale by the gullible German; and, as has been seen, he is incorrect as to the place of castration. But he shows very well from what suffering this great art sprang.

A propos of Archenholz may be quoted here another strange anecdote he has to tell about a castrato: "A very particular accident happened a few years ago to a singer of the name of Balani. This man was born without any visible signs of those parts which are taken out in castration, he was, therefore, looked upon as a true-born castrato; an opinion, which was even confirmed by his voice. He learned music, and sung for several years upon the theatre with great applause. One day, he exerted himself so uncommonly in singing an arietta, that all of a sudden those parts, which had so long been concealed by nature, dropped into their proper place. The singer from this very instant lost his voice, which became even perceptible in the same performance, and with it he lost every prospect of a future subsistence." This strange occurrence was apparently observed in the San Carlo opera house, Naples, in about 1765; where, not long before, another unfortunate accident had taken place. The young castrato Luca Fabbris, straining after a top note of exceptionally dizzy altitude, collapsed and died on the stage, to the consternation of the composer Guglielmi, who had induced him to attempt it.

A typical daily curriculum of study for a singer was remarkable, not only for the amount of hard work it entailed, but also for its thoroughness and comprehensiveness. That followed in youth by Caffarelli, for instance, was as follows:

In the morning
    1 hour singing passages of difficult execution,
    1 hour study of letters,
    1 hour singing exercises *in front of a mirror*, to practise deportment and gesture, and to guard against ugly grimaces while singing, etc.

In the afternoon
    ½ hour theoretical work,
    ½ hour of counterpoint on a *canto fermo* (in other words, practice in improvisation),
    1 hour studying counterpoint with the *cartella*,[1]
    1 hour studying letters.

The rest of the day was spent in exercise at the harpsichord, and in the composition of psalms, motets, etc. It is noticeable that the voice was not overburdened with too much use, and that as much attention was given to the theory of singing, and all its ramifications, as to its actual practice. Under the heading of 'letters' one of the main points stressed was the value of words, and how they should be sung so as to bring out their meaning rather than obscuring it.[2]

The anecdote of Porpora, who is said to have confined Caffarelli for five or six years to exercises written on a single sheet of paper, and then to have dismissed him with the words, "Go, my son: I have nothing more to teach you. You are the greatest singer in Europe", has been quoted and requoted in numerous

[1] The *cartella* was a sort of glazed tile with music-staves, on which exercises could be written, and then erased at will. Thus it served the purpose of a school slate.

[2] One rule that came to be observed was that elaborate divisions should only be executed on the sound 'a', as pronounced in Italian, as this suffered less from distortion than the other vowels.

works of reference; yet it seems singularly improbable. Many more of Porpora's *solfeggi* have survived to this day—and they must be but a small percentage of the total—than could possibly be written on any sheet of paper of a likely size; could it, perhaps, be that someone misunderstood the meaning of the word *cartella*?

While on the subject of Porpora, there is another interesting question that has been raised in connection with his work. To quote Frank Walker[1]: "The very moderate range employed by Porpora even when composing for the greatest singers who ever lived is remarkable. We have it on Quantz' authority that Farinelli had a compass of nearly three octaves, and yet Porpora rarely asks for more than one octave and a fifth, and generally for less. 'Lusingato dalla speme', sung by Farinelli in 'Polifemo' (1735) falls wholly within a single octave. The singer's ornaments, judging from authentic examples given by Haböck, would not add more than a tone to this."

One reason for this may be the fact, not always realised, that the castrati were able to extend their range by means of the falsetto, in the same way as natural male singers. Tosi lays it down that "A diligent Master, knowing that a male Soprano, without the Falsetto, is constrained to sing within the narrow Compass of a few Notes, ought not only to endeavour to help him to it, but also to leave no Means untried, so to unite the feigned and the natural Voice, that they may not be distinguished; for if they do not perfectly unite, the Voice will be of divers Registers . . . the extent of the full natural Voice terminates generally upon the fourth space, C . . . or D. Among the Women, one hears sometimes a Soprano entirely *di Petto*, but among the Male Sex it would be a great rarity should they preserve it having passed the Age of Puberty." He also remarks: "Many Masters put their Scholars to sing the Contr'alto, not knowing how to help them to the Falsetto, or to avoid the trouble of finding it."

It seems, therefore, as if Porpora may have been anxious to keep Farinelli within his 'natural' register—in so far as his voice was natural at all—which was no doubt stronger and richer in

[1] In 'A Chronology of the Life and Times of Nicola Porpora'.

tone. On the other hand, it is possible that singers transposed
some notes up by an octave from the written score, like tenors
who attempt the famous high C in 'Di quella pira' from 'Trovatore'—a hurdle never envisaged by Verdi. However, the eighteenth century as a whole does not seem to have been particularly
interested in voice of enormous range, or in top notes of dizzy
altitude, and it is rare, even, to find a singer's exact range mentioned. Lucrezia Agujari, called La Bastardina, was a woman
singer celebrated for her high notes, yet according to Kelly
Mozart's sister-in-law Aloysia Lange had an even wider range,
and the music written for her—in particular the role of Kon-
stanze in the 'Seraglio', while still considered difficult, does not
now appear phenomenal. But all this is something of a digression.

One function of the conservatorios that must have provided
the young singers with a welcome break from routine, apart from
their duties as singers in church and at funerals, was that of
providing the choir for the Teatro San Carlo, whenever an opera
was given that required it: the governors of the institutions were
not at all enthusiastic about the idea, and in 1759 those of the
Pietà dei Turchini petitioned the King to put a stop to the
practice.[1] They complained that the *figlioli* got into bad company
and habits, kept assignations with ladies of the ballet, learnt to
play cards, and racketed about the town until all hours. The King
had other things to think about (for it was in this year that he

[1] Another quarrel between the San Carlo and a conservatorio was with
S. Onofrio in 1761. The impresario Grossatesta announced that "to make up
the company of *musici* the last part is missing. I propose Luigi Costa . . . who
has sung in this theatre and in Venice with Guarducci. As the above mentioned
Costa was here, he took advantage of the School of Naples, and entered the
Conservatorio of S. Onofrio." To which the Conservatorio replied "that
Luigi Costa was received into this Conservatorio in 18th October, 1760, with
the obligation to serve for six years. The following April Luigi C. said that
by order of H.M. he had to sing at the Teatro S. Carlo: but we have found
that no such order was ever given, and that Costa's intention was to defraud
the Conservatorio, which ought to profit from the perfection of his voice."
They therefore demanded that his salary should be paid straight to them; and
thus, apparently, it was decided over the unfortunate *musico*'s head.

inherited the throne of Spain from his half-brother, and left Naples for ever), and took no notice. The governors later repeated their plea to the ministers of the young King Ferdinand, but to no greater effect. Discipline became more and more unpopular and difficult to impose as time went on, until in 1782 the students staged a full-dress revolt, which it took government intervention to appease. Evidently, the castrati were among the participants in this outbreak, for the Rector gave orders that they should share in the general punishment, and that in future "they should be liable to the same duties [such as in the army would be called 'fatigues'] as the other *figlioli*". The French invasion completely undermined whatever authority was left to the conservatorios, and they never really recovered their prosperity or reputation.

Eventually, at some age between fifteen and twenty, a castrato who had retained and embellished his voice, and passed the various tests with more or less distinction, was considered ready for his début, and contracted to some opera house. He would, often, be seen first in a female part, for which his youth and fresh complexion would render him particularly apt. His looks and unfamiliarity would, perhaps gain him a greater success than his as yet immature art would in itself have deserved, to the rage and envy of his senior colleagues, both male and female: but, braving their black looks, he would take his bows, and with elaborately simulated condescension pick up the flowers and *billets doux* that fell at his feet. His name would henceforth be made; a band of supporters—'fans'—would gather round him, going *en masse* to the theatre every time he sang and hanging on his every note as if it were of pure gold, barracking the other singers and refusing to admit that, beside their idol, these miserable braying donkeys could be said to sing at all. There would be an exchange of sonnets, satires and pasquinades between the new star's devotees and the rival cliques; aristocratic ladies and gentlemen would imagine themselves in love with him and engineer a piquant interview, and nothing else would be talked about for the next few weeks.[1]

[1] The success of Lorenzo Girardi, known as 'il giovane fenomeno', at Venice in 1737 is an instance. We read that: "The theatre of S. Cassiano,

Back-stage, the same warfare might rage with even greater
virulence; yet sometimes, too, the singers were sensible enough to
recognise one another's merits and become friends. But, if the new
hero were too insolent and puffed up with his success, he might
end, one dark night, with a knife in his ribs; the envious prima
donna, perhaps, had persuaded her protector to have him killed,
that worthy Duke or Cardinal had called in some assassins—members of a respected and business-like profession—and, at a charge
fixed according to the circumstances, had had the deed despatched.

Perhaps, however, the young castrato would not please. He
might be wooden in his acting, tasteless in his embellishments;
or, like so many of his tribe, he might have grown unconscionably
tall and gawky,[1] or, conversely, enormously fat—and the men's
costumes then in vogue on the stage were anything but becoming
to an unfortunate figure. The poor wretch might then decline to
the touring of small provincial opera-houses—the 'sticks' of
eighteenth-century Italy—or hide his head in some church choir;
where, to keep his spirits up, he would choose all the latest and

property of the Tron family, at which in 1737 was given Hasse's 'Demetrio'
with Metastasio's poetry, could not succeed in attracting the public, despite the
excellence of the music, because Girardi was not singing there. 'Tutto buono,
tutto bello—qui però non c'è il puttello.'"

Count Francesco Zambeccari, impresario at Naples, in a letter dated 28th
August, 1708, refers to a singer's resounding failure: "Regarding the *musico*
you mention called Silvestro, I know him very well and assure you that he is
an excellent person, though he comes from Modena. But in the theatre he is
no good at all; the last time I was in Venice I heard him sing at S. Angelo and
everyone shouted 'off the stage!' [*dentro!*], and made horns at him with their
candles every time he came on."

1 Of Farinelli in London it was elegantly written: "If thou art in the environs
of St James', thou must have observed in the Park with what Ease and Agility
a cow, heavy with calf, has rose up at the command of the milkwoman's foot:
thus from the mossy bank sprang the divine Farinelli."

Parini, a convinced enemy of the castrati, wrote:

> Abborro in sù la scena
> un canoro elefante
> che si strascina in pene
> e manda per gran foce
> di bocca un fil di voce.

flashiest operatic arias, have them reset to sacred words, and with them startle the angels on the reredos and the martyred saints on the frescoed ceiling. The congregation did not mind—they liked a good tune, whatever its associations—the priest probably did not notice; and it was left to some conscientious visiting prelate or musical pundit to recall to the errant singer some conception of the intended dignity of his calling.[1] For all that, the poor castrato could not but sigh for the applause and excitement of the stage; and no doubt, sooner or later, he would leave his present employment and go to Bologna, "which", says Archenholz, "is the mart of all Italian musicians, castratos, and comedians, out of employ. Application is made hither from all countries, for people of that description." The town was infested with agents and other habitual appurtenances of theatrical life, and there was always some post or another going free.

Success had its pitfalls, and the castrati came in for a good deal of scurrilous and unkind abuse, of an all too predictable sort. Already in 1640, we find Della Valle, in his 'Discourse', defending them in the following terms: "I cannot subscribe to the common assertion that Evirati are all cowards, devoid of genius for literature, or any solid study; and that even the voice, for the melioration of which they are so inhumanly treated, is inferior to that of a woman or boy"; and, as their fame increased, so did the hatred of them. Salvator Rosa, a fanatical patriot in an age when such sentiments were almost freakish, seems to have seen in the castrati a sort of symbol of his country's degradation, and in his 'Satire' on music vented the bitterest venom of his spleen upon them[2]; while Foscolo attacks Milan (why Milan in par-

---

[1] Salvator Rosa remarks:

> Ond'è che ognun si scandalizze e tedia,
> Cantar sù la Ciaccone il *Miserere*
> E con stili da sfarzi, e da Comedia
> E Gighe e Sarabande alla distesa. . . .

[2] As, for instance, in the following passages, chosen largely at random:

> Sol di Becchi, e Castrati Italia abonda.
> E i Cornuti e i Cantor vanno a Centurie;
> Turba da saltinbanchi vagabonda,

ticular is not clear) as a "città d'evirati cantori allettratice". They were often castigated as evil creatures who lured men into homosexuality—and there were admittedly homosexual castrati, as Casanova's accounts bear witness. In 1745 he writes: ". . . an abbé with an attractive face walked in [to a café]. At the appearance of his hips, I took him for a girl in disguise, and I said so to the abbé Gama; but the latter told me that it was Bepino della Mamana, a famous castrato. The abbé called him over, and told him, laughing, that I had taken him for a girl. The impudent creature, looking fixedly at me, told me that if I liked he would prove that I was right, or that I was wrong."

In 1762, Casanova was again in Rome, and writes: "We went to the Aliberti theatre, where the castrato who took the prima donna's role attracted all the town. He was the complaisant favourite, the *mignon*, of Cardinal Borghese, and supped every evening *tête-à-tête* with His Eminence.

"In a well-made corset, he had the waist of a nymph, and, what was almost incredible, his breast was in no way inferior, either in form or in beauty, to any woman's; and it was above all by this means that the monster made such ravages. Though one knew the negative nature of this unfortunate, curiosity made one glance at his chest, and an inexpressible charm acted upon one, so that you were madly in love before you realised it. To resist the temp-

---

Fatta vituperosa in su le scene,
D'ogni Lascivia, e disonor seconda,

  . . . . .

Agamemnone mio, se tu lasciasi
Oggi per guardia alla tua Moglie un Musico,
Quant' Egisti cred'io che tu trovassi?

  . . . . .

Solo in un caso il musico è prezzabile;
Che quando intuona a Prencipi la Nenia
Se ne cava un diletto impareggiabile.
Mà del restante poi gia! Antistenia
Sentenza grida, c'ha per impossibile,
Che sia buon Huomo, e sia Cantor Ismenia.

tation, or not to feel it, one would have had to be cold and earth-bound as a German. When he walked about the stage during the *ritornello* of the aria he was to sing, his step was majestic and at the same time voluptuous; and when he favoured the boxes with his glances, the tender and modest rolling of his black eyes brought a ravishment to the heart. It was obvious that he hoped to inspire the love of those who liked him as a man, and probably would not have done so as a woman.

"Rome the holy city, which in this way forces every man to become a pederast, will not admit it, nor believe in the effects of an illusion which it does its best to arouse."

Goethe, however, shows that one did not have to be a castrato to indulge in this sort of thing. In his account of the famous Roman carnival he writes: "The masks now begin to multiply. Young men, dressed in the holiday attire of the women of the lowest classes, exposing an open breast and displaying an impudent self-complacency, are mostly the first to be seen. They caress the men, allow themselves all familiarities with the women they encounter, as being persons the same as themselves, and for the rest do whatever humour, wit or wantonness suggest. Among other things, we remember a young man, who played excellently the part of a passionate, brawling untameable shrew, who went scolding the whole way down the Corso, railing at everyone she came near, while those accompanying her took all manner of pains to reduce her to quietness." But this taste was enormously prevalent in Italy at that time, and there is no indication that castration of the kind practised had any effect whatever on the sexual urge. Many of the castrati were famous lady-killers; and they were of course much in demand by the opposite sex, for their embraces could not lead to awkward consequences.[1] We read, for instance, that Matteuccio "could not bear to stay for long away from this city [Naples], where he was loved by all, and particularly by the ladies, as much because he was handsome and a eunuch, as for his sweet and sonorous voice".

[1] Not, however, in France. When the castrati taking part in Luigi Rossi's 'Orfeo' arrived in Paris, they looked forward to making ravages in all hearts;

But the most common accusation against them—and one of the reasons often cited for their ultimate downfall—was the insufferable conceit and unreasonableness with which their name has become coupled in many people's imagination.[1] There were certainly some among them—Caffarelli and Marchesi, to name a couple—whose tantrums and absurdities were classics of their kind; but it is surely unjust to attribute to them an exclusivity, or even a superiority, in this particular line of country. No castrato could have equalled the famous Caterina Gabrielli, for instance, whose caprices turned all Europe upside-down; and there were many who were remarkable for their good sense and freedom from affectation. But they formed an obvious Aunt Sally, like the Jews under Hitler, and everything was thrown at them.

They were subject to further measures of discrimination. The Catholic Church, for instance, does not permit eunuchs, or those known to be impotent, to marry,[2] and this rule was applied to the castrati. One of them, Cortona (q.v.), was determined to marry an attractive female singer, Barbaruccia, who was also in the service of his master, the Duke of Modena, and made special application to the Pope. This was, however, refused, even though

but they were coldly received, and were whimsically addressed by an anonymous versifier in these lines:

> Je connais plus d'un Fanfaron
> A crête et mine fière
> Bien dignes de porter le Nom
> De la Chaponardière.
> Crête aujourd'hui ne suffit pas,
> Et les plus simples Filles
> De la crête font peu de cas
> Sans autres Béatilles.

[1] "When he is with singers and particularly with *castrati*, the composer will always give them his right hand, and will remain with his hat off, a little behind them, reflecting that the most lowly of these gentlemen is at least, in the opera, a general or a captain of the guards of the King or Queen." (Marcello).

[2] As did the Lutherans, on the advice of the theologian Gerhard. Marriage was, it was argued, a sacrament designed for the procreation of children. If that was manifestly impossible, there was no excuse for not remaining in a state of virgin innocence.

the Duke himself lent his authority to the request, and Cortona perforce remained a bachelor. Evidently, His Holiness was frightened of creating a precedent. One castrato, Bartolomeo de Sorlisi, endured much hardship in his truly heroic determination to remain with the woman he had surreptitiously married, a German girl called Dorothea Lichtwer. All their endurance was in vain, and in the end Sorlisi died broken-hearted (1672): another castrato, Filippo Finazzi (1710–76), successfully married Gertrude Steinmetz, a Protestant girl from Hamburg, while the marital adventures of Tenducci (*q.v.*) are both famous and noteworthy.

In this connection may be quoted a strange flight of whimsy against the castrati, indulged in by Marcello, author of the 'Teatro alla moda', in the form of two burlesque madrigals with accompanying comments, and entitled 'Il flagello dei Musici'. He begins: "The first madrigal is sung by tenors and basses, who inform the castrati of a most terrible disgrace. The latter, hearing the fatal decree, and without waiting for its reason, interrupt on the highest possible note to show their peculiar quality. This is, that they constantly seek to reach the extremest altitudes with their voice, flattering themselves that, the higher a *musico* ascends, the greater is his price and reputation. On hearing the evangelical reason, for which they must burn in eternal fire, they can do nothing but shriek ahi! ahi! as if they were already among the flames." The first madrigal goes as follows:

> (*per due tenori e bassi*)
> So, che lassù ne' cori almi e beati
> Non entrano castrati,
> Perchè è scritto in qual loco
> (*i soprani interrompono*)
> Dite, che e scritto mai?
> (*tenori e bassi rispondono*)
> Arbor che non fa frutto arda nel fuoco!
> (*i soprani gridano*)
> Ahi! Ahi!

Then Marcello continues: "The second madrigal is sung by

the soprani and contralti, to the confusion of the tenors and basses and their own justification, and tries to prove that they too are blessed ("delle sacre parole"). They begin, therefore, on a cheerful note and in a lively tempo, though the words are grave and serious, to show that they sing everything in a joking manner. . . . In the adagio, they sing with passages which *they* claim to be in good taste and in the best manner, so clashing with the regular notes of the counter-point and producing unbearable discords. . . ." The second madrigal follows:

> (*per due soprani e due contralti*)
> So che laggiù nell'erebo profondo
> Ove alle fiamme vassi
> Cadran tenori e bassi,
> Perchè scritto fu già da' sacri vati:
> Quei che castrati son, saran beati.

So much for the sufferings and slights which the castrati had to endure. But there was much to recompense them, and they could look for rewards more tangible and lasting than the acclaim of an idle and capricious society, whose passion was novelty, and which would scarcely maintain its enthusiasm for a new singer even through one of the short 'seasons' then given by Italian opera-houses. A castrato, or any other singer, who had enjoyed a passing vogue in Rome or Venice and could for a while make capital of that success, would, if he were wise, seek a more reliable position and a more assured income, by attaching himself to some music-loving court, and becoming *virtuoso da camera* to some crowned Maecenas.

Among notable seventeenth-century patrons of singers both male and female was Queen Christina, particularly after her abdication and exile to Rome. There, unburdened with the cares of state, she could devote herself wholeheartedly to the enjoyment and cultivation of her pleasures, of which one of the chief was music. She was notorious for her feuds with other employers—particularly the Duchess of Savoy, whom she accused of enticing her best singers away, while at the same time herself trying to tempt them back, with others who had never been in her employ. Two castrati, Bianchi and Ciccolino, formed a special bone of contention between the two ladies, whose mutual vituperation fell far below the level of dignity to be expected from such illustrious persons. Among others of Christina's pet castrati were Siface and Cortona, the foremost singers of their time; and she provided a refuge and rallying-point for all the artists thrown out of work by Papa Minga's high-minded offensive against the theatres. She was a woman of unpredictable temper, and when one of her *musici*, Alessandro Cecconi, died suddenly, she was accused—with much probability—of having had him murdered for some real or imagined misconduct. Not that there was anything unusual in having people murdered in Italy at that time; it was an accepted custom, furnishing honourable employment to large numbers of persons.

In Italy, too, such princes as the Dukes of Parma and Modena were lavish supporters of the opera: but the field where the richest prizes were to be won was Germany, with its multitude of courts each trying to outdo the others in splendour and extravagance, its freedom from the nationalistic obsessions that kept foreign musicians out of France, and its relative lack of home-grown talent (for there were few German singers of note in the eighteenth century).

The Italian governments of the day may have been arbitrary, unenlightened, and reactionary; but they seem almost benevolent beside those of Germany with their ponderous and feudal tyranny and the rapacity of their extortions, made all the easier by the supine acquiescence of the population. Foreign visitors to the capital cities of the numerous Electors and Margraves—cities reached by roads execrable even by eighteenth-century standards, through an almost desert countryside—noted that, on an average, half of their population consisted of the prince's servants, retainers and dependants, collectively battening on the other half, who could be told at a glance by their dejected and downtrodden appearance. The princes squandered incredible sums on the construction, upkeep, and embellishment of their Ludwigslusts and

Montplaisirs and Residenzen—to the benefit of posterity, which can admire their beauty without having had to pay for them—and one of the principal items in their expenditure was very often the opera; for many of them were genuine and knowledgeable music-lovers, and themselves first-rate musicians.

The Dukes of Württemberg, the Electors Palatine and those of Bavaria, and Frederick the Great were all fanatical lovers and protectors of music, whose court operas employed the leading singers and composers of Europe, and were famous for the meticulousness and high artistic level of their productions and the excellence of their orchestras—a quality most rare at the time. The martinet mind of Frederick, and his virtually exclusive admiration for the operatic compositions of Graun, as for the instrumental music of Quantz, made the Berlin theatre somewhat hidebound in its procedures; yet it enjoyed great fame in his day. Mannheim had the best orchestra, under the direction of the celebrated Stamitz, while Stuttgart[1] under Jommelli was the scene of that composer's interesting reform of Metastasian opera.

But perhaps the most important among these dynasties of melomaniac sovereigns were the Electors of Saxony, who for long years held also the resounding but largely meaningless title of King of Poland. Dresden in the mid-eighteenth century was fast usurping the place of Paris as the intellectual centre of Europe, and as the city where luxury and refinement were carried to their most elegant extreme. The opera, under Hasse's direction, fully kept pace with this fastuous life, and in 1755 it had among its contracted artists half the famous singers of Europe,[2] as well as an enormous number of other first-class musicians. Such glory, however, was too good to last, and in 1756 came the Seven Years' War, in which Saxony suffered ignominious defeat and devastation at the hands of the Prussian monarch, and, after years of

[1] When Burney was there in 1772—at a time when the Duke was attempting to economise (!)—he still had fifteen castrati in his service.

[2] According to Burney: 10 sopranos, 4 contraltos (in each case both male and female), 3 tenors, and 4 basses—among them Faustina, Pilaia, Mingotti, Monticelli, Pozzi, Annibali, Amorevoli, and Campagnati.

occupation, was left humiliated, enfeebled, and in abject poverty. Dresden was little more than a heap of ruins, and there was no money left to support the opera.

At Mannheim, Berlin, Dresden, and various other places, no money was ever taken at the opera-houses, and any decently-dressed person was admitted free; so that, in effect, the exchequer subsidised the pleasures of the well-to-do—a curious state of affairs that seems to have been peculiar to Germany. The public there, who did not have to pay for their entertainment, could scarcely venture to express their opinion but in private; and the opera was entirely dependent on the caprice of the monarch; so that, should an economy-minded prince come to the throne, or one insensible to the charms of music, the theatre would rapidly be shut or turned over to other uses, and the singers and musicians, often arbitrarily deprived of their salaries and appointments, would be dispersed in all directions in search of another place. The Imperial Free Cities—commercially-minded and more or less democratically governed—were not as a rule much given to expenditure on the arts; the richest of them, Hamburg, supported an opera for some seventy years, but eventually even this succumbed to financial difficulties and was forced to close down. The intellectual, not to say highbrow, bourgeoisie which were later to contribute so much to German artistic life had scarcely yet emerged, and the good merchants of those days were more interested in solid comfort, and the pleasures of bed and board—particularly, perhaps, the latter.

In other countries too—England, Spain, Russia,[1] and Sweden—where opera was mainly an exotic importation dependent on the court and aristocracy, it was almost confined to the capital cities: and since these nations, unlike Germany, had only one capital each, the openings for singers were limited in number. The

---

[1] Among castrati who went to Russia was one Torcchino, who was in Moscow when the French entered the city. He sympathised with their ideas, and accompanied them on their disastrous retreat. Captured by Cossacks, he at first melted their hearts with his singing, but afterwards was murdered by a drunken soldier, and his body eaten by the wolves.

salaries paid in London and Madrid were as good as anywhere, but the total number of singers employed at a given moment was necessarily small.

A virtuoso engaged by one of the court operas, perhaps through the medium of one of the talent scouts who used to be sent to Italy from time to time to look for promising singers, or to sign up some established name that was temporarily without a situation, would often be contracted for a number of years at a fixed salary: but he would generally demand a clause limiting his obligation towards his principal employer to a certain proportion of each year. For the rest of the time, he was free to do as he pleased, and to supplement his income by appearances at 'commercial' opera houses in other towns and countries: and, while foreign countries provided a safe and easy livelihood to a large number of Italian singers, their own country was still the mainstay of the majority. In Italy, opera was the amusement of all classes of society save the very poorest, and every town that was much above the size of a village would have its own opera house. In the Papal States alone, in about 1780, there were more than forty towns that did so, and the figure for the whole of Italy must have been something like one hundred and fifty at least.

So the years would pass, and the virtuoso would move from town to town and country to country, remaining, perhaps, for some years at some royal or electoral court or preferring absolute freedom of movement; attaining gradually the highest plateau of his mastery, remaining there for some glorious years, and then gradually declining again, as age robbed his voice of its brilliance, and himself of his looks and the stamina to sustain the ardours of an *aria di bravura*. If he had been a soprano, he might make a new career, in his later years, by confining himself to those lower notes that remained unimpaired and singing as a contralto; if he were already a contralto, of course, this resource would be denied him. In any case, however, it is as a rule the highest notes that show the first signs of decay, and the contralto, not possessing them, could not suffer from their loss.

Some enemies of castration have claimed that the practice

brought upon its victims an early loss of voice and an untimely death; while others have affirmed, on the contrary, that castration prolonged the life of the vocal chords, and even of their owner. There seems, however, no evidence at all for either contention: the castrati as a rule lived neither a shorter nor a longer time than their contemporaries, and retired, on the average, at about the same age as other singers. The operation appears, for all its cruelty, to have had surprisingly little effect on the general health and well-being of the subject, any more than on his sexual impulses and intellectual capacities. The hurt was very largely a psychological one, in an age when virility was accounted a sovereign virtue.

Eventually, if he had sense, the eminent castrato like every other singer would decide that the time had come for him to quit the stage for good, before the memory of his earlier triumphs should be tarnished by later and inferior performances. He would retire to some luxurious villa to enjoy a well-earned repose, entertaining himself with his memories, with the reception of music-loving visitors from far and near, and with the deploring of the execrable taste of the younger generation—save, perhaps, for one or two budding singers who had taken his fancy, and whom he would consent to teach. Then he would die, much mourned or already almost forgotten; he could found no dynasty to keep his memory alive, nor were there gramophone records to record his voice for posterity, and only the inadequacy of the printed word remained, to give some faint idea of his vanished art.

IV

THEATRICAL CONDITIONS

STENDHAL has a famous picture of the way in which the average small-town Italian opera-house was run, in the early years of the nineteenth century when Rossini's fame was at its height: "The mechanism of the Italian theatre is as follows. The manager is frequently one of the most wealthy and considerable persons of the little town he inhabits. He forms a company, consisting of a prima donna, tenore, basso cantante, basso buffo, a second female singer, and a third basso. He engages a maestro, or composer, to write a new opera, who has to adapt his airs to the voices and capacities of the company. The libretto, or poem, is purchased at the rate of from sixty to eighty francs from some unlucky son of the Muses, who is generally a half-starved abbé, the hanger-on of some rich family in the neighbourhood. The character of the parasite, so admirably painted in Terence, is still to be found in all its glory in Lombardy, where the smallest town can boast of five or six families with incomes of three or four hundred a year. The manager, who, as has been already said, is generally the head of one of these families, entrusts the care of the financial department to a registrario, who is generally some pettifogging attorney who holds the situation of his steward. The next thing that generally happens is, that the manager falls in love with the prima donna; and the progress of this important amour gives ample employment to the curiosity of the gossips.

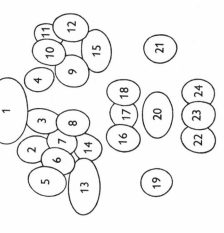

Key to plate 3: 1 Bernacchi, la Tesi, Farinello, la Bulgari, Pistocchi. 2 Cav. Ferri, Caffariello. 3 Bordoni. 4 Egiziello. 5 La Taiber, Carlini. 6 Elisi. 7 Tibaldi. 8 Cav. Matteucci, Aprile. 9 Manzuoli, Cav. Guadagni. 10 Amorevoli, Guarducci. 11 Carestini. 12 Raaff, Millico. 13 Mafeoli, la Gabrielli, Monbelli, Babbi. 14 la Pilaia. 15 Caselli, Tenducci, la Bastardina. 16 Pacchierotti, Mazzanti. 17 Ansani. 18 Damiani, Babbini. 19 Marchesi, la Billinton. 20 la Catalani, la Morichelli, la Todi, And. Martini. 21 Crescentini, la Banti. 22 De Amici, la Silva. 23 la Grassini, David. 24 la Bertinotti, la Marra.

(*Names as given on plate*)

3. FAMOUS SINGERS OF THE XVIIITH AND
EARLY XIXTH CENTURIES
from an engraving by Antonio Fedi

"The company, thus organised, at length gives its first representation, after a month of cabals and intrigues, which furnish conversation for the whole period. This is an event in the simple annals of the little town, of the importance of which the people of large places can form no idea. During months together, a population of eight or ten thousand persons do nothing but discuss the merits of the forthcoming music and singers, with the eager impetuosity which belongs to the Italian climate. This first representation, if successful, is generally followed by twenty or thirty more of the same piece; after which the company breaks up. This is what is called a *stagione,* or season, the last and best of which is that of the carnival. The singers who are not engaged in any of these companies are usually to be found at Milan or Bologna, where they have agents, whose business it is to find them engagements, to manœuvre them into situation when opportunity offers."

By that time, the castrati had been superseded by tenors and basses, and the same Metastasian librettos were no longer made use of, over and over again; but, for the rest, the account would no doubt be equally true for the conditions of a century earlier. At Venice, in the 1780's, according to Archenholz (though he is, admittedly, a somewhat splenetic observer), things were if anything, even more haphazard: "A set of singers, dancers, and musicians join in a body, and borrow of Jews and Christians a certain sum limited by the permission of the government, at twenty, thirty, or more per cent. This is intended as a security for the payment of the performers they hire. Frequent are the disappointments they meet with, for they seldom engage above one singer to act the same part, of course the least indisposition of one of the principals, or any other little accident, may ruin the whole body of those heroes, and frustrate all their hopes." At Naples, the San Carlo was of course a royal theatre, and the King met any deficit that might accrue from the year's operations; yet in theory it was supposed to 'break even', and woe betide any Intendant who got too far into debt. Kotzebue, visiting Naples in 1804, writes that "the theatre San Carlo is usually committed to

3

some speculator called *impresario*[1]; but since the actors both male and female demand and receive enormous salaries . . ., it is scarcely possible for any proprietor to satisfy the public without injuring himself! For that reason no person has been found disposed to embark in it for the present year; and several noblemen have in consequence been obliged to combine."

Since, at that time, the singers *were* the opera to a far greater extent even than in, say, the age of Bellini and Donizetti, an impresario would economise on anything rather than on their salaries; for he knew that, while a good voice or two could make up for any number of shortcomings in other directions, a production without them could not hope to please, be it never so lavishly mounted and visually splendid.[2] The interest of Italian audiences in elaborate decorations and 'effects' was far less great in the eighteenth century than it had been in the late seventeenth, and in the Metastasian type of opera the same backcloths and wings of a baroque palace, or a formal garden with statues, could be used

[1] Among the most original of eighteenth-century impresarios was undoubtedly Andrea del Po, who married the notoriously ugly soprano Anna Strada—she was known as 'the pig' in London—to avoid having to pay her 2,000 ducats which he owed her at the end of a season at Naples. I cannot resist quoting a reference to him in one of Zambeccari's letters: "Andrea del Po is making a tour of Italy to look for women, as he wants to put on 'The Life of St Ursula', and is unable to find eleven thousand virgins in Naples. . . . If you know anyone who really is a virgin, you might let her know: if she can prove it on examination, she is bound to be taken. But I think it unlikely that he will find so many."

[2] According to Riccoboni: "Formerly, the most able and celebrated Musicians at *Venice* received one hundred Roman Crowns for performing for the whole Autumn and Carnaval; and if their Appointments reached to one hundred and twenty Crowns, or six hundred *French* Livres, it was considered as a Mark of great Distinction and a Proof of superior Merit. But for these thirty Years past, a fine Singer, either Man or Woman, has always had upwards of one hundred Golden Sequins, Sancta Stella, Faustina, Cuzzoni and Farinelli, were all paid on this Footing; but these prodigious Expences have ruined all the Undertakers of the Opera at *Venice*, and drained the heaviest Purses in *Italy*. On this Account, and in order to raise the vast Sums that are paid to their Performers, they have for some Time past retrenched their expensive Machinery."

for almost any conceivable situation. In theory, the re-use of old scenery was much frowned on, as the spectators would have been furious had they seen last year's set from 'Semiramis, Queen of Assyria' making do for 'Tamerlane' or 'Sulla'; but often they were tricked by a little refurbishing, and simply did not notice. A visitor to the opera at one of the less important towns, Rimini, Livorno, or Taranto, would have heard some excellent singing from one or two *virtuosi* in costumes of their own devising, amongst dingy and tattered surroundings, and accompanied by an undisciplined scratch orchestra composed largely of violins, and with the woodwind appallingly out of tune.

The salaries paid to the most famous castrati were very great, and it may be of interest to quote some of them. Matteuccio, in 1695, for singing one season in the Empress's Chapel, was paid 3,000 scudi. At Naples in the 1730's, the regulation fee, per season, for a top-line singer was between 600 and 800 Spanish doubloons —a figure which would have been considerably augmented by the proceeds of the virtuoso's customary 'benefit'. Carestini even held out for 1,100 doubloons, but he did not get it, and the place went to Caffarelli who asked only 500—an untypical piece of modesty which he afterwards deeply, and most vociferously, regretted. Senesino, when he visited Naples in 1738, was paid 800, or, in the local currency, 3,693 ducats. The other singers in the company for that season had the following 'onorarii':

La Strada	.	.	D. 600
Amorevoli	.	.	D. 1,053
La Cataneo	.	.	D. 1,108
Francesco Tolve	.	.	D. 750
Manzuoli	.	.	D. 613
Teresa Baratti	.	.	D. 1,004

The composers of the operas given were paid 200 ducats each: whilst in the previous year Vittoria Tesi, the foremost woman singer of her day, got 2,812—considerably less than Senesino.

Often, however, the leading woman would be paid as much as

the *musico*. When, for instance, la Tesi sang with Farinelli in Hasse's 'Siroe' at the Formagliari theatre in Bologna (1735) they were each paid 2,500 lire bolognesi. Caffarelli, also in the cast, got 2,000, and Anna Peruzzi only 1,200. In Leo's 'Siface' (1737) at the same theatre, we find that the composer received L.1,575, as against 2,880 for Carestini, 1,800 only for Salimbeni (though his fame was very great), and 1,500 for the tenor, Amorevoli. In 'Eumene' in 1742, Gius. Appiani received as much as 3,400, while the tenor Babbi was paid 1,980.

Caffarelli, when he went to England, was paid 1,000 guineas for a season, plus 100 for the expenses of the journey; Farinelli earned as many as 1,500, not counting innumerable presents of money, jewellery, snuff-boxes, etc., and when he took up his famous Spanish engagement, his salary amounted to the equivalent of £3,000 a year—an enormous sum for those days. At Rome, where the seasons were particularly short, "the principal singers receive from eight to nine hundred zecchini, and are lodged in the house, or rather confined, in order that they may not catch cold, or suffer any other accident". On the other hand, there were long periods of the year when it was impossible for free-lance singers to earn very much: "The musicians do nothing during the time when the theatres are shut, or join together in small companies to go to Reggio, to the fair at Alessandria, or to other second-rate towns, and sometimes even, during the autumn, into the country, where many of the nobility are in *villeggiatura* at their chateaux."[1] There were, too, more adventurous troupes, who wandered far afield over the face of Europe; Burney met with such a band while he was staying at Brescia in 1770. "In the next room to mine," he says, "there was a company of opera singers, who seemed all very jolly; they were just come from Russia, where they had been fourteen or fifteen years. The principal singer among them, I found upon enquiry to be the Castrato Luigi Bonetto. He is said to be still very rich, though he lost in the night at play ten thousand pounds of the money which he had gained *con la sua virtù*. He is a native of Brescia; was

[1] De Brosses.

welcomed home by a band of music, at the inn, the night of his arrival, and by another the night before his departure."

The enormous popularity of the opera in eighteenth-century Italy was largely, as has been mentioned earlier, the result of an almost complete lack of competition from other forms of entertainment. There was little 'straight' theatre, and what there was was mostly bad; the café—that mainstay of present-day life in Latin cities—had to wait for the broad boulevards and gaslight of the nineteenth century to attain its fullest flowering; whilst entertaining in private houses was little practised, save in the largest towns and among the highest classes of society. The incessant routs, salons and soirées of London and Paris were scarcely known; the opera-house took the place of all of them—and made, it must be admitted, an excellent substitute. There were gambling and refreshments of every kind in the anterooms of the theatre, which must have resembled the Assembly Rooms at Bath during a ball, or the Albert Hall during the Chelsea Arts; everywhere, and particularly at Venice, it was customary to attend the opera masked, and there, indeed, only foreigners were allowed entrance with uncovered face[1]—and they rarely availed themselves of this

---

[1] The Council of Ten had literally dozens of spies in all the Venetian theatres, whose task was to find out everything about everyone. There still exist large numbers of their reports, often on the most trivial subjects, and particularly about ladies who came unmasked to the theatre, pretending to be foreign— either wishing to show off their beauty or to meet genuine foreigners (for it was a heinous crime for any Venetian patrician to have anything to do with what would now be called the Diplomatic Corps.) The love-life of the Princess Ercolani, wife of the Austrian Ambassador, gave the Inquisitors some headaches. She used the opera-houses for her assignations, and, her husband being of a jealous nature, it was feared that he might surprise the guilty pair in her box, and kill the lover outright. We read in another denunciation that one Lazzari "is admitted on to the stage by a ballerina who is his mistress. But this ballerina also has a rich Englishman after her, who has given her quite considerable presents; and as Lazzari never leaves her alone, the Englishman has protested that he must go away. As I am sure the Englishman carries firearms, I foresee that some mishap may arise from this young man's anger." In 1760, the spies reported that the singers and dancers of the S. Benedetto and S. Moisè theatres had allied themselves against those of S. Angelo, with the

privilege, so convenient was the incognito. The gambling-tables were often in the hands of nobles, for counts, marquises, and barons were disproportionately numerous and needy, while prejudice and the law, as much as their own pride, precluded them from the majority of gainful occupations.

The larger boxes, assigned to the leading nobles and dignitaries, were fitted up very much as drawing-rooms "with valuable tapestries, chandeliers, looking-glasses and sophas, according to the taste and means of the proprietor"—or lessee, depending on the arrangements in force—and were used, too, very much as drawing-rooms. Half of the spectators probably cared nothing for the music, which was to them like the three-piece orchestra in an hotel foyer at tea-time. Every writer of the period lavishes abuse on those who come merely to be seen, on "the people who have no better means of passing the time, and buy, for four or five *paoli*, four or five hours' boredom". Archenholz laments that "the foolish custom to play at cards during the opera is here [Florence] as common as in other cities of Italy: the noise which it causes, and the continual rambling from one box to another, annihilate frequently the pleasure of the other spectators whilst the best ariettas are sung. It is *bon ton* among the Italian ladies to pay no attention to the play, they leave this to the wives of the tradesmen.[1] Some even effect the greatest insensibility at the most beautiful songs, which are sung by the best singers, and choose the moment when all is silence, to have a loud conversation. . . . The ruling passion of the Florentines, as of all other Italians, is singing and buffoon tricks. They hate every sort of theatrical

help of two young patricians who were the protectors of two ballerinas, and intended to break up the performances at the latter theatre altogether. The government, however, did nothing and the plot fizzled out.

[1] It will be recalled how, in the palmy days of the 1880's and 1890's the box-holders of the Metropolitan were opposed to the performance of most of Wagner's operas and of 'Trovatore', not because they particularly disliked these works (which they probably were unable to distinguish from 'Carmen' or 'Lucia di Lammermoor'), but because they took place mainly at night; and a darkened stage prevented their jewels from glittering to the best advantage.

production, that requires thought, and put up with all their gross senses. During my stay, 'Didone abandonata', written by Metastasio, was to be acted; but the first singer, who had the part of Dido, was suddenly taken ill, this did not hinder the performance of the opera. Dido was left out, and they acted Dido without Dido". This performance must certainly have been curious in the extreme; but as to the ladies, there are many today who have no need to *affect* such insensibility.

De Brosses has a long and entertaining account of the opera at Rome, which agrees very much with the serious-minded and rather scandalised German: "As soon as the theatres are opened here, the assemblies at Princess Borghese's, at Casa Bolognelli, etc., cease. The general meeting-place is at the opera, which lasts from eight or nine o'clock, until midnight. The ladies hold court in their boxes, and those of their acquaintances who are in the audience go and pay them little visits. I have already told you that everyone has a box rented in advance: and as there are four theatres in use this winter, we have clubbed together to have a box at each, at the rate of twenty sequins per box. You feel quite at home on arriving there. You look about with your lorgnette to see who is there that you know, and visit them if you feel inclined. The taste these people have for the theatre and for music is much more evident from the fact that they are there, than by the attention they pay to it. After the first few performances, when everyone is fairly silent, even in the pit, it is not done to listen, except at the most interesting points." In Kotzebue's words, "When a favourite piece of music commences, a sudden stillness ensues . . . as a flock of geese are still for a moment on the discharge of a gun, but to recommence their gabbling with double violence afterwards. In the recitatives a particular scene has now and then the credit of reducing them to silence; but there must then be a dreadful screaming on the stage, or otherwise the scene passes unnoticed."

De Brosses continues: "The principal boxes are well furnished and lit by wall-brackets. Sometimes one gambles in them, but more often one chats, sitting in a circle all round the box; for that is how the chairs are placed, unlike France, where the ladies embellish the spectacle by sitting in rows at the front of the boxes; from which you will conclude that, despite the magnificence of the individual boxes, the general coup d'œil is infinitely less fine than at home." Marcello, similarly, in his mock advice to members of the audience, remarks: "They will come to the theatre every night, but will stay not more than a quarter of an hour, so that they take a dozen successive evenings to see the whole opera. They will frequent those theatres to which they are admitted without paying, and will pay attention only to part of the Prima Donna's aria. . . ." The rest of the time would no doubt be spent in the *sala da ridotto* of the theatre, playing faro or piquet.

Things were still much the same at Milan in 1819, according to Lady Morgan: ". . . the most scrupulous ladies of the highest ranks came alone in their carriage to the opera. As soon as they enter their box, and have glanced their eye along the circles . . . they turn their backs on the scene, and for the rest of the night, hear and see nothing out of their own society; except when apprised by the orchestra that some scene in the ballet, or some *aria* or *duo* in the opera is about to be performed which it is good taste or good fashion to listen to and admire. Then indeed the most rapturous attention is lent; but, the scene over, the 'Crocchio ristretto' as they call it (or private chit-chat) is resumed, and it is only interrupted by the ingress and egress of visitors."

Foreigners, again, are unanimous in their surprise at the admiration shown by the Italians for their ballets,[1] which were often substituted for the *intermezzi*, or supplemented them, between the acts of the serious opera; the audience showed more interest in them than the whole of the rest of the performance put together, yet they seem as a rule to have been execrable—at least until the days of the famous choreographer and dancer Viganò, so much

---

[1] Ballets were sometimes on the most surprising subjects. In Venice, 1796, Mayr's 'Lodoiska' was accompanied by a production called 'Cook, ossia gl'Inglesi in Othaiti', whilst, the following year, the Milanese were regaled with a choreographic representation of Pope Pius VI and the Consistory making up their minds to sign the Treaty of Tolentino.

admired by Stendhal. Lord Mount Edgcumbe, speaking of Italy, writes: "The passion for music cannot be so great in that land of song as we are apt to suppose: for on enquiring in any town if the opera was good, I was uniformly answered, Oh! si; bellissimi *balli*! and indeed in general the dances are more thought of, and attended to in greater *silence*, than the opera itself, in which, if there is one, or at most two good performers, and as many good songs, it is quite sufficient, and the rest may be as bad as possible without giving offence."

The pit of the theatre was filled with a heterogeneous mass of more or less disreputable characters—servants, gondoliers, young rakes on the loose—who had a fine time behaving exactly as they thought fit, shouting and bandying insults, chattering loudly, searching for some gallant adventure, and occasionally staging a riot (as on a famous occasion in 1763 their English counterparts did at Covent Garden). Among them wenches circulated, hawking refreshments and themselves, while the bottom row of boxes was given over to women of doubtful character, who were often admitted free by the management as an added attraction, and with whom assignations could be made during the performance. Honest tradesmen and their families took refuge in the topmost boxes, whilst the nobility alone could, in many places, occupy the principal tiers. Lady Morgan, visiting Turin in 1819, remarks of the Opera there: "Long deemed the private property of royalty, it has undergone the general purification which followed the Restoration, and is exclusively set apart for the noblesse; the Queen presiding over the distribution and prices of the boxes. Her list decides the number of quarterings requisite to occupy the aristocratic rows of the first and second circles, and determines the point of *roture*, which banishes to the higher circles the *piccoli nobili*."

In Rome, the theatres were full of *abbati*—the innumerable semi-ecclesiastical hangers-on of the Holy See—who were notorious as the most ruthless critics in Italy. They were quicker than anyone to spot a plagiarism, conscious or otherwise, in a new opera, and would ironically chorus 'Viva Leo!', 'Viva Pergolesi!'

or whatever master they considered to have been raided, while
the unfortunate composer cowered trembling at the harpsichord,
and debated whether to flee; things were still the same in Rossini's day, and the first night of the 'Barber' is a classic among
theatrical disasters. The *abbati* would nose out the slightest faults
in a singer's technique,[1] even in a violinist's bowing, and their
pleasure was that of the ancient Romans turning down their
thumbs and condemning some gladiator to death. The high
dignitaries of the Church and the secular nobility did not dare to
question their judgment, or express a divergent opinion, for fear
of seeming ridiculous; and, the day after a première, the *abbati*
would meet again at their favourite coffee-house and discuss the
affair in every possible light. Did they intend once and for all to
break the composer's reputation, so that he should never again
dare to put his music forward in Rome (though of course it might
be tolerated in such ignorant places as Naples and Venice), or
would they be magnanimous, and merely treat him with indiffer-
ence? Or even, possibly, would they decide that they had been a
little unfair, and give the man another chance? They prided
themselves on giving praise where praise was due, and were
capable of acclaiming a singer though condemning what he sang,
or vice versa: "bravo Farinelli, a basso Porpora", etc., etc. Yet
there was a certain check on their exuberance—the *cavaletto*. A
spectator making too much of a nuisance of himself "is seized by
the police or guards, with which the theatre is filled (for the most
military government in Europe is the Pope's), and he, is carried
to the Piazza Navona, where he is mounted on a sort of stocks
and flogged. He is then carried back, and placed in his seat, to
enjoy the rest of the opera 'with what appetite he may'. On the

---

[1] It is recorded that a certain *succès de scandale* was once gained at Rome by a
tenor called Gabrielli, brother of the famous Caterina Gabrielli. When hissed
by the abbati for his singing, which was in fact, abominable, he addressed them,
saying, "I quite agree with your opinion: and, in fact, in every other town
where I've sung, I've had an even worse reception." His false notes and in-
competences became the fashionable joke of the hour, and everyone flocked
to hear him, on the principle of 'Young England' in London in the 1930's,
or Mrs Foster Jenkins.

13th of January, 1820, the strict enforcement of this penalty was recommended in the 'Notizie del Giorno'."

In court theatres, at least when the King, Duke, or Elector was present, manners were far less free. The *bis* was the sovereign's prerogative, and even applause was frowned on, and sometimes forbidden. Dullness has ever been the bane of courts, especially if they followed the traditions of Spain (as those of eighteenth-century Italy mostly did); and Casanova recalls with wry amusement the spectacle of Don Philip, Duke of Parma, and all his entourage nearly choking themselves in an effort not to laugh at a comic opera of Galuppi. At Naples, however, we are told, "On the last night of Carnival, [King] Ferdinand would go to the beautiful theatre San Carlo, and, ordering a dish of macaroni to be brought him, scalding hot, and mixed up with oil, cheese, beef gravy, and what not, from one of the upper boxes, when the pit was crowded with spectators, all attentive to the opera or ballet, he would throw the greasy mess, by handfuls, on his loving subjects; and those who wished to be particularly noticed by the monarch, would tumble head over heels, and scramble to pick up some of it to eat. All of which the king would heartily enjoy, and would laugh most immoderately at those who appeared concerned and vexed at beholding the unctuous marks of royal favour on their holiday suits."

Stage *management*, and anything that could be called production, is of course a fairly recent development, and at that time the singers were free to behave on stage almost exactly as they pleased, while every other consideration was sacrificed to their whims. The prima donna's mother, for instance, would often be ensconced on the stage,[1] accompanied by a posse of the lady's protectors and admirers, and would have about her the vinaigrettes, mirrors, sweets, gargles, combs, etc., etc., of which her daughter might suddenly have need—in the middle of someone

---

[1] De Brosses, it is true, remarks: "The spectators are never allowed on the stage, either at the comedy or in the opera; it is only in France that this ridiculous custom is followed." But he spoke mainly of Rome, and the usage no doubt varied from town to town.

else's aria, if possible. The anecdote is familiar, of the singer who stipulated that her first song should contain the words 'felice ognora', which she felt showed off her voice to the best possible advantage, whilst Marchesi insisted on making his entrance descending a hill on horseback, and wearing a helmet with multi-coloured plumes at least a yard high. He must be announced by a fanfare of trumpets, and must begin by singing one of his favourite arias—most often 'Mia speranza, io pur vorrei', written expressly for him by Sarti—whatever character he was representing, and whatever the situation in which he found himself. Many singers had such signature tunes, which were known as 'arie di baule'— 'suitcase arias'—because they were constantly being carried about from place to place.

Some idea of the strange principles of staging in favour, based not so much on theatrical effectiveness as on the vanity and competitive spirit of the performers, may be gathered from a letter written by Metastasio to the Abb. Giovanni Claudio Pasquini, theatre manager at Dresden:

"Vienna, 10th February, 1748.

"Most dear friend,

I hasten to answer your letter of the 5th, and to return your kindness by enclosing the arrangement of the positions which I allocated to the characters in 'Demofoonte', when it was presented at this Caesarean theatre . . .

ACT I

SCENE I

RIGHT	LEFT
Matusio	Dircea

SCENE II

RIGHT	LEFT
Dircea	Timante

SCENE III

Adrasto	Demofoonte	Timante

SCENE IV
Timante

SCENE V

Creusa   Cherinto

SCENE VI
Creusa   Timante   Cherinto"

and so on: in one instance we have the remark "Demofoonte may cross to the centre for his aria". The final *ripieno* is disposed as follows:

Demofoonte
Dircea   Cherinto
Matusio   Adrasto

"This", continues Metastasio, "was how I regulated the characters' positions at the Imperial theatre. At moments, when the action necessitates it, the more illustrious [*degno*] character may be at the left, but this does not produce the least inconvenience. In the first place the right hand is not considered the most eminent position by every nation; and, even if it were, the character could make the left the most distinguished merely by walking across the stage."

These sagacious considerations evidently did not satisfy Pasquini, for in a second letter Metastasio writes: ". . . if in view of such considerations and necessities the more illustrious character is on the left, and the lowlier one on the right, they can be distinguished in various ways, for instance by placing the former a few steps ahead of the other, or placing him in the middle of the stage facing the audience, and the other a long way from him and further back, sideways on to the audience and facing his superior. . . ."

There follows a really ludicrous discussion as to "who should demand respect, Dircea of Creusa, as being the principal role, or Creusa of Dircea as a princess in disguise"; the whole business

sounds not so much like stage-management, as the heart-searching
of an anxious ambassadress faced with a ticklish point of protocol.
At another point in his correspondence, Metastasio satisfies an
inquirer, who had desired to know which should be considered
the best role in his 'Adriano in Siria' : "All I can say with sincerity,
is, that if I were a first man singer, I would represent the part of
Adriano, and if a female singer, it would please me more to be a
Roman Empress, full of generosity and virtue, than a slave,
enamoured like a cat."

The most comic picture of all this absurdity is found in Marcello's famous satire, and it is difficult to resist the temptation of
quoting it all. So much of it—and particularly, perhaps, his sage
reflections on theatrical mothers—is as applicable today as the day
it was written : but here we must confine ourselves to his remarks
on the castrati, who were his pet aversion. "If he [the singer] has
a scene with another actor, whom he is supposed to address when
singing an aria, he will take care to pay no attention to him, but
rather bow the people in the boxes . . . in order that the audience
may clearly understand that he is the *Signor Alipio Forconi,
Musico*, and not the Prince Zoroaster,[1] whom he is representing."
This ironical advice of 1720 is echoed, sixty years later, by
Arteaga : "Here Eponina turns her back on the Emperor
Vespasian[2] who is still on stage, without regard to the respect due

[1] A character with this name occurs in the opera 'Semiramide' (music by
C. F. Pollarolo), given at the Teatro S. Giovanni Grisostomo, Venice, in 1714—
a few years before Marcello's book appeared. The role was sung by one
Giovanni Paita; and it would be interesting to know whather Marcello had
him in mind. 'Forcone' means, among other things, a pitchfork; whilst
'Paita' suggests some connection with 'paglia' meaning straw. But perhaps
this is rather far-fetched : Paita, too, is sometimes described as a tenor.

[2] It seems probable that Arteaga, when he says 'Vespasian', means that
emperor's son Titus, who figures along with Epponina among the *dramatis
personae* of Sarti's 'Giulio Sabino', one of the most popular operas of the
period, first given at Venice, where Arteaga lived, in 1781. On this occasion
the Titus was Giacomo Panati, and the Epponina, Anna Pozzi, who was such a
flop when she came to London. In Casti's 'Prima la musica e poi le parole',
there are also frequent allusions to this work: The prima donna claims to have
sung Epponina at Cadiz.

him, and entertains herself by walking slowly about, as if she were there for any purpose other than that of holding the audience's attention and simulating passion. Eventually she begins to sing, in a manner so unconvincing, inanimate, and ridiculous that she seems to intend an insult to the audience's good sense. And meanwhile Vespasian, who is listening—what is he doing? His Imperial Majesty is most genially affecting that air of amiability of which he is so fond, looking as a rule at the multifarious coiffures and multicoloured and lofty plumes that are moving about in the boxes, greeting his friends and acquaintances in the pit, smiling at the prompter and the orchestra, fiddling with his watch-chain . . ." and so on, and so forth.

We read of Pacchierotti in London, returning "the perpetual bows made him from almost every box in the house."

To return to Marcello: "All the while the *ritornello* of his aria is being played, the singer should walk about the stage, take snuff, complain to his friends that he is in bad voice, has a cold, etc., and while singing the aria he must bear in mind that at the cadence he can pause as long as he likes and introduce runs and ornaments according to his fancy; during which time the leader of the orchestra will leave his place at the harpsichord, take a pinch of snuff, and wait until the singer is pleased to finish." Every writer attacks the interminable length of the *ad lib.* passages interpolated by vain and tasteless singers, and at their descending to the imitation of agile instruments like the flute, while they leave expression to fend for itself. "The Presumption of some Singers", says Tosi, "is not to be borne with, who expect that a whole *Orchestra* should stop in the midst of a well-regulated Movement, to wait for their ill-grounded Caprices, learned by Heart, carried from one Theatre to another, and perhaps stolen from some applauded female Singer, who had better Luck than Skill, and whose Errors were excused in regard to her Sex. . . . It was thought," he continues, "not many Years since, that in an Opera, one rumbling Air full of Divisions was sufficient for the most gurgling Singer to spend his Fire; but the Singers of the present Time are not of that Mind, but rather, as if they were not satisfied with transforming them all with a horrible Metamorphosis into as many Divisions, they, like Racers, run full speed, with redoubled Violence, to their final Cadences, to make Reparation for the Time they think they have lost during the Course of the Air. . . . The study of the Singers of the present Times consists in terminating the Cadence of the first Part with an overflowing of Passages and Divisions at Pleasure, and the Orchestra waits; in that of the second the Dose is increased, and the Orchestra grows tired; but on the last Cadence, the Threat is set going, like a Weather-cock in a whirlwind, and the Orchestra yawns." Yet there were castrati—Guadagni and Rubinelli among them—remarkable for the simplicity and plainness of their vocal style, and the *reductio ad absurdum* of meaningless execution was reached by the early nineteenth-century diva, Angelica Catalani, noted for singing Rode's violin variations and other similar idiocies.

In no country in Europe, and in no theatrical *genre* in the eighteenth century, was the slightest attempt made at historical accuracy in the costumes and scenery, despite the vogue for exotic settings such as Persia, Mexico, and China. The décors for the serious opera were of the same general 'Bibiena' type, evolving gradually throughout the period from rigid symmetry to a freer and more varied arrangement, but always of much the same components; and the costumes were merely much-bedizened variants of the current modes, both civil and military. The sight was familiar, at Drury Lane, of Banquo's ghost in a powdered wig; and, had there been at that time an opera on the subject of Macbeth, the same oddity would doubtless have been perpetrated. Lord Mount Edgcumbe, taken when very young to hear Gabrielli as Dido, could remember nothing about her but "the care with which she tucked up her great hoop as she sidled into the flames of Carthage", and Mann writes of the Bagnolese as Andromache "in a black velvet gown covered with bugles".

A *musico*, singing the same part at Rome, is pictured by a diarist dying "in snow-white gloves, disappearing amid the immensity of a most sumptuous guard-infanta, and overshadowed by a vast wig adorned with feathers, flowers and birds"; while

Jacopo Ferretti writes: "I remember to have seen, at the Teatro Argentina, Julius Ceasar falling stabbed at the foot of Pompey's statue, shod in elegant ox-tongue shoes with blood-red heels and paste buckles, silk stockings with flowers embroidered in colours up the sides, olive-green knee-breeches with emerald fastenings, and an incipient rain of ringlets falling all about his face." It was one way of making an audience feel at home in remote ages and places. . . .

Another most entertaining picture of theatrical customs of the period is given by the Venetian playwright Simone Sografi in his two comedies 'Le Convenienze teatrali' and 'Le Inconvenienze teatrali', written respectively in 1794 and 1800.[1] Both of them hinge on the production of an opera on Metastasio's libretto of 'Romolo ed Ersilia', and the frightful perplexities endured by the impresario in trying to please everyone without reducing the piece to absolute nonsense. In the first comedy, Sografi informs us that, above all else, the castrati love a mad scene, a sacrifice, and a scene in chains, all of which are calculated to arouse the spectators' pity and sympathy; and they try to insist that some, and if possible all, of these items are included in every opera. The *maestro* is represented in despair, because the *musico* Giuseppino is determined to wear chains when he acts the scene of Romulus' victorious return to Rome: "In the third act Romulus comes on in triumph and sings in the midst of the chorus. All the people are hailing Romulus—and this animal wants to sing his rondo in chains!"

In the 'Inconvenienze', it is one Procolo who is to sing the part of Romulus. This *musico* is not so set on chains, but instead he demands that his triumph be greeted with a salvo of artillery, that the scene-painter devise a décor including the Arch of Constantine and some Egyptian colonnades, and that he himself be given a velvet cloak and boots with spurs. The other actors,

---

[1] Sografi was himself by no means guiltless of theatrical absurdities, to judge from his ridiculous adaptation of Goethe's 'Werther' as a prose drama. He also, among other things, provided the libretto for Cimarosa's 'Gli Orazii ed i Curiazii.'

meanwhile, "appear richly dressed with much magnificence, and resplendent with gold and silver, precisely because this is so inconsistent with the simplicity of new-born Rome."

"The actor who is to take the part of Romulus", continues Sografi, "will turn his back on the public and walk to the back of the stage; he will then turn back again, and have a conversation with the other actors. Next he will look round at the boxes, waving at several people, and after blowing his nose will again approach the footlights. There, turning to the prompter, he will demand 'the words!' and will thereupon sing:

> Son guerriero e sono amante
> Son di stirpe al mondo ignota;
> Fin l'America remota,
> In tal dì faro tremar."

There are many more satires in a similar vein: among them Goldoni's well-known comedy 'L'Impresario di Smirna', in which the poet promises to ensure that the two leading ladies' roles are of identically the same length, down to the last syllable; Girolamo Gigli's little *intermezzo* 'La Dirindina' and Casti's 'Prima la musica e poi le parole'. In the latter, one of the high points is the production and rendering of the following burlesque aria:

> Se questo mio pianto
> Il cor non ti tocca,
> Se questo mio canto
> Che m'esce di bocca
> Ancor non espugna
> Quel barbaro sen;
> Via sfodern, impugna
> Quel spietato
> E quanto castrato
> Trafiggimi almen.

Metastasio did not disdain to parody himself, in the intermezzo 'La cantante e l'impresario', whilst Calzabigi has a comic-opera libretto 'L'Opera seria', which begins with a chorus that might have come straight from the 'Barber':

> Oh che bell'opera!
> Che bella musica!
> Che stil drammatico!
> Che stil cromatico! etc.

Such were the shortcomings of opera in the days of the castrati; yet opera has always possessed an almost unique capacity for, so to speak, absorbing its own absurdities, and turning them from defects into an added attraction. The operatic composer or producer who seeks to banish absurdities too thoroughly is doomed to failure: and, in any case, just as the ghost in 'Hamlet' demands that celebrated 'suspension of disbelief' so opera has always demanded the suspension of that strict and unimaginative logic that ends by turning everything into tedium. Then, as today, when a great singer sang, all the absurdities must have seemed as nothing, and only beauty remained.

The strange mixture of levity and idolatry of individuals, with which the eighteenth-century Italians received their contemporary artistic creation, may seem deplorably frivolous and worldly: yet at least they were free from hypocrisy. Too many people, nowadays, will sit grimly through an opera, a symphony, or a classical drama, hating every moment of it, but pretending to everyone— and even sometimes to themselves—that they are undergoing a wonderful and rare experience. They emerge vaguely resentful, or weltering in bogus ecstasy, their mind soggy and blurred, their senses numbed. Yet they feel they have done something in some way noble and good, and preen themselves over it.

The eighteenth century, whatever may be said about it, was on the whole honest with itself, and did not ask for 'moral values' or 'spiritual sustenance' in art. It knew what beauty was and passionately admired it, realising that it must be worth while for its own sake, or not at all. And it knew how to enjoy itself with what it had, without constantly sighing for the unattainable.

V

CAREERS OF SOME
WELL-KNOWN CASTRATI

ANNIBALI, Domenico

ENDLESS confusion has arisen as between this singer and his almost exact contemporary, the tenor Annibale Pio Fabri; both of them are on occasion referred to as 'Annibalino', and it is often difficult to discover which is meant.

Domenico Annibali was born, probably at Macerata in the Marches, in about 1700, and is first heard of at Rome in 1725. His principal fame, however, was at the court of Dresden, where he went in 1729, and remained until 1764. He sang in all, or almost all, of the numerous operas of Hasse, as well as those of other composers, and had a particular success in Terradellas' 'Astarto' in 1736. In the same year he also visited England to sing in Handel's company, appearing in 'Arminio', 'Poro', and 'Berenice' of that composer, as well as in some of his oratorios. His principal *forte* seems to have been his coloratura, and his voice was an exceptionally high one, attaining F *in alt*.

It is almost certainly of Annibali that Gorani in his 'Mémoires secrets' recounts the following story: "Mengs [father of the famous painter] was one day at a house where there was a concert. A famous *musico* sang so exquisitely that this man, hard to the point of ferocity, was moved. He went up to the new Orpheus, who saw with pleasure the results of his talent, and asked him to begin again. 'I will agree,' answered the musician, 'but only on one condition.' Mengs in his turn agreed. 'It is,' said this humane man, who had heard of the cruelty with which the other treated his children, 'that you will allow me to do so at your house, before your entire family; and I insist that apart from my presence nothing be changed from the usual condition of your household. I wish to see your children, and to have them share in the pleasure you have experienced.'" The musician, who had his plans laid, took with him several persons, who found the young children in a state of indescribable fear and weakness. As a result of this visit, the Elector interested himself in the children, and finding one of them had a taste for painting, had him sent to Italy; and it was thus that Raphael Mengs was started on his brilliant career. His fine portrait of Annibali may well have been painted as a token of his gratitude.

Annibali, on leaving Dresden, was granted a pension of 1,200 thalers a year, on which he retired to Rome. He is known to have been alive in 1779, but probably died soon afterwards.

APPIANI, Guiseppe (Appianino)

This pupil of Porpora was born at Milan in 1712, and made his début at the Teatro S. Giovanni Grisostomo, Venice, in Predieri's 'Scipione il Giovane' in 1731. The following year he sang again in Venice, in Giacomelli's 'Epaminonda' and in Hasse's 'Demetrio'; in 1733 he was at Genoa in 'Arsace' and 'Tito Manlio', and in 1734 back in Venice in Galuppi's 'La Ninfa ed Apollo'.

Appianino continued his round of Italian cities—Milan 1735 in Giacomelli's 'Cesare in Egitto', Venice 1737 in Lampugnani's 'Ezio'—until 1738, when, after singing again in Milan he was invited to Vienna. He must have made a great success there, for when he returned to Italy in 1742 and sang at Bologna in 'Eumene', a *pasticcio,* he was paid the enormous sum of 3,400 lire bolognese. Carestini, five years earlier, had been paid only

2,880; and, even allowing for a possible depreciation of the currency, Appiani was evidently well on the way to becoming a top star.

It was also his swan-song; for, in the words of Quadrio, "this worthy man finished living from erysipelas at Cesena in 1742, when he was only twenty-eight, leaving the cities of Ferrara and Venice where he was headed and awaited, with the regret of seeing themselves prevented for ever from hearing so admired a singer". In point of fact, Appiani would have been thirty in 1742; and according to other authorities he died at Bologna.

Nothing seems to be known of Appianino's private life or character[1]; and he must be classed among the great 'might-have-beens' of the operatic stage.

APRILE, Guiseppe

There are two schools of thought as to the place and date of this great singer's birth; the one placing it at Martina Franca in Apulia, and in 1732; the other at Bisceglie, also in Apulia, in 1738. As Aprile died in the former place, it certainly seems likely that he was born there too; one would hardly have retired to so remote a place if it were *not* one's birthplace.

Aprile was a *figliolo* of the Pietà dei Turchini conservatorio at Naples, and in after years returned there as a teacher, being held in high repute; among his pupils was Cimarosa, and he also composed music himself which was admired at the time.

Aprile's fame as a singer was very great, and he was known as 'il padre de' tutti cantanti'. He seems to have sung principally in the Kingdom of Naples, where few singers were more admired; but he was also very popular at Stuttgart during the years 1756–66 in the operas of Jommelli. Schubart, who heard him there, wrote: "In him art and nature were marvellously combined . . . he sang with the purity of a bell up to E above the treble stave, and had a

[1] For a piece of guesswork concerning him, see the article on Salimbeni page 183.

profound knowledge of vocal technique, as well as a warm and sympathetic personality." In 1766, however, Aprile realised that the Duke was bent on economy, and would be unlikely to pay him his arrears of salary; so he absconded, leaving considerable debts.

Burney, who heard him in 1770, in Jommelli's 'Demofoonte' was more impressed by his technique than by his voice, which he thought rather weak. Kelly has much to say about him. The famous castrato took a fancy to the young Irishman, and gave him every help and encouragement. Engaged to sing in Sarti's 'Alessandro nell'Indie' at Palermo, he took the boy along with him, and even arranged for him to sing in public for the first time, at an open-air religious festival. Returning to Naples, Aprile was among the singers in the cathedral, during the celebrated and absurd ceremony of the liquefaction of the blood of St Januarius, on one alarming occasion when the miracle refused to work. The Archbishop was new at the game, and nervous, and nearly died of terror when the *lazzaroni*, fishwives, and others who filled the church began to shout and curse, calling the saint 'Porco di San Gennaro', 'Cane gialutto', etc., etc., and apparently proposing to lynch the prelate as well, as if that would have helped.

Aprile, seeing the danger, executed a few spectacular *roulades* and trills, which diverted the attention of the maddened crowd for a few seconds, just sufficient time to heat the glass vase with the warmth of his hands, and disaster was averted.

After ceasing to sing, Aprile continued for many years to teach, privately as well as at his conservatorio,[1] but finally retired to Martina Franca, where he died in 1813.

BERNACCHI, Antonio Maria

Few eminent singers have aroused such varying reactions as Bernacchi. Even his warmest admirers admitted that his voice, in

[1] Lady Hamilton was one of his pupils, though Milliro, too, taught her singing. A friend of hers found that "Aprilli [*sic*] was quite the gentleman in

itself, was nothing special, but contended that his marvellous technique more than made up for his deficiencies in sheer sensuous beauty of tone. Others, however, were not at all impressed by him; they allowed him to be a brilliant vocal acrobat, but thought him inartistic and inexpressive. They reproached him, particularly, for introducing *instrumental* execution into his cadenzas, imitating flutes and oboes and other agile but inhuman agencies such as the song of birds; all of which reminds one of those Viennese ladies of today who decorate the waltzes of Johann Strauss with a froth of elaborate but meaningless coloratura in a piercingly high register. Even his own teacher, Pistocchi, on hearing him after a number of years, is said to have remarked: "Tristo a me, io t'ho insegnato a cantare, e tu vuoi suonare!"

Bernacchi was born at Bologna in 1685, and is first heard of at the court of the Elector Palatine in 1701. He continued in Germany for a number of years, both at Mannheim and at Vienna in the Imperial service, and returned to Italy about the year 1712, when he was heard in Venice in Ruggeri's 'Arato in Sparta'.

The following year, Bernacchi returned to his native city, where he sang in Gasparini and Orlandini's 'Carlo Re d'Alemagna', and in 1716 he went to England for the first time, without, apparently, making any particular impression. Back in Venice the year after, he remained for the most part in that city until 1724 and gained an immense popularity; one of the most notable occasions on which he sang elsewhere being at Pesaro in 1718, when he took part in a gala performance of Pallavicino's 'Vespasiano' in honour of the Old Pretender, who was staying there at the time.

In 1727, Bernacchi was again heard in Bologna, when he had his famous contest with Farinelli in Orlandini's 'La Fedeltà coronata'. The younger singer, thinking to astonish by his agility, put his all into a most elaborate cadenza; but Bernacchi, whose aria followed, exactly imitated all Farinelli's graces, executing them with superior polish and ease, and added some extra

public society, except when he spoke on music, and thereby instantly discovered himself to be of the neuter gender"—one wonders exactly in what way.

fioriture of his own. On this occasion, there is no doubt that Bernacchi won the day, though it is likely that the fact of his being a local boy contributed to his success. The event was commemorated by a grand banquet, and a sonnet composed in the Bolognese dialect[1]: but it is to the credit of both Bernacchi and Farinelli that they became firm friends,[2] and sang together again on several occasions—soon afterwards at Parma in Vinci's 'Il Medo' and Giacomelli's 'Scipione in Cartagine', and in Bologna again in 1731, in Porta's 'Farnace'. Bernacchi passed on some of his secrets to Farinelli, and seems to have given him a passing taste for excessive ornamentation, until the Emperor Charles VI's famous advice turned him once more towards simplicity.

In 1728, Bernacchi was engaged for Naples with Carestini, but the season was not a happy one. In Zambeccari's words, "The Viceroy [Cardinal d'Althann], who likes Bernacchi well enough, told him that he was determined to have him remain for the coming year (1729). Bernacchi replied that he would agree, on condition that all his stipulations should be fulfilled; among which were that the Merighi should stay, and that Carestini, his enemy of the rival party, should be dismissed. The Viceroy gave orders to the impresario (Carasale) that all this should be done, and that the contract should be signed. The ladies and gentlemen of Carestini's party at once made a fuss, and went in a body to the Viceroy, protesting that they should not be absolutely deprived of Carestini. The Viceroy now found himself in a difficult position, and ordered the impresario to set about settling the affair, saying that he (the Viceroy) wanted no part in it, that he wished to know nothing further about the theatre, and that he would no

[1] It is perhaps worth quoting a few lines, if only as an example of this eccentric patois, which looks so strange in print:

"In favore del musico Bernacchi, e contro il Farinelli:

        Avrè ch'am dsersi coss'è mai gran fiacch
        Ch'fa al person can st'al voster Farinel!
        Per Crest, av'degh ch'avì pere al zervel:
        E me v'so dir ch'al canta mai Bernacch!" etc.,

[2] When Bernacchi died, Farinelli arranged an elaborate memorial service in his honour.

longer grant it the usual subsidy. When Bernacchi heard about this, he went to the impresario saying that he was a man to make conditions, and not one to accommodate himself to them; that he would not stay in a country where he was not liked, and that he would have no part in such foolishness. . . ." Thereupon, Bernacchi left for Milan, taking the Merighi with him (she was apparently his mistress), and afterwards returned to Bologna, where he was made a member of the Accademia Filarmonica.

In 1729, Bernacchi was engaged by Handel, and again came to England; and this time he was frankly a failure. A small number of connoisseurs were ecstatic over his facility and impeccable style; but the general public disliked him, and it was largely for this reason that Handel's 'La Partenope', considered by many his masterpiece, came off after only a few performances.

Bernacchi returned to Italy, where his popularity continued to be great. As mentioned above, he once more disputed the palm with Farinelli in 1731; he was acclaimed at Venice in 1732, and went on singing until 1736. In that year he was heard at Modena in Hasse's 'Demetrio' and 'Artaserse', and afterwards retired, though he continued to sing occasionally in private.

He had begun to give lessons in 1727, and on his retirement from the stage he established his famous school of singing, whose pupils, including Guarducci, were many and notable. He was a leading figure in the musical life of Bologna, and a close friend of both Metastasio and Padre Martini; and he is said to have induced the latter to undertake his great History of Music, though the work was not begun until after Bernacchi was dead. He also composed some music, and gave help and encouragement to many aspiring musicians; he died, much regretted, in 1756.

Bernacchi's character was in general noble and generous, and historically he is one of the most important singers who ever lived; were it possible for us to compare him with his immediate predecessors and older contemporaries, such as Nicolino and Senesino, he would no doubt sound noticeably more modern, more like the singers of today. His influence was partly for the good, and his cultivation of flexibility and ease brought a vast improvement to the art; yet he must, too, be made ultimately responsible for the imbecile warblings and trills of the typical tasteless prima donna. Still, every progress has its disadvantages; and for all that it is none the less a progress.

BERNARDI, Francesco (Senesino)

It is tiresomely confusing that three well-known castrati should have been born at Siena, and should all, because of it, have been known as 'Senesino'; but the singer at present under consideration is decidedly the most famous of the three, and the one most usually referred to by the pseudonym—the others being generally known by their real names.

Nothing seems to be known of Senesino's early life. He is generally supposed to have been born in about 1680; but as his name occurs in no extant cast-list before the year 1714 (in Venice, in Pollarolo the elder's 'Semiramide'), he may well have been a good deal younger. The following year, the impresario Zambeccari writes of him: "Senesino continues to comport himself badly enough; he stands like a statue, and when occasionally he does make a gesture, he makes one directly the opposite of what is wanted. He expresses himself abominably in recitatives, unlike Nicolino who used to do them admirably; as for the arias, he sings them well when in voice. But yesterday evening, in the best aria, he was two beats ahead of time.

"Casati is really insufferable, both for the tediousness of his pathetic singing and for his great pride; he is in league with Senesino, and they have no respect for anyone. So no one can [bear to] see them, and almost all Naples considers them, if at all, as a couple of —— conceited eunuchs. They have never been mine, unlike so many opera *musici* who have been in Naples; only these two have never been mine. And so I have the consolation of seeing them ill-considered by everyone."

We next hear of Senesino in 1719, when he was singing at the Court theatre at Dresden; and he was still there the following year when Handel visited the city to engage singers for the newly-constituted Royal Academy of Music in London. It seems strange that the composer should have gone to Germany to look for Italian singers, even though Dresden was a great centre of Italian opera; but Handel seems always to have had ideas of his own on the subject of singers, choosing, for instance, Carestini in preference to Farinelli. On this occasion, he selected Senesino along with Berenstadt, Boschi, and Margherita Durastanti.

Senesino remained with the Academy until its failure in 1728, and sang the principal roles in all the operas of Buononcini, Ariosti, and above all Handel; but his relations with the latter great composer were continually strained.[1] Despite their differ-

[1] To be fair to Senesino and Handel, it must be said that the worst trouble was caused by the rival prima donnas, Cuzzoni and Faustina (who actually came to blows on the stage during a performance of Buononcini's 'Astianatte'), and by the factions in the audience who supported one lady against the other, and Handel against Buononcini, largely for political reasons. Handel was the Tories' candidate, and Buononcini the favourite of the Whigs.

Senesino was in this juncture on leave of absence in Italy, after an illness, and the poet Rolli (another born troublemaker) writes to him, enclosing a satirical comment on the situation, in the form of a poem:

> I concerti di città
> si preparano a gran fatti
> gabbia amplissima di matti
> e la musica si fa.
> Londra è già divisa tutta,
> i partiti non an freno
> chi vorrà il mercato a fieno
> chi 'l mercato della frutta
> Aman qui le contenzioni
> come i lor campestri balli
> non sarà pero di galli
> ma battaglia di capponi.

To which Senesino, who was not without wit, replied:

> Farinello è un gran campione
> della musica moderna,
> e con spada e con lanterna
> può venire alla tenzone

ences, however, Senesino was re-engaged by Handel in 1730[1] to supplement the inferior company with which he had resumed operatic management; but their relations were even less happy than before, and culminated in a total breach in 1733. It was, in fact, very largely the personal animosity between Handel and Senesino[2] that led to the foundation of the 'opera of the nobility' in opposition to Handel's company, with Porpora as composer. Senesino naturally took part in it, along with Cuzzoni; and they were soon joined by Farinelli, who, being a soprano, complemented the older singer rather than competing with him. These two castrati seem to have got on together very well, contrary to expectations, and there is a famous anecdote of the effect that Farinelli's singing had on Senesino, when first he heard it (see p. 99).

The absurd warfare between the rival companies ended inevit-

> Nell'antica a merto equale,
> perchà brava educazione
> nella prima sua lezione
> gli die il Porpora immortale.

All of which refers to a proposal to bring Farinelli over at that time, and so provide the Londoners with the spectacle of a battle between rival castrati, which promised to be even more furious than that between Cuzzoni and Faustina. But the plan fell through, and when Farinelli did finally come to England, it was to sing for Handel's rivals.

[1] In January 1729, Rolli writes again to Senesino, who had once more returned to Italy: "Heidegger came back, saying he could find no singers in Italy, and protested that he would not undertake anything without the two Ladies, speaking only of them, and proposing Farinelli . . . but Handel was not lulled to sleep by the music of such a flute. He showed up the craftiness of his rival [presumably Heidegger, though Handel and he were actually partners], his vain and ridiculous journey, his thoughts of gain alone; he said that there was need of variety, and that the former system of changing the singers should be readopted. . . . Faustina is not wanted; you seem to be wanted up to a point; they want Farinello and the Cuzzoni if she does not stay at Vienna. . . . They propose 4,000 pounds in all for the singers, with two at 1,000 each and a benefit performance. . . ." However, when in 1729 Handel himself went to Italy, he did not at first engage Senesino, until Bernacchi had been tried and found wanting.

[2] Handel is said to have particularly enraged the singer by making the part of Zoroastro in 'Orlando' as good as his, the title role.

ably in the ruin of both, since London could not possibly have been expected to support two permanent opera companies, especially with the added competition of the ballad operas, then at their apogee. The end came in 1737, and Senesino at last returned to Italy, where for the season of 1738–9 he was engaged by the San Carlo Theatre, Naples, for the *onorario* of 800 doubloons, reserved for the greatest stars. He did not, however, particularly please the Neapolitans, who found that he sang 'in an antique style', and he was not re-engaged.[1]

After this, the singer returned to his native Tuscany, where at Florence in the same year, 1739, he had the dubious honour of singing a duet with Maria Theresa, already Grand Duchess of Tuscany and soon to become Empress, as well as appearing in two operas of Orlandini—'Arsace' and 'Arianna'—apparently his last public professional performances. He then seems to have relapsed into obscurity, and the date of his death is as vague as that of his birth.

Of Senesino's voice and manner, Quantz has the following praise: "He had a powerful, clear, equal and sweet contralto voice, with a perfect intonation and an excellent shake. His manner of singing was masterly and his elocution unrivalled. Though he never loads adagios with too many ornaments, yet he delivered the original and essential notes with the utmost refinement. He sang allegros with great fire, and marked rapid divisions, from the chest, in an articulate and pleasing manner. His countenance was well adapted to the stage, and his action was natural and noble. To these qualities he joined a majestic figure; but his aspect and deportment were more suited to the part of a hero than of a lover." Others, however, while admiring his voice, continued to find his acting painfully wooden and unconvincing

---

[1] Says de Brosses: "Le célèbre Cénazino [*sic*] faisoit le premier rôle [in Sarro's 'La Partenope']; je fus enchanté du goût de son chant et de son action théâtrale. Cependant je m'aperçus avec étonnement que les gens du pays n'en étoient guères satisfaits. Il se plaignoient qu'il chantoit d'un style *anticho*. C'est qu'il faut vous dire que les goûts de la musique changent ici au moins tout les dix ans."

and his movements awkward; his character seems never to have been notable for amiability, though his emotion on hearing Farinelli sing is a sympathetic trait.

BROSCHI, Carlo (Farinelli)

The career of this extraordinary man is unique in many ways, and among them are the circumstances of his very birth; for, unlike any other castrato of whom knowledge exists, he came from a noble family. He was born at Andria in Apulia on January 24th, 1705 (though for some reason he always claimed, and perhaps believed himself, to be a native of Naples), and his father was Royal Governor of the towns of Maratea and Cisternino from 1706 to 1709. The latter survived until 1717, when he died at Terlizzi, and devoted his later years to the composition and teaching of music: but however fanatically he may have been addicted to the art it seems astonishing that he should have consented to his son's being castrated. It is possible that in this case the excuse so often made use of was true, that the operation had had to be performed to ward off some threatened sickness.

The nickname Farinelli was a family, rather than personal one, since the singer's brother—a composer of some standing—was also known by it, but it has never been satisfactorily explained: the Broschis had no connection with milling or baking, as sometimes supposed, nor were they related to the French violinist brothers Farinel. "Farinello" in Italian means a thorough rascal, a rogue; is it, then, possible that the father first earned himself the sobriquet in carrying out his official duties? The Austrians conquered the Kingdom of Naples in 1707 and in general replaced all existing functionaries with creatures of their own, thus Broschi Senior must have been a pretty wily customer to remain in office even till 1709; whilst his later abandonment of public life suggests the likelihood of a disgrace. In any event, Farinelli seems to have come to Naples as a very small boy, perhaps when so young that he did not remember Andria at all, and soon was applying himself assiduously to the study of music; his principal master being Porpora, in many of whose operas he was afterwards to sing. Despite their long association, however, Porpora seems to have preferred Caffarelli as a singer, for all his dislike of him as a man.

Farinelli made his début in the *serenata* 'Angelica e Medoro', with music by Porpora, at Naples in 1720. The book was by Metastasio, and by a remarkable coincidence was his first operatic work as well[1]; so that perhaps the most famous singer and the most famous librettist that ever lived made their début on the same occasion. Their friendship was immediate, and lasted with increasing warmth throughout their lives; by force of circumstance they seldom saw one another, but their correspondence was voluminous and unceasing, and they always addressed one another as 'caro gemello'—'dear twin'—in memory of their double appearance before the world. For many years the coincidence was declared to be a fallacy; but modern research has shown it to be true, and Metastasio himself, in his dedication to Farinelli of his drama 'La Nitteti', makes mention of the fact:

> Appresero gemelli a sciorre, il volo
> La tua voce in Parnaso e il mio pensiere.

Soon after this, Porpora took his pupil with him to Rome, where he was to compose an opera for the Aliberti Theatre, and in which he had arranged for Farinelli to appear. Some have thought that this work was 'Eumene' (1721), but apparently the singer was not in Rome till the following year, when at the same theatre, Porpora brought out his 'Flavio Anicio Olibrio'; and it was perhaps in this work that occurred the famous contest with the German trumpet-player described by Burney. "He was seventeen", he writes, "when he left that city [Naples] to go to Rome, where during the run of an opera, there was a struggle every night between him and a famous player on the trumpet, in a song accompanied by that instrument; this, at first, seemed amicable and merely sportive, till the audience began to interest

---

[1] His first completely original *opera seria*, as opposed to a mere *serenata*, was 'Didone abbandonata' (1724); in the interval, however, he produced 'Siface' which was a thorough remodelling of an older libretto.

4. DOMENICO ANNIBAL
from the portrait by Mengs

themselves in the contest, and to take different sides: after severally swelling a note, in which each manifested the power of his lungs, and tried to rival the other in brilliancy and force, they had both a swell and shake together, by thirds, which was continued so long, while the audience eagerly waited the event, that both seemed to be exhausted; and, in fact, the trumpeter, wholly spent gave it up, thinking, however, his antagonist as much tired as himself, and that it would be a drawn battle; when Farinelli, with a smile on his countenance, shewing he had only been sporting with him all that time, broke out all at once in the same breath, with fresh vigour, and not only swelled and shook the note, but ran the most rapid and difficult divisions, and was at last silenced only by the acclamations of the audience. From this period may be dated that superiority which he ever maintained over all his contemporaries."

Farinelli's fame rapidly became prodigious; he was known as 'Il ragazzo'—'the boy'—and, being handsome as well as a phenomenal singer, he was a particular success with the female part of his audiences; yet amorous intrigue does not seem to have been among his interests, and not a single anecdote of gallantry is attributed to him.

In 1724 Farinelli went for the first time to Vienna, and the following year was heard in Venice, in Albinoni's 'Didone abbandonata', after which he returned to Naples to sing with Vittoria Tesi. He continued to wander between the various cities of Italy; in 1727 at Bologna he had less than his usual success, singing in Orlandini's 'La fedeltà coronata' along with Bernacchi, who was not only a fabulously accomplished singer but a native Bolognese, and was preferred to Farinelli (see page 88). Farinelli himself was evidently much impressed by the older *musico*, who graciously consented to pass on to him some of his technical secrets, and seems to have influenced him towards an exceedingly, perhaps excessively, florid style of singing. Farinelli was again in Vienna in 1731, and it was on this occasion that he had his famous interview with the Emperor Charles VI, who advised him to give up trying to astonish his hearers, and instead to set about engaging

4

their emotions. Farinelli took the advice, and soon became as
famous for his pathos as he already was for brilliance and
agility.

It was in 1734 that Farinelli first came to England, to sing for
the Opera of the Nobility; Handel had preferred Carestini to him[1]
after hearing them both in Bologna, but must soon have regretted
his decision. Great a singer as Carestini was, he could not rival
the other's popularity, and Farinelli aroused positively hysterical
enthusiasm in everything that he sang. "In the city," says Sir
John Hawkins, "it became a proverbial expression, that those who
had not heard Farinelli sing, and Foster preach, were not qualified
to appear in genteel company." His salary was 2,000 guineas, and
at his benefit he earned unprecedented sums—200 guineas from
the Prince of Wales, 100 pounds from the Spanish Ambassador,
50 from the Austrian, and from the Duke of Leeds, and so on
through half the nobility of England; so that he was estimated to
make, all told, some £5,000 a year while in London.

The poet Rolli, the crony and fanatical supporter of Senesino,
had evidently been asked by that singer to go and hear Farinelli,
while on a visit to Italy some years before, and had written: "I
cannot, because of his merit, forbear to say that Farinelli has surprised me so much that I feel as though I had hitherto heard only
a small part of the human voice, and now have heard it all. He
has, besides, the most amiable and polite manners, and I take the
greatest pleasure in his acquaintance."

Senesino himself, however, had apparently never heard Farinelli (or had not heard him for a long time) until the rehearsals of
the first opera which they were to sing together—'Artaserse', a
pasticcio with music partly by Hasse and Farinelli's brother, Ric-

---

[1] Farinelli was a soprano, whilst Carestini, like Senesino, was a contralto:
and it may be that Handel preferred the latter type of voice. There were others,
however, who were less than overwhelmed by Farinelli's singing; if he had a
fault, one would guess it to have been a certain lack of fire and temperament.
His extreme placidity and gentleness of character would no doubt have rendered him somewhat ineffective in moments of vehement drama, and in expressing the more strenuous passions. Again, he seems to have made little attempt
at acting, and generally remained stock-still while interpreting an aria.

cardo Broschi, and partly by various other composers. At the first rehearsal, the orchestra forgot to play, so astonished were they at Farinelli's virtuosity; and at the first actual performance occurred the famous incident reported by Burney, when "Senesino had the part of a furious tyrant, and Farinelli that of an unfortunate hero in chains; but in the course of the first air, the captive so softened the heart of the tyrant, that Senesino, forgetting his stage-character, ran to Farinelli and embraced him in his own". It was perhaps on this occasion, too, that a lady of fashion uttered that memorable phrase, "One God, one Farinelli!" which Hogarth introduced into his 'Rake's Progress'. "The world", says Hawkins, "had never seen two such singers upon the same stage as Senesino and Farinelli; the former was a just and graceful actor, and in the opinion of very good judges had the superiority of Farinelli in respect of the tone of his voice; but the latter had so much the advantage in other respect, that few hesitated to pronounce him the greatest singer in the world." About the same time, the 'Gentleman's Magazine' complains that "so engrossing are the *Italians*, and so prejudiced the *English* against their own country, that our Singers are excluded from our very Concerts; *Bertolli* singing at the Castle, and *Senesino* at the Swan, to both their shames be it spoken; who, not content with monstrous Salaries at the Opera, stoop so low as to be hired to sing at the Clubs!"

Farinelli remained in England, save for one brief excursion to France, until May 1737; yet even his art could not save the opera from falling into decline. The foolish warfare between the rival companies was prejudicial, and in the long run fatal, to both, and, says Cibber, "within these two years we have seen even Farinelli sing to an audience of five-and-thirty-pounds". Despite this unfortunate state of affairs, however, Farinelli fully intended returning to England the following year; but an invitation at once more lucrative, more flattering, and more surprising induced him to change his mind, and he never in fact returned to England.

Philip V of Spain suffered from incurable melancholia, and

could scarcely be induced to attend even to the most pressing matters of state; he had already abdicated once in favour of his son Louis, but on the young man's speedy death had been prevailed upon to resume the throne. Now, however, even his life was despaired of: but his second wife, the ambitious and energetic Elizabeth Farnese, was determined that he should not die. She enjoyed being Queen, and dreaded the condition of a dowager relegated to obscurity, religion, and cards: besides, the heir apparent was her stepson Ferdinand, whom she hated, and her own son Charles was far away governing Naples. She conceived the idea of inviting Farinelli to Madrid in the hope that his singing might assuage the anguish of the King's sick mind; and, on his arrival, she stage-managed the encounter with much adroitness, so that Philip should hear the singer as if by chance, and in another room. Everything went exactly as she had planned; the monarch was entranced and quite forgot to mope, and in fact was spared for another nine years of life—a life whose only solace was to be the voice of Farinelli. That solace was valued at some £3,000 a year, which was the singer's salary—no doubt augmented by many valuable presents and perquisites.

During those years, as everyone knows, Farinelli is said to have sung the same four songs nightly before the King, who would suffer none but his immediate entourage to hear the miraculous voice. Two of the four were, according to Burney, 'Pallido il sole' and 'E pur questo dolce amplesso', both from Hasse's 'Artaserse'[1]; but it does not appear whether Farinelli sang *only* this strangely restricted repertoire, as is usually supposed, or whether he gave a varied programme which included one or more of the four, as a sort of 'theme-song'. The latter certainly seems the more probable supposition.

Farinelli soon came to acquire, over the court of Spain, an influence comparable only to that of Rasputin over the last Tsar

[1] Hasse set 'Artaserse' at least twice, in 1730 and 1740, and according to some authorities it was from the second setting that Farinelli chose his arias; in which case, of course, he could not have sung them at all during his first three years or so in Spain.

of Russia, though far excelling that in beneficence, as it exceeded in duration. The former opera-singer turned his attention to such subjects as the dredging and canalisation of the river Tagus, and its use for irrigation purposes, and the importation of horses from Hungary to improve the Spanish strain: for this latter purpose he applied to his perennial confidant Metastasio, and the poet's letters on the subject are decidedly comic, with their minute considerations as to the best way for the horses to be shipped, what wages to pay the men in charge of the string, etc., etc., all expressed in his habitual, somewhat gushing and high-faluting style.

On the accession of Ferdinand VI in 1746, Farinelli's influence became, if possible, even greater than it had been under Philip; and in 1750 he was made Commander of the Order of Calatrava —a signal honour reserved for those of noble blood. Yet, for all that, Farinelli's character was such that even the umbrageous Spanish grandees could not find it in their hearts to resent or dislike him. "The Spanish minister plenipotentiary Don Antonio de Azlor", writes Mestastasio in one letter, "has arrived, and is very much liked. He is questioned by everyone concerning you, and his answers are most gratifying. He assured us that the gentleness and moderation of your character has in no way suffered from your high position. . . . He says that, though raised to so enviable a situation, you have no enemies. To be forgiven for your eminence, I can well imagine how prudent, disinterested and beneficent your conduct must be." There are, too, many anecdotes of Farinelli's generosity and consideration towards those less fortunate than himself, but they are perhaps too familiar to bear retelling. In 1754 he had a difficult time over the disgrace of the minister Ensenada, with whom he was suspected of sympathising; but he weathered the storm, and fully recovered his power and influence.

He had meanwhile, since the accession of Ferdinand, had a chance to try his skill as theatre-director, for the new Queen, Barbara of Portugal, was devoted to opera. A court opera-house was opened, and a first-class company of singers collected together over whom he ruled with great firmness, though not with in-justice. "According to his regulations," says his biographer Sacchi, "no one, even of the highest rank, was allowed access to the actors' dressing-rooms. He wished the women's dresses to be decently long . . . and would not permit the introduction of ballets." He was sometimes blamed for excessive rigour, particu-larly in the case of outside engagements, and there is a well-known anecdote of the pregnant wife of a Spanish duke who longed for a song from the famous Caterina Mingotti, then among Farinelli's company. It was only by the King's express command that Farinelli could be induced to allow Mingotti to sing for her, and he was criticised for his obduracy; no doubt he felt that this occasion would prove the thin end of the wedge, so that before long his singers would be taking engagements all over the place and overtaxing their voices.

All the operas performed under Farinelli's supervision were on texts by Metastasio (save one, 'Armida') and several of the poet's dramas were specifically written for Madrid. Their correspon-dence at this time contains some interesting discussions about the *mise-en-scène*, Farinelli being particularly proud of a new method he had invented for simulating rain, though he does not describe exactly how it was done: on another occasion, Farinelli had ap-parently wished to introduce a fairground with illuminated booths on the stage, and a scene in which a fort should be taken by assault with scaling-ladders, etc., but Metastasio demurred. "I dare not", he wrote, "mention either *Fair* or *Shop* in my directions for shifting the scenes: as it would be giving a handle to the flippant impertinence of the little Roman Abate."

When the Queen died, Farinelli once more found himself the only refuge of a monarch distraught with grief and melancholia, and he tried without success to interest the wretched man again in life. But Ferdinand was inconsolable, and would wander about the gardens of Aranjuez unshaven and in his nightshirt, refusing to listen to anyone; soon afterwards he died.

That year, 1759, was a fatal one for Farinelli, and the end of his active career. Ferdinand was succeeded by his half-brother

Charles III: who, relinquishing his Neapolitan dominions and his enormous unfinished palace of Caserta, came back to Madrid to fulfil his mother's dearest wish, that her son should be King of Spain. He was by no means hostile, as some have made out, to Farinelli; one of his first acts in his new royal capacity was to continue the singer's pension, remarking, "I do so willingly because Farinelli has never abused the benevolence and generosity of my predecessors", and the latter went to meet him at Saragossa to thank him for his generosity. Nor was Charles, though indifferent to music, at all averse to singers, and on several occasions at Naples he had personally intervened to save Caffarelli from the consequences of his grosser acts of insolence; yet he decided, for reasons that can only be guessed, that Farinelli would be better out of Spain. One explanation often given is that Farinelli favoured Austria at the expense of France, and Charles wanted the policy changed. In 1759, however, France and Austria were busy fighting together as allies against Prussia in the Seven Years' War, as a result of the dramatic switchover of French policy engineered by Madame de Pompadour some years before; thus Farinelli could not have been taking sides, in a rivalry that was for the moment in abeyance. In all probability, Charles merely felt the need for a clean sweep; Farinelli, as a native of Apulia, had been technically his subject while he was King of Naples, but instead of serving him had been the mainstay of his brother-in-law, with whom he, Charles, had always been on awkward terms. It appears, moreover, that in 1766 Farinelli was still employed by the Duke of Medinaceli, Intendant of the Madrid Opera, to look for singers in Italy, whilst in the previous year there had been talk of his returning to Madrid to direct the performance in honour of the Infant's wedding.

In all events, Farinelli's days of glory were over. His letters to Metastasio betray his depression, and his resentment at the false friends who, though so recently they had praised and flattered him, had no use for him now that his power was gone; and he seems, in fact, to have caught something of the kingly melancholy he had so long worked to assuage. According to Sacchi, "A true friend said to him, 'How, Signore, can you be surprised at this ingratitude and instability of men, which your great friend Metastasio predicted so many years ago?' 'When', said he, 'did he make such a prediction?' The friend replied, 'When he was writing the first scene of his 'Artaserse', which he intended as a warning of what has now befallen you.' The words which the friend meant were these:

> L'altra turba inconstante
> Manca de' falsi amici, allor che manca
> Il favor del Monarca. Oh quanti sguardi
> Che mirai rispettosi, or soffro alteri!

Five years later, Metastasio himself was still writing to Farinelli of these afflictions. "Your last letter", he says, "really consoled me. From the serenity and gaiety that colours it from beginning to end, I see that you have at last found the secret of wiping from your mind that cursed soot which has blackened it so long."

Farinelli left Spain for ever, and returned to Italy. He first visited Parma, where he was received with much distinction by the Duke, younger brother of the monarch who had dismissed him from Madrid; after that, he made a visit to Naples, where he was feted as a national hero and thought of settling. In the end, however, he decided against it, and established himself at Bologna, where he lived quietly for the rest of his days.

Some strange reasons have been invented for Farinelli's choice of Bologna as a residence; Burney states that he was 'ordered' to live there, and nowhere else, by Charles, and Vernon Lee, going one better, implies that the Spanish King chose the place deliberately, out of spite, as the town in Italy which he knew Farinelli most disliked. Actually, Bologna was a very natural place for Farinelli to have chosen; at that time it rivalled Naples as the musical capital of Italy, and was the home of Padre Martini, Farinelli's friend and one of the most distinguished musical personalities of his age. In point of fact, too, it appears that the great castrato had all along intended to settle there when he should retire: for an entry by the Bolognese diarist Antonio Barilli, dated as long ago as September 22nd, 1732, reads: "I hear that the famous *musico* Farinelli is resolved to take up residence here, and is acquiring a fine property." Just over a month later, the same writer adds: "The famous *musico* Farinelli was granted citizenship by the Senate, and is acquiring a property for twenty-eight thousand lire in ready cash." During his years in Spain, Farinelli, though at a distance, had supervised the construction of a fine villa on his property, and it was now ready to receive him.

Another diarist, Galeati, records his arrival at Bologna to take up residence, and the honours then granted him, in an entry dated July 6th, 1760: "Carlo Broschi called Farinelli arrived at Bologna, and went to his house outside the *Lamme*.[1] The next day he was visited by Senator Count Francesco Caprara wearing his Fleece, it is said on the Emperor's part. At eight o'clock he paid a visit to Count Odoardo Pepoli ..." and so on, concluding with Farinelli's reception by the famous Philharmonic Academy. Evidently, the establishment of so eminent a person in their midst was quite an excitement for the good Bolognese.

At his villa, Farinelli lived a life which, though retired, was by no means that of a recluse. Burney has a famous account of his meetings with him in 1770. "It will give pleasure", he begins, "to every lover of music ... to learn that Signor Farinelli still lives, and is in good health and spirits. I found him much younger in appearance than I expected. He is tall and thin, but seems by no means infirm." He met the singer on several occasions, during one of which "Signor Farinelli, pointing to Padre Martini said, 'What *he* is doing (i.e. writing his history of music) will last, but the little I have done is already gone and forgotten'. I told him, that in England there were still many who remembered his performances so well, that they could bear to hear no other singer; that the whole kingdom continued to resound to his fame, and I was sure tradition would hand it down to the latest posterity."

Burney's account of his visit to Farinelli's villa, too, is well known, but it is worth quoting: "This day I had the pleasure to spend with Signor Farinelli, at his house in the country, about a

[1] The Porta delle Lame or Lamme, one of the city gates.

mile from Bologna, which is not yet quite finished, though he has been building it ever since he retired from Spain . . . Signor Farinelli has long left off singing, but amuses himself still on the harpsichord and viol d'amour: he has a great number of harpsichords made in different countries, which he has named according to the place they hold in his favour, after the greatest of the Italian painters. His first favourite is a piano forte, made at Florence in the year 1730, on which is written Rafael d'Urbino; then, Coreggio, Titian, Guido, etc. He played a considerable time upon his Raphael, with great judgment and delicacy, and has composed several elegant pieces for that instrument. The next in favour is a harpsichord given him by the late Queen of Spain, who was Scarlatti's scholar, both in Portugal and Spain; it was for this princess that Scarlatti made his first two books of lessons. . . .

"Signor Farinelli was very conversable and communicative, and talked over old times very freely, particularly those when in England; and I am inclined to believe, that his life were it well written, would be very interesting to the public, as it has been much chequered, and spent in the first courts of Europe; but, as I hope it is yet far from finished, this seems not to be the place to attempt it. . . ." Some doubt was cast on the truth of Burney's whole account by the discovery of a letter from a certain William Parsons, an English harpsichord-player of some repute, written from Bologna to a friend in Rome in 1772. In this, among other matters, the Englishman remarks: "I had almost forgotten to mention that everything said by Doctor Burney in his book about Signor Carlo Broschi is a tissue of lies, and the Signor Padre Maestro (Martini) never introduced him to him at all. . . ." It seems probable, however, that it is Parsons who was telling the lies, perhaps out of spite towards Burney, who failed to mention him in his 'History of Music'; and it is significant that neither Farinelli nor Padre Martini, who lived respectively until 1782 and 1784, ever attempted to correct the statements made by Burney, which they must certainly have seen.

A less sunny account of Farinelli's later years is that of Casanova, who writes: "At this point, the Electress of Saxony arrived in

Bologna, with the sole object of seeing the famous soprano Farinelli. He gave the princess an excellent luncheon, after which he played an air of his composition on the piano. I was present at the performance, and saw, not without surprise, the electress rushing ecstatically to embrace the singer; she told him, in a state of exaltation, that henceforth she could die content, for she had heard him. . . . Farinelli, at this time, was an old man of about seventy; he was in good health, but idleness made him bored and boring.

"One day while I was speaking to him of Spain, he burst into tears; his heart was still set on the high position he had lost. Ambition is a passion livelier even than avarice. Yet the sorrows of Farinelli had another cause, which he hid so well that in the end he died of it. He had married his nephew, the heir of all his fortune, to a young girl of good family and great beauty; and, old and worn-out though he was, poor Farinelli fell in love with his nephew's wife—and, what was worse still, was jealous of the nephew. The fair niece made but a poor response to such a passion with white hair; how could an aged, wrinkled creature such as the soprano dare to take the place of a young and ardent husband, who could serve her as much as she liked in every way? The thing was ridiculous. And what was even more ridiculous, was that Farinelli, enraged by the contempt with which he was treated, sent his nephew off on a voyage and shut the young wife up in her apartments; fearing to lose sight of her, he never left the house."

The whole of this passage seems suspect at first sight, and is not made the more convincing by a quite fallacious account (omitted here) of the reasons why Farinelli left Spain. In the first place, it is barely credible that Farinelli, in giving a luncheon for an Electress, should have invited such a character as Casanova; and Corrado Ricci has dug out some interesting evidence, that seems to throw light on the reality of the affair. Galeati, the same diarist who had recorded Farinelli's arrival in Bologna to take up residence, has an entry for February 9th, 1771: "Prince Xavier Augustus of Saxony . . . with his wife of the house of Spinuzzi of Fermo, arrived from Florence incognito under the name of —— and took lodgings at the inn of S. Marco"—at which Casanova, too, was staying, at the time. The diarist goes on to record that a gala concert was got up in honour of the prince, despite his disguise, and of the two young princes of Holstein-Eutin who were being educated at Bologna, for which a number of singers and musicians were collected from various neighbouring towns; the opera-house at Bologna was apparently not functioning, but a season was in progress at Reggio d'Emilia, not far away. It seems not unlikely that Farinelli would have attended, and that it was then that Casanova heard him play; and, as will have been noticed, the lady was far below an Electress in rank, being the morganatic wife of a prince who was not even the heir apparent. Others, it is true, have supposed that it was the famous bluestocking ex-Electress Maria Antonia, who was in Italy in 1772 : yet the evidence points to the other explanation.

With regard to Farinelli's supposed infatuation for his nephew's wife, Casanova appears to have been indulging in pure fabrication, to judge from the provisions of the singer's will. This long and elaborate document, dated February 20th, 1782, deals at length with the marriage of Farinelli's nephew, Don Matteo Pisani, "the son of Don Giovan. Domenico Pisani, *razionale della Regia Camera di Napoli,* and my sister Donna Dorothea Broschi"; "I condescended to lend myself to the renewed instances made me by distinguished persons far and near, to give ear to the various proposals of marriage made to the aforementioned Don Matteo Pisani, with the aim of doing good to relatives and friends. On this occasion, defending myself with my constant maxim of not letting myself in for anything, or of standing bail for events and for reciprocal good relations between the parties to the marriage; and finally with the conviction that each of them would know how to perform their duty, and at the same time to provide me in the last years of my life (in which I have done good to others) with the presence of company of the persons who should be grateful to me for the good which I did them without any obligation to do so, and on the basis of the good behaviour and good education which they boasted of to me: for these reasons I agreed to the marriage of Don Matteo Pisani with the Signora Anna Gatteschi, subject to the cautions, conditions and reservations set out in my hand in a document of June 13th, 1768, which begins as follows: 'In Dei Nomine Amen. I agree with full satisfaction to the marriage which Don Matteo Pisani wishes to contract, etc.' Which document, sealed with my arms in red sealing-wax of Spain, is deposited with their original marriage-deeds in the Archives of Pistoja; and of this marriage there was born in this my country house Maria Carlotta Pisani, held by me in holy baptism and provided with a dowry according to the Act of the notary Sig. Lorenzo Gamberini. . . ."

A certain nuance of righteous indignation can be read between these lines; and from the continuation of the will it is evident that Farinelli both disliked and mistrusted his niece: "In order to spare the same Don Matteo Pisani the fatigue of thought and anxiety inseparable from marital, family, and other claims [*seduzioni*], I command and will that neither Siga. Donna Anna Gatteschi his wife, nor any other member of the Gatteschi family shall directly or indirectly have any access, management, disposal or influence on any part of my fortune." He goes on to observe that the niece's dowry had never in fact been paid, but that he will not further labour the point, and implied that her extravagance would in any event have rapidly dissipated the sum.

The Pisanis, in fourteen years of marriage, had had only the one daughter, and to her, in the last instance, all Farinelli's fortune was to go; if Matteo Pisani predeceased his wife, the widow, on condition of not remarrying, was to receive an annual pension of 1,200 Bolognese pounds. "I leave to the Siga. Anna Gatteschi", adds Farinelli, "all that I have given her during my life as listed in an inventory drawn up by me in 1775, I say 1775; all of which is to remain in her possession, save the diamond ring in the shape of a heart, a rosary of gold, and a chocolate-pot, cup and saucer."

It is difficult to interpret the querulous reiteration of the date 1775, and two of the items excepted by Farinelli from his presents to his niece can have had little else than sentimental value; it is just possible that he had nourished a hopeless passion for the lady, which had afterwards turned to bitterness. A typical quarrel between in-laws seems, however, much the most likely explanation.

Metastasio died early in 1782, and his correspondence with Farinelli, maintained over six decades, was at last cut off. The latter continued, during the short remainder of life allotted him, to write to his friend's young and brilliant protégée, Signora Martinez (of whom Burney thought so highly), speaking nostalgically of old times when he and the poet were still earning their laurels; but on September 16th he, too, suddenly died. He was buried with much pomp at the nearby church of the Capucin monks; but his tomb did not long survive. When Napoleon invaded Italy, the monastery was secularised and the church pulled down; and even the exact position of his grave was soon forgotten. His villa, however, is still in existence, though the suburbs of Bologna have spread out all round it and encroached upon its privacy.

Farinelli, incidentally, shares with Maria Malibran the distinction of being one of the only two opera-singers about whom an opera has ever been written; he appears, too, among the dramatis personae of Auber's 'La Part du Diable', whose libretto is one of Scribe's oddest effusions. The other work, with music by Barnett, was given at Drury Lane in 1839; the title-role—vocally, one would have thought, more suitable for a woman—was allotted to a tenor, and was taken by the composer Balfe. The plot deals with Farinelli's miraculous cure of King Philip, but makes his return to Italy immediately after effecting it, instead of remaining in Spain for twenty-two years as in fact he did. As a specimen of this dramatic curiosity may be quoted the singer's opening words:

> 'Gia riede primavera,'
> In Spain's fair capital behold us!
> Our entré, in good sooth, is most auspicious.
> What charming weather!

The reference to the weather is explained by the stage directions, which specify that it is pouring with rain.

CARESTINI, Giovanni (Cusanino)

This singer was born at Monte Filottrano near Ancona in 1705 —the same year as Farinelli. He made his début at Rome in 1721, in Buononcini's 'Griselda', and was an immediate success; and in 1723 he was invited to Prague for the almost unbelievably lavish celebrations in honour of the coronation of the Emperor Charles VI. The opera—Fux's 'Costanza e Fortezza'—was performed in the open air, with vast orchestras and choruses rather in the manner of the Verona amphitheatre today, and the soloists had to exert themselves very greatly to be heard at all.

In 1728–9, Carestini was at Naples in company with Bernacchi; they fought like cat and dog, and it was Carestini who came off the better of the two—either because, or in spite of, the fact that he was much the younger man. In 1733, Handel heard both Carestini and Farinelli at Bologna, and chose the former, while the 'opera of the nobility', Handel's deadly enemies, grabbed the more famous singer. Carestini remained in England until 1735, earning great applause.[1] "His person", according to Burney, "was tall, beautiful, and majestic. He was a very animated and intelligent actor; and having a considerable portion of enthusiasm in his composition, with a lively and inventive imagination, he rendered everything he sung interesting by good taste, energy, and judicious embellishments. He manifested great agility in the execution of difficult divisions from the chest in a most articulate and admirable manner." His voice was an exceptionally deep and rich contralto. "Metastasio", says Vernon Lee, "let his conception of a part be influenced by the individuality of the performer. Thus in his passionate proud Aetius we can recognise the superbly strong and florid Carestini."

[1] He appeared in a number of Handel's operas, among them 'Arianna', 'Il pastor fido', 'Ottone Re di Germania', 'Ariodante' and 'Alcina'. It was in the latter work that he was to sing the aria 'Verdi prati', but refused to, on the grounds that it did not suit his voice; at which Handel is said to have exclaimed "You tog! Don't I know petter as yourself vaat es pest for you to sing? If you vill not sing all de song vaat I give you, I vill not pay you ein stiver!"

After his return to Italy, Carestini entered into negotiations with the management of the Teatro S. Angelo at Naples (for the San Carlo was not yet opened), and showed that a considerable portion of the enthusiasm, attributed to him by Burney, was directed towards himself. "To have the good fortune of serving this city," he writes, "you will give me eight hundred doubloons of Spain, otherwise I pray you to leave me at liberty; for I have other contracts waiting to be concluded, and I hope that you will not want to harm my interests. For you know very well that today in Italy I am unequalled (solo), and can earn one thousand one hundred doubloons. . . ." He proceeds to insinuate that, for him to be really satisfied, his *onorario* should be made up to that figure by the addition of a travelling allowance.

On receiving this none too modest epistle, Carasale, the impresario at Naples, angrily remarked: ". . . he should remember that we have Caffarelli . . . and for *his* onorario he asks only five hundred doubloons; and he should also remember that he is no longer the Carestini that he used to be, for he has lost much of his voice." The latter comment was probably pure spite; but in any case Carestini did not get the job, and sang in Bologna instead, with Amorevoli and Salimbeni.

Carestini did, however, sing at Naples the following year, in Sarro's 'Alessandro nell'Indie' and Leo's 'Farnace'; he pleased the public, but not the powers that be, who found him 'intolerably insolent', though in quite what way is not recorded. After, this date, he sang for many years in the principal cities of Italy, with great success, until the year 1755 when he went to Germany, scoring a great success in Berlin in Graun's 'Orfeo' (1752), though Frederick the Great does not seem to have liked him very well, and his health was bad; and from there to Russia. Returning from St Petersburg to Italy in 1758, he retired, and died at the place where he was born in 1760. His pseudonym, relatively little used, is said to have been derived from the noble family of Cusani, who patronised and encouraged him at the outset of his career.

CECCHI, Domenico (Cortona)

It was not until the 1670's or thereabouts, when opera-houses became widespread throughout Italy, and common in Germany, that something approaching the modern international star system could begin to arise. It soon became a well-organised and lucrative business; and among the first to take advantage of it was the generation of singers born around the year 1650.

Of these, one of the most famous was Cortona, born in the town of that name in Tuscany about the middle of the seventeenth century, or a little later. His début was at the Teatro dei Formagliari, Bologna, in 1673, in an opera called 'Nino' by an unknown composer; and soon afterwards he became attached to the court of the music-loving Duke of Mantua.

At Mantua, he felt the bitterness of his situation; for, according to d'Ancillon, "one of the principal musicians of the Duke of Mantua, called Cortona, having wished to marry a very pretty musician in the same Prince's service, called Barbaruccia, they were obliged to ask permission to do so of the Pope, who refused it absolutely and without return."[1] This was possibly the tiresomely puritanical 'Papa Minga' (Innocent XI), who was so inexorable a foe of music and musicians in every form; in any event, Cortona soon came under the protection of Queen Christina at Rome, and any enemy of the Pope's was a friend of hers. He also, perhaps disgusted with women, became for a time the favourite *mignon* of Gian Gastone de' Medici, subsequently the last native Grand Duke of Tuscany. He may, too, perhaps be identified with the castrato Cecchino de' Castris, who obtained such an ascendancy over Gian Gastone's brother Ferdinand, so that the latter's wife, Violante Beatrice of Bavaria, was heard to remark, "I would marvel greatly if matters were properly conducted at Court, while they are regulated by a *castrone*." Things

---

[1] He is said to have written, in the margin of the petition, the words "che si castri meglio".

got to such a pass, that the Prince's father, the Grand Duke
Cosimo III, was reduced to approaching his son on the subject of
his extravagances via the castrato, who, says Harold Acton in
'The Last Medici', "took upon himself to promise that the
Prince should in future be obedient . . . a treaty was thus entered
into between the Grand Duke and Hereditary Prince with a
eunuch as guarantee of its observance."

In 1688, Cortona went to Munich, where he sang with great
success; and, returning to Italy, he obtained an even greater
triumph at the great annual fair of Reggio d'Emilia, of which
operas formed an important part, and where he sang in Ballarotti's
'La Caduta de' Decemviri'. He became proverbial for his acting
in the part of a lover.

Cortona seems to have been something of a tough customer;
for when he came to Naples in 1697 the following circumstance is
reported of him: "When the carnival was over, and the theatre
shut, an Englishman came to Naples bringing with him a bear,
with which he played many amusing tricks. The Englishman
wanted a room in which to present himself to the public, and,
very sensibly, thought that that of S. Bartolommeo (the predecessor of the S. Carlo theatre) would suit him very well. He went to
the theatre, found the *musico* Cortona, who lived with the others
in one of the adjoining apartments, and told him of his wishes.
Cortona got in a rage, and accused him of gross insolence in
daring to think of 'so magnificent and royal a theatre for the
vulgar buffooneries of an animal'. The poor Englishman, thus
insulted, gave as good as he got. Whereupon Cortona ordered
his servants to break his head in; and they did so, with blows and
the flats of their swords. The Englishman was carried, seriously
injured, to the Hospital of S. Giacomo. Cortona, who prided
himself on the business as if he had been a great prince, and
defended his servants 'who had only carried out his orders', was
taken by the Spanish patrol to the guardroom of the Palace; but
from there he escaped (or, some say, was allowed to escape by
the Viceroy) and returned to his own country." This Viceroy
was the Duke of Medinaceli, protector of the prima donna known

as la Giorgina[1]; and it seems not impossible that the 'Barbaruccia' whom Cortona had attempted to marry was her sister Barbara Voglia (for the date of his application to the Pope is unknown). This would have accounted for the Viceroy's clemency to him.

After a short but brilliantly successful visit to Vienna, Cortona sang in Venice in 1707, in Gasparini's 'Flavio Anicio Olibrio' and after this retired to his native town, where he died in 1717.

CONTI, Gioacchino (Gizziello)

Gizziello, one of the most admired contemporaries of Farinelli and Caffarelli, was the very antithesis of everything that a castrato is popularly supposed to be. Far from being boastful and self-assertive, he carried timidity and diffidence almost to excess; so much so that, when he first heard Farinelli sing, he fainted away from despondency. He felt he could never bring himself to sing again, after hearing a master whom he considered so superior to himself; and it took all Farinelli's encouragement[2] and powers of persuasion to induce him to fulfil his engagement, which he finally did with the greatest success.

Gizziello was born at Arpino, about half-way between Rome and Naples, in 1714, and is alleged to have been castrated as a baby to save him from severe illness; but this is an oft-told tale, and one to be taken with a pinch of salt. At any event, he was taken to Naples at the age of eight, and placed under Domenico Gizzi, himself an eminent singer, with whom he studied seven years, and whose name he took for his usual pseudonym.

Gizziello's début was at the Teatro delle Dame, Rome, in 1730, in Vinci's 'Artaserse'; he caused an immense sensation, which reached the ears of Caffarelli—and, if the story is true, prompted that umbrageous virtuoso to one of his rare acts of generosity. The famous singer travelled post haste to Rome and went straight to the theatre, which he entered incognito. Gizziello sang, and

---

[1] See page 29.
[2] Which he freely gave, though he was engaged by the rival company.

Caffarelli cried in a loud voice: "Bravo, bravissimo, Gizziello! è Caffarelli che ti lo dice!", after which he left the theatre, and returned directly to Naples. Yet when the management of the San Carlo, a few years later, invited Gizziello to sing for a season there in Caffarelli's stead, he did not dare to go for fear of his possible spite.

Gizziello went to London in 1736, to sing in Handel's 'Ariodante', on which occasion he first heard Farinelli. "His voice", says Burney, "was then a very high soprano, and his style remarkable for pathos, delicacy, and refinement." His manner of singing is said to have had a considerable effect in modernising the character of Handel's opera arias, in the direction of the lighter Neapolitan style.

In 1743, Gizziello was invited to Lisbon, where he remained, with occasional visits elsewhere, for the next ten years (including one visit to Naples in 1747, by which time he must have overcome his fear of Caffarelli).[1] He left Lisbon in 1753, and did *not* return to take part in the celebrated performances of 1755 for the opening of the new theatre; which renders impossible the picturesque and much-quoted story that, appalled by the destruction and terror of the Lisbon earthquake, he henceforth shunned the world, and retired into a monastery. He does in fact seem to have retired in 1753, shortly on returning from Lisbon, first to his native town and then to Rome, where he became more and more addicted

[1] The two singers were heard together in a setting (probably Jommelli's) of 'Achille in Sciro'—and argument raged as to which was the better—apart from some other compositions. Mann, writing from Florence, relates that "our second opera begins on Sunday, and will be acted in a hurry, to give time to Caffarelli to get to Naples by the latter end of October, to prepare for the great Cantata which is to be performed among the proposed rejoicings for the birth of the Duke of Calabria . . . the Cantata is to be a Duo by Caffarelli and Egiziello, and a trio, by adding Babbi. Caffarelli swears he will make Egiziello sing out of tune. . . ." In a later letter he adds, "You have heard of the great doings at Naples, and the rivalship between Caffarelli and Egiziello, which luckily did not, as was expected, disturb the festa. Upon Caffarelli's arrival at Naples, Egiziello went to make him a visit, and was received by that saucy creature upon a stool, where he sat during the whole visit. The affair was made up by mediators and afterwards they appeared good friends."

to religion, but the reason seems to have been ill-health. He had never been strong, and according to Mann had narrowly missed dying at Florence in 1742, on which occasion he had ingeniously taken advantage of the *da capo* arias by leaving out all the repeats to save his strength. On the eve of his retirement he was said to be singing better than ever, and amazed everyone by his performance in Perez' 'Didone abandonata'. He died in Rome in 1761.

CRESCENTINI, Girolamo

Crescentini, one of the last great castrati, was born at Urbania near Urbino, in the Marches, in 1762; but, apart from this fact, little seems to be known about his early life. He studied at Bologna, and made his début at Rome in 1783, at the age of twenty-one—rather later in life than the average castrato. He followed up this first appearance with visits to other Italian cities, and was brought over to England the following year; but, says Lord Mount Edgcumbe, he "was thought so moderate a performer, and so little liked, that before the season was half over, he was superseded by Tenducci". The Englishman, however, adds in extenuation: "It is but fair to Crescentini to add, that when he was here he was very young, and had not attained that excellence which has since gained him the reputation of a first-class singer." Londoners had no opportunity of modifying their opinion, for Crescentini never returned to England.

On the Continent, however, the young singer made rapid headway, being admired for his sweet, pure, and agile voice and his expressive singing: he wanted only a degree more of power to have made him the equal of Pacchierotti, and soon came to be thought absolutely superior to Marchesi, at least by all who valued taste, judgment and spontaneity above mechanical brilliance and execution. Crescentini had a great success in Naples in various operas, among them Guglielmi's 'Enea e Lavinia', singing as a rule with David, the most famous tenor of his day; at Bologna in 1791 in Borghi's 'La morte di Semiramide'; at Venice, and elsewhere. In 1795, again at Bologna, we read that "On June 6th, in this theatre [the Communale] was given the benefit performance for the famous singer Signor Girolamo Crescentini, who on this occasion received from the whole theatre, not only repeated and well-deserved applause, but also more tangible evidence of the esteem in which his rare skill and knowledge is held; for this was one of the most profitable benefits that ever was given in this city." Soon after this, governments might well have regarded this castrato as the prophet of doom. In Milan, in January 1796, he created the hero's role in Zingarelli's 'Giulietta e Romeo', to immense applause, and by May the Austrian viceroy had fled, and the French had occupied the city: the following winter, in Venice, he starred in another notable première—that of Cimarosa's 'Orazii'—and again, by May, the Republic had fallen, and the French were in command. Nothing daunted, he adopted Romeo and Curiazio as his favourite roles and sang them constantly throughout his career, both in Italy and elsewhere.

There is a pleasing anecdote of Crescentini, again in Venice, at the very end of the eighteenth century. The impresario Crivelli and the managing committee of the Fenice theatre were at loggerheads as to the artists who should be engaged for the forthcoming carnival; Crivelli wanted to spend money on a first-rate prima donna, preferably the Grassini,[1] while the *Presidenza* was in favour of engaging a first-rate castrato. Eventually the impresario gave in, and Crescentini was engaged, though very much against the grain as far as Crivelli was concerned. At the first rehearsal, Crescentini was prodigal of *fioriture*, and Crivelli was heard to complain: "With all this agility, where does the singing come

---

[1] Giuseppa Grassini, the celebrated contralto who afterwards caused such a sensation in London, particularly when she sang with Mrs Billington in Winter's 'Il ratto di Proserpina'. Crescentini did actually sing with her at Venice, in Cimarosa's 'Orazii' and other works. Among other successes of Crescentini's about this period were: Cherubini's 'Artaserse' at Livorno; Sarti's 'Didone abandonata' at Padua; and Tarchi's 'Il ritorno di Bacco dall'Indie' at Turin.

in?" "But surely agility is an essential part of singing?" replied the *musico*.

The impresario said nothing at the time; but, when Crescentini came to sign his contract, he found it so covered with writing that only a minute space remained free, and this too was inky. "With all this ink," said Crescentini, "where am I expected to sign?" "You'll admit, though, that ink is an essential part of the business?"—and Crivelli was much pleased at his own smartness.

The singer, seeing the point, remarked, "I know the essential part of the business, as far as you are concerned, is the graces of the prima donna."

"Better profit by her graces, than by another's disgrace."

"I daresay you know a remedy for my disgrace—to substitute yourself for what I lack."

Soon after this, Crescentini went to Lisbon where he remained four years, as singer and a director of the opera. He returned to Milan, where he was applauded in Mayr's "Alonso e Cora' and Federici's 'Ifigenia in Aulide', and then went on to Vienna, where he earned the praises of the 'Allgemeine Musikalische Zeitung' and of the youthful Schopenhauer, who wrote in his diary: "His supernaturally beautiful voice cannot be compared with that of any woman: there can be no fuller and more beautiful tone, and in its silver purity he yet achieves indescribable power . . .", etc. He was still in Vienna in 1805 when the French occupied the city, and it was there that Napoleon heard him, was enchanted by his voice, made him Knight of the Iron Cross of Lombardy, and invited him to Paris. The singer arrived in 1806, and remained six years in France, during which time he sang incessantly at the Tuileries before the glittering *parvenu* audiences of the Imperial Court; and it is strange that one of the last of the castrati should have been the first really to conquer France. "It will be remembered," says Fétis, "that at the court of Napoleon, which was never thought excessively given to sensibility, this virtuoso reduced the prince, the courtiers, and all the assembly to tears when he sang in the role of Romeo."

Alfred de Vigny, in his 'La canne de jonc', has a description of a performance at the court theatre, which is worth quoting not only for its reference to Crescentini, but for its ludicrous picture of the etiquette so laboriously mastered and observed by the Emperor's vassals, who were none the less subservient for being called kings and princes: "As soon as I arrived in Paris, I determined to see the Emperor. I had the chance to do so at the court theatre, to which I was taken . . . it was at the Tuileries. We took our seats in a little box opposite the imperial box, and waited. There was no one in the theatre so far, save the kings. Each of them was sitting in one of the first row of boxes, surrounded by his court, and in front of them were their aides-de-camp and the generals with whom they were on familiar terms. The kings of Westphalia, Saxony, and Württemberg, and all the princes of the Confederation of the Rhine, were in the same row. Near them was Murat, King of Naples, standing, speaking loudly and quickly, and shaking his black hair . . . further away were the King of Spain and, very much by himself, the Russian Ambassador, Prince Kourakine, with diamond epaulettes. The *parterre* was filled with a crowd of generals, dukes, princes, colonels, and senators; above them were everywhere the naked arms and uncovered shoulders of the court ladies.

"The box surmounted by an eagle was still empty; we watched it without ceasing. After some time, the kings got up, and remained standing. The Emperor came into his box alone, walking quickly, threw himself into his seat, and looked about through his eyeglass; then he remembered that the whole audience was standing and awaiting a look from him, nodded his head twice, brusquely and ungraciously, and allowed the queens and the kings to sit down. . . . Crescentini was singing 'Les Horaces',[1] with a seraph's voice that came from an emaciated and wrinkled face. The orchestra was soft and weak, by order of the Emperor; who perhaps wished, like the Spartans, to be appeased by the music, rather than excited. . . ."

In 1812, Crescentini asked Napoleon for leave to return to

[1] This performance of Cimarosa's opera took place on January 18th, 1810: the first public performance of the work in France was not, however, till 1813.

Italy, as the climate of France was injurious to his health; and the Emperor, most unwillingly, was induced to grant it. Crescentini established himself at Rome, where he stayed until 1816, apparently no longer singing, at any rate in public. In the latter year he went to Naples, where he taught singing for many years at the Royal College of S. Pietro a Majella; he found the institution in a sorry state, and bitterly complained to Spohr, who visited Naples in 1816, about the decline in the musical standards. There, in 1846, he eventually died, at the respectable age of eighty-four.

Besides his prowess as a singer, Crescentini is sometimes credited with the composition of several arias, particularly the once-famous 'Ombra adorata aspetta' in Zingarelli's 'Giulietta e Romeo'. It seems, however, improbable that the singer did more, at the most, than indicate to Zingarelli what kind of aria he wanted at some point in the drama, a practice then common among influential virtuosi.

DAL PRATO, Vincenzo

Mozart's 'molto amato castrato Dal Prato' was born at Imola, near Forli, in 1756, studied with Lorenzo Gibelli, and made his début at the small town of Fano, in the Marches, in 1772. Invited to Stuttgart in 1779 to sing in honour of the Russian Crown Prince, afterwards the Emperor Paul I, Dal Prato was spotted there by one of the Elector of Bavaria's talent scouts, and immediately secured for Munich.

Dal Prato sang constantly at the Bavarian capital between 1780 and 1805, and there in 1781 created the part of Idamante in Mozart's 'Idomeneo'. A gentle, agreeable, and good-looking man, he was beloved by all; his singing was admired for its grace and polished execution, though it was never remarkable for power or dramatic qualities. With his essentially intimate gifts, he made a particularly good 'serious lover' in comic operas, and was fond of singing such roles, in which he could temper his lyricism with some nicely-judged touches of comedy.

After his retirement, Dal Prato continued to live in Munich, on a pension from the Elector, until his death in about 1828, remaining in touch with all the latest musical developments, and being horrified by the vocal writing in Beethoven's 'Missa Solennis', though he understood and admired the composer's genius.

FERRI, Baldassare

This remarkable man, who can be called the first of all the star castrati, was born at Perugia in about 1610, and at the age of eleven entered the service of the wealthy dilettante Cardinal Crescenzi at Orvieto. Ferri stayed with him until 1625, when he took up a stage career, with enormous success.

He was tall, handsome, and very attractive to women, and was fêted everywhere he went; it is related that, when he went to Florence to sing in an opera of Monteverdi, he was received three miles from the city gates by a numerous cortège of the town's most eminent citizens, and escorted in triumph through the streets to his lodging.

After this, he went to Poland, and sang for three of its kings— Sigismund III, Ladislas VII, and John Casimir. During the reign of the first of these monarchs, Queen Christina wrote to him, though their respective countries were at war, begging him to allow her Ferri for a fortnight, since she had heard so much about him and would give anything to hear him. Her request was granted, and the singer was passed between the lines of the opposing armies, an armistice being declared for the occasion, and was received in Stockholm with extraordinary enthusiasm, a medal being struck in his honour.

In 1655, Ferri was invited to the court of Vienna, and stayed there twenty years,[1] after which he retired, immensely rich, to

[1] The Emperor Leopold I had the singer's portrait hanging in his bedroom, with the inscription: 'Baldassare Ferri, Re dei Musici'.

his native town. He died in 1680, leaving 600,000 scudi for a charitable institute to perpetuate his name.

A story is also related of a visit of his to London, to sing the part of Zephyrus in an opera; one night after the show, in which he had been much acclaimed, a masked woman approached him and put an enormous emerald ring on his finger, and then disappeared without a trace. The whole business, however, appears more than dubious; the character of Zephyr appears in the opera 'Psyche', with words by Shadwell and music by Locke and Draghi, but it was not produced until 1673, at which date Ferri must have been at least sixty years old—hardly an age, one would have thought, to inspire so vehement and mysterious a passion.[1] It is by no means certain, in any case, that Ferri ever came to England at all; his almost contemporary biographer, Andrea Bontempi, is much more remarkable for his imagination than his respect for accuracy, and may well have invented the whole journey.

GRIMALDI, Nicolò (Nicolino)

This great singer is historically important, not only for his own sake, but because he was, perhaps, more than any other single person responsible for the popularity of Italian opera in England, if not for its actual introduction. He was, too, the finest artist of his generation, and an altogether remarkable character.

Nicolino was born at Naples in 1673. For long, the Venetians claimed him as a compatriot, and he never personally disabused them, for, had he done so, his popularity at Venice must inevitably have suffered; but it is nevertheless certain that he was a Neapolitan. He came of a poor but respectable family; his brother Antonio-Maria became a distinguished tenor, often appearing with him in Naples, whilst his sister Caterina-Speranza

---

[1] According to another account, his performance was at Whitehall on June 3rd, 1669; but in what opera does not appear.

married the composer Fago, known from his birthplace as 'il Tarantino'.

Nicolino was something of an infant prodigy, and was early noticed by Provenzale, then the leading Neapolitan composer, who wrote a page's role into a revival of his opera 'Stellidaura'[1] (1685) specially for the boy; so that Nicolino made his début at the tender age of twelve. The maestro also took charge of his teaching, and gave him every help and encouragement in his career: at seventeen, Nicolino was given an appointment at the Cappella di Tesoro of S. Gennaro, and soon afterwards was singing at the Royal Chapel.

Meanwhile, he was by no means neglecting the stage; and before long he became identified with the success of Alessandro Scarlatti's operas, among them 'La caduta de' Decemviri' (1697), 'Muzio Scevola', and 'Il prigioniero fortunato' (both 1698). Other works in which he shone at this time were C. F. Pollarolo's 'Tito Manlio' and Manzo's 'Partenope', and he was acclaimed as much for his fine appearance and stage presence and superb acting as for his singing; in after years such theorists of opera as Algarotti were to cite him as the ideal combination of singer and actor.

In 1699, Nicolino was for the first time applauded outside Naples—at Bologna—and the following year he went to Venice, the city that was to become his second home. He remained there, with occasional visits to other towns, until 1708; and so much was he admired that, in 1705, he was awarded the title of 'Cavaliere della Croce di S. Marco' for his singing in Gasparini's 'Antioco'.

In 1708, Nicolino took the—for that time—sensational step of journeying to England, a country only just beginning to savour the charms of Italian opera. He was by no means the first Italian singer to be heard on the London stage—for Baldassare Ferri had perhaps made an isolated appearance there many years before, whilst Margherita de l'Épine had been in London since 1692[2]—

---

[1] The full title of the work was 'Difendere l'Offensore, o La Stellidaura vendicata', and it was first given probably in 1670.

[2] Siface, on his visit in 1687, does not seem to have sung in public or on the

but he was certainly the first top-ranking castrato to come over for any length of time, and but for him it is probable that the Italian opera would have proved no more than a passing vogue, as it had in France, and would have succumbed before a combination of national prejudice and the fact that it was in a language incomprehensible to the majority of the audience.

In point of fact, the first production in which Nicolino appeared, in December 1708, was in a mixture of Italian and English, as was the nationality of the participants. The opera was Alessandro Scarlatti's 'Pirro e Demetrio' (originally given at Naples in 1694) and it was a very great success, to the shocked surprise of Steele in the 'Spectator', and other persons who prided themselves on their devotion to reason and logic. No one, however, thought to ridicule Nicolino himself, and admiration of his art was general even among those who considered the opera an absurdity.

"For my own part," says Steele, "I was fully satisfied with the sight of the actor, who, by the grace and propriety of his action and gesture, does honour to the human figure. Every one will imagine I mean Signor Nicolini, who sets off the character he bears in an opera by his action, as much as he does the words of it by his voice. Every limb and every finger contributes to the part he acts, inasmuch that a deaf man may go along with him in the sense of it. There is scarce a beautiful posture in an old statue that he does not plant himself in, as the different circumstances of the story give occasion for it. He performs the most ordinary action in a manner suitable to the greatness of his character, and shows the prince even in the giving of a letter, or despatching of a messenger. . . . Our best actors are somewhat at a loss to support themselves with proper gesture, as they move

stage at all. The first castrato to fix himself in England for any length of time was Valentino Urbani: but he was not a singer of anything like the same calibre as Nicolino. Quadrio lists him as 'Musico del Duca di Mantova', and as having first appeared during the 1680's, so that he was probably born in about 1660. He is recorded as having sung at Bologna in 1691, and again in 1695 with Pistocchi, in Perti's 'Nerone fatto Cesare'.

from any considerable distance to the front of the stage; but I have seen the person of whom I am now speaking enter alone at the remotest part of it, and advance from it with such greatness of air and mien as seemed to fill the stage, and at the same time, commanded the attention of the audience with the majesty of his appearance."

After this, operas began to be performed entirely in Italian, the first being 'Almahide', with music probably by Buononcini: but Nicolino's biggest London success was in Mancini's 'Idaspe fedele', in which occurred the ridiculous scene of the *musico*'s combat with the lion—the delight of ordinary audiences, and the butt of every satirist down to Carey, in his enchanting 'Dragon of Wantley' of 1737. "This scene", says Hogarth, "must have had a most whimsical effect on the stage. Hydaspes addresses the lion in a long bravura song, 'Mostro crudel, che fai?' full of divisions and flourishes; first calling on the 'cruel monster', in a tone of defiance, to come on, and then telling him, with a sentimental air, and in a *largo* movement in the minor key, that he may tear his bosom, but shall not touch his heart, which he has kept faithful to his beloved. The exhibition of Nicolino, altern-ately vapouring and gesticulating to a poor biped in a lion's skin, then breathing a love-tale in the pseudo-monster's ear, and at last fairly throttling him on the stage, must have been ludicrous in the extreme, and sufficient to throw ridicule on the Italian opera." Doubly ludicrous, in fact, for the whole scene was generally encored, and the vanquished animal had to be revived, and slain all over again. Lady Mary Wortley Montagu, in a letter, refers rather mysteriously to the scene: "I was last Thursday at the new opera, and saw Nicolini strangle a lion with great gallantry. But he represented nakedness so naturally, I was surprised to see those ladies stare at him without any confusion, that pretend to be so violently shocked at a poor *double entendre* or two in a comedy; which convinced me that those prudes who would cry fie! fie! at the word *naked*, have no scruples about the thing."

The 'Spectator' even goes so far as to take Nicolino to task for appearing in 'Idaspe'. "I would not be thought", says Addison,

". . . to reflect upon Signor Nicolino (which is exactly what he is doing) who in acting this part only complies with the wretched taste of his audience. He knows very well that the lion has many more admirers than himself; as they say of the famous equestrian statue on the Pont Neuf at Paris, that more people go to see the horse than the king who sits upon it. On the contrary, it gives me a just indignation to see a person whose action gives new dignity to kings, resolution to heroes, and softness to lovers, thus sinking from the greatness of his behaviour, and degraded into the character of 'The London Prentice'." It is, by the way, sometimes stated that Nicolino had written the libretto of 'Idaspe' himself, as well as that of Gasparini's 'Ambleto'; but this is not strictly accurate. Nicolino was directing the Haymarket Theatre, and his name was therefore printed on the librettos of operas presented there; but the former drama was actually by Cicognini, and the latter by Zeno and Pariati. Nicolino, of course, may have revised them.

In 1711, Handel arrived in London, and produced his 'Rinaldo' with enormous success, despite many absurdities in the *mise-en-scène*. Nicolino was among the cast, and is portrayed by Addison "exposed to a tempest in robes of ermine, and sailing in an open boat upon a sea of paste-board". The following year, the singer returned to Venice, where he performed to rapturous applause in Albinoni's 'Gare generose', Gasparini's 'La verità nell'inganno', and other works. A contemporary notice reads as follows: "A few days ago, the most virtuous Cavalier Nicolino Grimaldi returned here, after we had sighed for him for many years, during which time, with the harmony of his more than earthly voice, he has been the idol of the first courts of Europe, and at that of England has earned an excess of graces from H.M. the Queen. It is said that, along with other valuable gifts, he has brought with him from London a most singular and priceless jewel whose quality we shall never know; we shall hear more certainly about it, perhaps, when he has recovered his health, for at present he keeps his bed."

This so-called 'jewel' was none other than the staff of St Joseph, "which flowered when he became betrothed to the Most Holy

Virgin", which Nicolino had somehow acquired while in England, and which became his most treasured possession. "Every year," according to a chronicler, "at the recurrence of the Saint's festival, he used to exhibit it in his own house, with the most excellent solemnity of ceremony and music."

Nicolino made a visit to Naples in 1713, and in the following year returned to London for a brief period, singing in a revival of the favourite 'Idaspe', in Handel's 'Amadigi di Gaule', and in 'Clearco', a *pasticcio*; but he soon returned to Venice, where he performed in Albinoni's 'Eumene', Buononcini's 'Astianatte', and Gasparini's 'Arsace'. Back in Naples in 1718, he was heard in Sarro's 'La fede ne' tradimenti' and 'Arsace', and in the *serenata* 'L'Andromeda' with Marianna Benti-Bulgarelli and Matteuccio.

The next few years were divided between Venice and Naples. In the former city he had a great success singing with Vittoria Tesi in Pollarolo's 'Arminio', and in the latter he was applauded in Leo's 'Arianna e Teseo' (1721). He took part, too, in the first performance of Metastasio's celebrated drama 'Didone abbandonata', set on this occasion, by Sarro: Nicolino singing Aeneas, Benti-Bulgarelli Dido, and the tenor Annibalino, Iarba.

By this time, Nicolino's voice was past its prime: but he continued to be admired for his superb acting and deportment, and to be given leading roles. He sang in Venice up till the year 1730, in which he performed in Vinci's 'Siroe Re di Persia' and Orlandini's 'Massiminiano'. The following year, at the age of fifty-eight, he was engaged for Naples, to perform in Pergolesi's 'La Salustia', and his name is printed in the libretto as taking part; but in fact he did not do so. After a quarrel with the impresario, he withdrew, and before it could be patched up, he had taken to his bed with a severe illness. He never recovered from it, and in January 1732 he died.

His will, a lengthy and verbose document dated January 1st, and dictated *in extremis,* contains the most minute directions for the disposal of his considerable possessions; and among its provisions is the following: "Item. Sig. Cav. D. Nicolò leaves to the

5.   GIOVANNI CARESTINI
from the portrait by Knapton

said Sig. Nicola Fago his brother-in-law, out of the love which he bears him, the famous relic of the Staff of St Joseph, which he obtained with so many hardships in England and removed from the hands of heretics, and which he has always kept in his house with so much veneration, solemnising his festival every year: beseeching and charging the said S.N. his brother-in-law to keep it in his house and to celebrate the festival in honour of the said glorious saint every year." He further gave instructions that Fago, on his death, should leave the relic to the Church; and this he must have done, for the staff is still to be seen at Naples, in the church of Real Monte.

It would, incidentally, seem superfluous to warn against confusing Nicolino with the composer Giuseppe Niccolini (1762–1842), in whose operas Velluti had such brilliant success, but for the fact that certain writers have done so.

GROSSI, Giovanni Francesco (Siface)

Siface, who with Cortona and Matteuccio formed a kind of musical trinity in the late seventeenth century, was born at a place called Uzzanese Chiesina, not far from Pistoia in Tuscany, in 1653. After studying at Loreto with Tommaso Redi of Siena, one of the foremost teachers of the day, he made his début at the Tordinona Theatre, Rome, in 1672. From 1675 to 1677, he must have interrupted his stage career, for he sang in the Papal chapel, but soon afterwards he entered the service of Francesco II d'Este, Duke of Modena.

It was at Venice in 1678 that he earned his nickname, from his success in the part of Siface (Syphax) in Cavalli's 'Scipione Africano'. He was again in Venice in 1680, singing in Augustini's 'Il Ratto delle Sabine', but soon returned again to Modena; for the Duke was constantly complaining that Siface was never there when wanted.

However, he soon got away again, and arrived in Rome. The Modenese representative, one Ercole Panciroli, in a letter of

5

October 19th, speaks of "the satisfaction of Christina of Sweden at having obtained Siface for her theatre", and, in another letter of the following February, he adds: "At every aria which he sings, the whole theatre resounds with applause, and cries of 'viva, viva'." Siface returned to Modena, where he seems to have stayed until the summer of 1683, having appeared earlier that year in the particularly splendid production of Pallavicino's 'Bassiano, o Il maggior impossibile'. He then returned to Rome and was put up by Cardinal Maidalchini—his prestige was by this time surprisingly great, and he was treated almost as a great nobleman—meaning to stay some time, and then go on to Naples, where he was engaged for the winter season. However, a passage of arms with the French Ambassador (whose brother, Cardinal d'Estrées, was a power in the ecclesiastical government) cut his visit short. In Panciroli's account, "When he arrived in Rome, they say that . . . the French Ambassador, who was anxious for him to sing in his forthcoming *serenata*, had him invited to this function; but when he left the Palace, it was reported to the ambassador that he (Siface) had said that he wanted doubloons for his singing, and not merely ices, which was all one ever got from the French." The affair made a great stir, the ambassador was furious, and Siface thought it prudent to leave in a hurry, and take refuge with his master at Modena.

The Duke, fearing political capital might be made out of the business, kept Siface confined to his quarters for some time (though he was never actually imprisoned, as legend would have it); but in the end the ambassador's rage abated, and, not wishing to look foolish, he wrote in person to Modena asking that Siface be released. By this time, the singer was urgently awaited in Naples, for rehearsals to begin; to reach that city, he had once more to pass through Rome, and Panciroli was in agonies of anxiety lest some further incident should occur. "Siface arrived on his way to Naples," he writes, "and I did not miss the opportunity of giving him a severe lecture, telling him to keep his mouth shut and not to discuss, whether for good or ill, the things that have happened; and to bear in mind the mortification these people have suffered, and even more the kind of people they are. He promised to do as I said, but I still hope he will leave here as soon as possible." In fact, nothing untoward happened, and Siface arrived safely at Naples.

His first appearance there was in Alessandro Scarlatti's 'Pompeo', and his success was immediate and prodigious; so much so that the Viceroy humbled himself to write a most obsequious letter to Modena, begging the Duke to extend the singer's leave of absence. This, however, Francesco d'Este refused to grant: he was determined to have his money's worth out of Siface, and ordered him to return by the date originally laid down. However, Siface returned to Naples again for the season of 1685–6, singing in Provenzale's 'Stellidaura', which was also incidentally, Nicolino's début. Again in 1686, Siface went to Florence, where he was heard in an opera called 'Cneo Marzio Coriolano', whose composer does not seem to be recorded: and on his return to Modena, he found a much longer journey awaiting him. He was to be sent to London, to entertain Mary of Modena, Queen of England and sister of his ducal master. The passport with which he was provided is an amusing instance of the official verbiage of the day, and shows also the somewhat exaggerated respect with which the singer was treated—enough, one would have thought, to have turned the head of the most sensible of men, which Siface most certainly was not: "Mandando Noi in Inghilterra per servire alla Maestà della Regina d'Inghilterra Nostra Sorella, Giov. Francesco Grossi detto Siface Nostro Musico, a Londra, abbiamo voluto accompagnarlo del presente Nostro Passaporte, in virtù del quale preghiamo i Regi, Potenti, Principi e loro Ministri, per li di cui Regni, Provincie e Stati gli occorre di transitare, a lasciarlo non solo libero e speditamente passare si nell'andare, come nel ritorno, con suo compagno, cavalli, servitore, robe ed armi; ma di fargli inoltre compartire tutte le grazie ed assistenze possibili in caso di suo bisogno, sicuri di rendersi sempre più verso di Loro obbligata la nostra ossequissima corrispondenza. Le stesso comandiamo che facciano li Ministri Ufficiali e sudditi nostri per quanto stimano la Grazia Nostra." In addition to this, he was provided with considerable sums of money, and numerous letters of recommendation.

In Paris, he was to be put up by Rizzini, the Modenese agent, who writes: "Siface arrived here, and is in every way a rare and excellent singer. There being no good *musico* who is not also a great coxcomb [*un gran fantastico*], I do not believe he will stay long in London." Siface dallied in Paris for some time, hoping to find favour at court; he was heard by the Dauphine, who praised him, but Louis XIV "could not be bothered to listen to him", and he got nothing for all his trouble. The French were decidedly not his lucky nation.

He arrived in London on January 16th, 1687, and remained until June 19th. His caprices during that time caused considerable annoyance: for a long time he pleaded the fatigue of the journey as a reason for refusing to sing, and then, when that excuse became too threadbare, decided that the climate was ruining his health and his voice—which of course may have been true. For all that, his success was immense whenever he did consent to perform, and nothing like him had ever been heard before in England; nor was it again till the arrival of Nicolino in 1708.[1] He seems, however, not to have sung at all in public, nor in any opera.

On his return, the Queen entrusted him with a letter for her brother, which is perhaps worth quoting:

"Windsor, June 16th, 1687.

"My dear brother,

This letter will be given you by Siface, who is returning to your service, as the air of this country is so little conformable

---

1 Evelyn, in his diary writes: "I heard the famous singer Cifaccio, esteemed the best in Europe. Indeed his holding out and delicateness in extending and looseing a note with incomparable softnesse and sweetnesse was admirable; for the rest I found him a mere wanton, effeminate child, very coy, and proudly conceited to my apprehension. He touch'd the harpsichord to his voice rarely well. This was before a select number of particular persons whom Mr Pepys invited to his house; and this was obtained by particular favour and much difficulty, the Signor much disdaining to shew his talent to any but princes."

with his genius and health that he could not stay here any longer. It is with my full leave that he is going, and I am more than satisfied with him; I believe him to be the finest *musico* in the world. Take good care of him, and remember that if after some time you should be willing to send him back to me, I should be obliged to you."

Siface did not, however, stay long at Modena, for in the autumn he was once more in Rome, on his way to Naples. While at Rome, however, he suddenly announced that he would go no further, "unless his claim were fulfilled for 800 scudi to perform in two operas, instead of the 800 lire for three operas which they wanted to pay him". Matters must have been settled to the satisfaction of both parties, for he was in Naples from December 1687 until March of the following year, after which he returned by dilatory stages to Modena. He stopped on the way at Florence, singing in an opera called 'Il Greco in Troja'; and from there he wrote to Francesco d'Este, perhaps as an excuse for the slowness of his journey, that "the horrible floods and winds have laid waste a large part of the countryside, and carried off more than thirty houses which were near the Arno". The tone he adopts when addressing his sovereign is, for that ceremonious age, remarkably informal and almost cheeky.

In the same year, 1688, he was applauded at Modena in Gabrielli's 'Maurizio', and in 1690 at Parma in Sabadini's 'Il favore degli Dei'[1]; after this date, however, nothing is heard of him for a number of years, and it is believed that he was suffering from ill-health. He turns up again, however, in 1696, singing at Reggio d'Emilia in Pollarolo's 'Almansor in Alimena', and his fame was clearly in no way abated.

It was Siface's prowess as a lady-killer that finally caused death

---

[1] This production was in honour of the wedding of Prince Odoardo Farnese and Dorothea Sophia of Neuburg—the parents of Farinelli's patroness Elizabeth Farnese, Queen of Spain—and became a byword for its lavishness. Apart from Siface, the cast included the castrati Pistocchi, Cortona, Valentino Urbani, and Francesco Balarini.

in the following year; for he was not, as Burney has it, killed in a quarrel with his postillion. He had been carrying on an affair with the Countess Elena Forni, *née* Marsilii (or Marsigli), the widow of a Modenese nobleman; but when her family (and that of her mother, the Duglioli) got to hear of it, they spirited her away to Bologna, her native town, and shut her up in the convent of S. Lorenzo.

Meanwhile, Siface had an engagement at Bologna, to sing in a *pasticcio* called 'Perseo', and refused to listen to the warnings of his friends and well-wishers. During rehearsals, he found means of getting himself admitted to the convent and continuing his tender interviews with the widow; and, far from keeping the matter dark, boasted fatuously of his exalted conquest all over Bologna. He had to leave the town for a few days on business, but persisted in returning; and, while on the road near Ferrara, he was attacked by the hired assassins of the Marsilii, and killed outright. He was buried in the church of S. Paolo at Ferrara, and his death was very much mourned, not only by the bereaved and unwilling cause of his death, but by all the music-lovers of Italy.

The investigations into this murder formed quite a *cause célèbre*, and the families responsible were implacably pursued by the Duke of Modena, though the crime had been committed on Papal territory, and many of the instigators were Papal subjects; an anonymous poet of the time, however, thought it more artistic to attribute the affair to Jupiter's jealousy, which he did in the following effusion, much admired when it first appeared:

> Mentre sul Po l'unica voce e chiara
> sciogliea Siface, e la virtù di lei
> udiasi in quelle sponde, uomini e Dei
> vaghi correan per ascoltarle a gara
>
> Giove allor ne giurò vendetta amara
> dicendo: 'chi è costui che i regni miei
> vuota e costringe? Or te, se pur non sei,
> te spoglierò della virtù più rara

E se l'alto saper d'ogni mortale
    maggior ti rende, il tuo sepulcro sia
    l'urna del Po, ch'è a' Numi ancor fatale!

Oggi la crudeltà sia legge mia;
    chè, per gloria del cielo, in me prevale
    all'usata equità la gelosia.

GUADAGNI, Gaetano

Unlike most of the castrati, Guadagni seems to have had little orthodox musical training in his youth, and began his career by touring round Europe as first *amoroso* in a buffo company. He was born at Lodi, near Milan, about 1725, and his first appearance was at Parma in 1747; in the following year he came to England, and attracted attention by his handsome appearance and potentially fine contralto voice, though his technique was at that time virtually nil.

He was, however, much taken up in the artistic circles of the day; by Handel, who gave him parts in some of his oratorios, (particularly 'The Messiah' and 'Sampson'), and by Garrick, who gave him lessons in acting. "During his first residence in England," says Burney, "he was more noticed for his singing in English than Italian", and adds that he made a particular success in 'The Fairies', an operatic version of 'A Midsummer Night's Dream' with music by Christopher Smith. Since 'The Fairies' was not produced until 1755 (on February 3rd, to be precise), Guadagni could not, as Burney has it, have left England in 1753; and it does not seem likely, either, that he could have been in Lisbon by April of the same year, for the famous gala performance of Perez' 'Alessandro nell'Indie' in which he is usually stated to have taken part.[1]

It seems, in fact, improbable that Guadagni ever was in Portugal at all, particularly if the story is true of his having been taught by

[1] Even without Gizziello and Guadagni, there still seems to have been an

Gizziello, who had retired to a monastery, but took a fancy to the young singer; for we now know that Gizziello left Lisbon in 1753, and never returned. It looks almost as if castrati were given to relating how they had *just* not been killed in the Lisbon earthquake, on the same principle as the Prince Regent boasting of having heard Wellington shout "Up guards and at 'em!" After leaving England, Guadagni appeared at various places in Italy, and particularly at Parma, where in 1760 he was heard in Traetta's festival opera-ballet 'La Festa d'Imaneo', in honour of the marriage of the future Emperor Joseph and Isabel of Parma.

We next hear of Guadagni at Vienna, where in 1762 he sang the part of Orpheus at the first performance of Gluck's famous opera; his style of singing was peculiarly suited to the great composer's music, and he sang also in several of his other operas. Possessing the grandeur and nobility that Gluck demanded, his powers of execution were not great enough to tempt him to introduce unsuitable *fioriture* or cadenzas, and thus mar the neoclassic severity of the conception.

Guadagni returned to England in 1769 as first singer at the serious opera, and at first proved a disappointment. "His figure", says Burney, "was uncommonly elegant and noble; his countenance replete with beauty, intelligence and dignity; and his attitudes and gestures were so full of grace and propriety, that they would have been excellent studies for a statuary. But though his manner of singing was perfectly delicate, polished, and refined, his voice seemed at first to disappoint every hearer. Those who remembered it when he was in England before, found it comparatively thin and feeble." He had extended his range to almost double its former extent, and from a contralto become a soprano, but in doing so had much dissipated its power and richness.

inexplicably large number of singers taking part. 'Alessandro nell'Indie' has only four male roles all told, yet four castrati, Caffarelli, Elisi, Manzuoli, and Veroli, and three tenors, Babbi, Amorevoli, and Raaff, are usually said to have sung in it. Perhaps the latter three alternated with one another; for in most settings there is but one tenor role.

"The music he sung", continues Burney, "was the simplest imaginable; a few notes with frequent pauses, and opportunities of being liberated from the composer and the band, were all he wanted. And in these seemingly extemporaneous effusions he proved the inherent power of melody totally divorced from harmony, and unassisted even by unisonous accompaniment. Surprised at such great effects from causes apparently so small, I frequently tried to analyse the pleasure he communicated to the audience, and found that it chiefly arose from his artful manner of diminishing the tones of his voice like the dying notes of an Aeolian harp. Most other singers captivate a swell or *messa di voce*; but Guadagni, after beginning a note or passage with all the force he could safely exert, fined it off to a thread, and gave it all the effect of extreme distance."

His art was, as may be imagined, not such as to captivate the multitude; yet he found many admirers among his more discerning auditors. He made, however, even more enemies, by his eccentric and unpredictable temperament, and by such actions as refusing to take curtain-calls after singing an aria—which *he* claimed was in the interests of dramatic propriety, but which the audience construed as a deliberate insult to themselves. His pride seems to have been not so much in his person as in his calling, and he talked much of 'the dignity of a singer'—a conception, in the general sense, then thought quite incomprehensible.

Guadagni left England in high dudgeon in 1771, and in the following year was heard at Verona. He then fell in with the blue-stocking Electress Dowager of Saxony, and accompanied her to Munich where she lived (for she had been a Bavarian princess), and where he remained until 1776. In that year he appeared on the stage for the last time, at Venice, and then retired to Padua; he had been attached to the church of S. Antonio there for some years, and had built himself a magnificent house.

Burney, visiting Padua in 1770, heard Guadagni sing in the church, at the time of year when he was not required in London, and writes: "There are eight castrati in salary, among whom is Signor Guadagni, who, for taste, expression, figure, and action, is at the head of his profession. His appointment is 400 ducats a year, for which he is required to attend only at the four principal festivals." Later visitors to Padua, too, speak of Guadagni, who had become quite an institution in the town. "In passing through Padua," says Lord Mount Edgcumbe of his tour in 1784, "I had the good fortune to hear a *motetto*, or anthem, sung by Guadagni, of whom I had heard very much. . . . He was now advanced in years . . . his voice was still full and well toned, and his style appeared to me excellent. . . . As he retained a great partiality for England, and had been much noticed by my family, he no sooner heard I was in the town than he came to call upon me, and insisted on my taking coffee at his house, where he entertained me not with singing, which I should have liked much better, but with exhibiting fantoccini on a little stage, in which he took great delight. I learnt lately that he died one year after I saw him." The latter piece of information was, however, false.

Kelly, too, had visited Guadagni a few years earlier, and had had both forms of entertainment in one; for the castrato had 'Orfeo ed Euridice' enacted by his puppets, and meanwhile sang the part of Orpheus behind the scenes. Guadagni all this time was very rich; but it appears that he carried charity to a point beyond the means of his purse. In 1785 or thereabouts he did not die, but found his wealth quite dissipated, and lived on in the greatest poverty. He died in the end, in 1792.

Goudar, who detested the castrati in general, admits that 'there is something to be said for Guadagni'—the only one that he thus excepts from his condemnation. He also tells a number of stories about him which, if but dubiously true, are at least reasonably *ben trovati*. "Guadagni", he begins, "used to be liked by men and adored by women, and a writer has said of him that he would have given great noblemen to France and princes to Germany, if the fatal knife which prevented him from being a man had not extinguished in him the germ of procreation. . . . Once, he made a powerful Monarch cool his heels in an anteroom. While he was speaking privately to his mistress, they came and told him that His Majesty was in the anteroom; he coldly replied, 'Let him wait. When I am ready, I shall come out.'" On another occasion, when a rich Englishwoman gave him 100 guineas to sing, he returned it to her after the performance, saying that he "had given an exhibition unworthy of himself and of her", and would take no money at all.

There are other anecdotes all of much the same tenor: but Guadagni was evidently something of a 'character', about whom legends accumulate, and it is difficult to know how much exactly to believe.

GUARDUCCI, Tommaso

Very little is known of the career of this singer, a modest and unassuming person who never seems to have had great success anywhere but in England. He was born at Montefiascone (prov. Viterbo), some fifty miles north-west of Rome, in about 1720 and studied under Bernacchi at Bologna. He sang at the San Carlo, Naples, in 1758–9 and again in 1762, with some success, but did not cause anything that could be called a sensation.

In 1767 he arrived in England, and at first was no more successful there. He was, says Burney, "tall and awkward in figure, inanimate as an actor, and in countenance ill-favoured and morbid; but with all these disadvantages, he was a man of great probity and worth in his private character, and one of the most correct singers I ever heard. . . . Guarducci's voice, though of much less volume than Manzoli's was clear, sweet, and flexible. . . . He soon discovered that a singer could not captivate the English by tricks or instrumental execution, and told me some years after that the gravity of our taste had been of great use to him. . . . He was the plainest and most simple singer, of the first class, I ever heard. All his effects were produced by expression and high finishing, nor did he ever aim at execution." It seems, from these rather inconsistent remarks that Guarducci had at first attempted to dazzle (and, whatever Burney may say, the English are not averse to being dazzled), but, lacking sufficient brilliance, had decided to try simplicity instead.

In any event, Guarducci's sincere and heartfelt style of singing soon gained him a big following, as did his obliging and easy nature. He would sing almost anything at the slightest notice, and without making a fuss; and he became much admired in English oratorios, being paid £600 for twelve—the highest salary ever paid for such employment until the time of Miss Linley. Meanwhile, the principal operas in which he sang while in London were J. C. Bach's 'Carattaco' and Vento's 'La Conquista del Messico'.

He left England in 1769, and retired to his native town, where Burney visited him the following year. "I visited Signor Guarducci," he writes, "who has here built himself a very good house, and fitted it up in the English manner, with great taste. . . . He was so obliging as to let me hear him, in a song of Signor Sacchini's composition, which he sung divinely. His voice, I think, is more powerful than when he was in England, and his taste and expression seem to have received every possible degree of selection and refinement. He is a very chaste performer, and adds but few notes; those few notes, however, are so well chosen that they produce great effect, and leave the ear thoroughly satisfied. . . . In Rome they still speak of his performance in Piccinni's 'Didone abbandonata' with rapture."

Though Guarducci's voice was evidently still in its prime, he does not seem to have sung again in public very much, and little more is heard of him; the reason was perhaps ill-health. "Guarducci", says Goudar, "continues to appear on the stage, despite a forty years' inflammation of the chest which gives him much trouble. His strong point is the *cantabile*, which he no longer sings, but only pretends to." The date of his death is absolutely unknown.

MAJORANO, Gaetano (Caffarelli or Cafariello)

Caffarelli, the almost exact contemporary and greatest rival of Farinelli, offers, as a man, the most striking contrast imaginable with that great singer. Where Farinelli was gentle, courteous, and unassuming, Caffarelli was capricious, proud, and quarrelsome; whereas Farinelli was the perfect courtier and the confidant of kings, Caffarelli cared nothing for any man, and his insubordination, in an age of flatterers, often landed him in serious trouble. He exhibits, in fact, the perfect type of the 'prima donna temperament', and it is doubtless his career, above all else, that has earned the castrati their reputation for ridiculous and insupportable vanity.

Gaetano Majorano was born at Bitonto near Bari in 1710, and not, as formerly supposed, at Bari itself in 1703. The accepted legend of his youth is still current: that the young Majorano, the child of poor but honest parents, was from the first passionately fond of music, and would haunt the churches to listen to the singing; that one Cafaro,[1] a musician, noticed his attentiveness, became interested in him, discovered in him the rudiments of a fine voice, and persuaded his parents for a certain financial consideration to put their child in his care; that Cafaro then took the boy to Norcia to be castrated, and afterwards to Naples, where in course of time he placed him under the tuition of the famous Porpora. According to this story, too, the boy took the name Caffarelli in gratitude for the—somewhat questionable—services rendered him by his first teacher.

Later research, however, has shown that Caffarelli's parents were quite comfortably off; his sister, on her marriage, brought a considerable dowry, and his family were of some substance in the little town of Bitonto. It is thus improbable that they should have more or less sold their child to a strange musician, to be castrated and trailed about like a sort of performing bear: yet the

---

[1] This could not have been the distinguished composer Pasquale Cafaro, who was only four years older than Caffarelli, having been born in 1706.

familiar fiction of the operation's having been necessitated by some illness seems never to have been made use of in Caffarelli's case. It appears not impossible that he was one of those strong-minded children who insisted on immolating themselves for the sake of their voice, like the Grassetto referred to by Burney. The 'bene-factor' has been identified as one Domenico Caffarelli, but his role must doubtless have been less Svengali-like in reality than in the legend.[1]

In any event, Caffarelli undoubtedly became Porpora's favourite pupil, and underwent a most thorough instruction in every branch of his art: and Porpora to his dying day considered him to be the greatest singer he had ever known, though he cared little enough for his character. Caffarelli's début was at the Teatro delle Dame, Rome, in 1726, in a feminine part: the opera was Sarro's 'Il Valdemaro', and the young castrato must have pleased, for his name was soon well known and his services competed for by the greatest theatres in Italy.

The next few years were spent in visits to various Italian cities, and in the consolidation of his reputation as an outstanding soprano. Among his successes were the following: Venice 1728, in A. Pollarolo's 'Nerina', after which he was heard in Turin, then in Milan in Sarro's 'Didone abbandonata'; in 1730, back in Rome, this time at the Teatro Capranica, in Porpora's 'Mitridate' and 'Siface'. Still in Rome, he caused a *furore* as Pirro in Hasse's 'Cajo Fabricio' and as Arminio in Porpora's 'Germanico'. He returned to Milan, and appeared with Amorevoli, la Tesi, and la Peruzzi in Lampugnani's 'Ezio', and was afterwards heard at Bologna in Hasse's 'Siroe'. In 1734, in Venice, he sang with Farinelli in Giacomelli's 'Merope', and their very different styles were equally admired.

In 1735, Caffarelli returned to Naples to succeed the aged Matteuccio at the Royal Chapel; and in that city he fixed himself for the rest of his life, though he continued to make frequent journeys abroad. In 1738 he essayed the conquest of London, but

[1] In fact, the records of the Naples conservatorios show quite a series of Majoranos who were known as Caffarelli; they were probably his brothers.

obtained little success; Farinelli was still the idol of the public, who were unwilling to own the merits of any other singer, while it seems that the English climate was unkind to Caffarelli, who was never at his best in London.[1] He stayed only one season, and immediately returned to Naples.

Caffarelli had been unaccountably modest there in his financial stipulations, asking only 500 ducats per season, although 800 was the accepted price for a star singer; but he more than made up for this restraint by his extravagant and overbearing behaviour, and made enemies in every quarter. The King, however, always retained a certain partiality for him (perhaps because of, rather than in spite of, his insolence, and not at all for his voice: for Charles, one of the more human of the Bourbons, was indifferent to music, and only supported the opera for the sake of prestige); and this fact alone, most probably, saved Caffarelli from the assassin's knife.

Already, when in Rome in 1728, he had had a narrow escape from death, when carrying on an intrigue with a woman of quality. The suspicious husband surprised Caffarelli with her one night, in a compromising situation, and the singer had to make his escape in the best farcical tradition. He hid all night in a disused cistern, caught cold, and took to his bed for some weeks: but the husband was still intent upon revenge, and the lady still enamoured; so much so that she provided Caffarelli with four bravoes, who accompanied him everywhere to protect him from the similar bravoes suborned by the injured spouse. Caffarelli soon decided that discretion was the better part of valour, threw up his engagement, and fled to Venice.

Elsewhere, his battles were professional rather than gallant. There is, for instance, an eyewitness account of a scene between Caffarelli and a rival singer that took place in 1739: "On the morning of June 8th, the orchestra was on hand in the church of

---

[1] He sang for Handel's company, after the warfare between this and the 'opera of the nobility' had ceased: the operas in which he performed were Handel's 'Faramondo' and 'Serse', Pescetti's 'La Conquista del Vello d'Oro', and Veracini's 'Partenio'; which last work pleased Caffarelli particularly.

Donna Romita, for the solemn celebration of Profession of a lady taking the veil, attended by large numbers of people of quality. Caffarelli was to sing a motet, and the violinist Crescenzo was distributing the parts; but, not being near enough to Caffarelli to give his to him in person, he asked the other *musici* to pass it to him, saying, 'Give this to Signor Don Gaetano.' Reginelli, hearing this and supposing it to refer to the priest D. Gaetano Leuzzi, who could not have sung the part as he was a tenor, asked who this D. Gaetano was. To which Caffarelli replied that he was Don Gaetano Caffarelli and was to sing it, saying this twice over and in a rude manner: Reginelli in his turn answered that, if Caffarelli was D. Gaetano, *he* for his part was Don Nicolò Reginelli. They proceeded to bandy insults, and to become more and more indignant, and Caffarelli struck Reginelli with a small cane which he had; Reginelli too raised his stick, but they were restrained by the other *musici*. Upon which, Caffarelli seized the bow of the double bass, while Reginelli, who had lost his stick, went behind the wainscoting to look for his sword. Not finding it, he took up a piece of wood which happened to be there and returned towards the orchestra. The two attacked one another, battering not only each other but also the onlookers who were trying to separate them. Eventually they were restrained, to the accompaniment of shrieks from the monks who were in the choir." As the upshot of this undignified scene, the quarrelsome castrati were haled before the ecclesiastical court and accused of sacrilege; but Caffarelli was due to be sent to Spain to sing at the wedding of Don Philip, the King of Naples' brother and later Duke of Parma, and the charge was dropped by royal intervention. Caffarelli got off with a solemn warning to mend his ways.

This, however, he by no means did; and on his return from Madrid his conduct became worse than ever. At a performance of Latilla's 'Olimpia nell'Isola d'Ebuda' he distinguished himself, according to the official report, by "disturbing the other performers, acting in a manner bordering on lasciviousness (on stage) with one of the female singers, conversing with the spectators in the boxes from the stage, ironically echoing whichever member of the company was singing an aria, and finally refusing to sing in the *ripieno* with the others". For these exploits, he was sent to prison, but released after three days, again by command of the King; the management of the San Carlo, however, decided on the strength of it that they needed a change of singer, and invited Gizziello to replace Caffarelli. The latter, a timid soul, refused to come, apparently fearing what Caffarelli might do to him, and the turbulent *musico* was perforce retained in the company, no other singer of equal calibre being available. Despite his outrageous behaviour, Caffarelli's singing continued to be admired, and among the operas in which he triumphed were Leo's 'Ciro riconosciuto' and 'Andromaca e Pirro', Hasse's 'Issipile', Sarro's 'Alessandro nell'Indie' (in which he divided the applause with an elephant, a present to the King from the Sultan of Turkey), and 'Demofoonte', a *pasticcio* composed by Sarro, Mancini, and Leo.

In 1744, the Marchese Obizzi, impresario at Padua, made a particular request to the King to allow Caffarelli leave of absence for a season, so that he might sing at Obizzi's theatre, and Charles was perfectly willing to grant it. Caffarelli, however, refused to go, alleging that his voice was out of condition—though the real reason was apparently his fear that, during his absence, another singer would captivate Naples, and he would lose his safe position. He did accept an invitation to Florence in 1747, where he sang in Caldara's 'Cajo Mario'—"divinely well", according to Mann—but then returned to Naples, and was soon up to all his old tricks. In January 1748, we find Saverio Donati, the Director of the San Carlo theatre, writing: "Yesterday evening at the Royal Theatre . . . when he came to the duet at the end of the second act, the *musico* Caffarelli began to sing the first two verses in a manner quite different from that written by the Saxon maestro [i.e. Hasse]; but the prima donna Astrua . . . though thus obliged to improvise, managed as well as she could, and the first and second sections were got through quietly enough. At the repeat, however, Caffarelli produced a new version different from his first one, and full of rhythmic variations and syncopations,

with the anticipation of a beat. When the Astrua, in respond-
ing, tried to get back into the proper tempo, Caffarelli had the
audacity not only to demonstrate, with his hands, how she should
keep time, but even suggested vocally how she should sing. This
was seen and understood by everyone, and I cannot tell you the
scandal that was aroused by the incident; there was a universal
murmur of outrage from the boxes and the pit. . . ." Caffarelli
detested prima donnas, and his aim had been to make the Astrua
look foolish; but his efforts only rebounded on his own head,
and once more he narrowly escaped imprisonment.

In 1748, Caffarelli was heard again in Rome, in Abos' 'Arianna
e Teseo', Perez' 'Semiramide riconosciuta' and other works, and
after this season went on to Vienna, where his reception was
mixed. Metastasio, writing to Farinelli, gives a slightly waspish
account of it: "You will be curious to know how Caffarelli has
been received. The wonders related of him by his admirers had
excited expectation of something superhuman; yet the first night
he completely displeased everyone. He claimed he was so disconcerted by the presence of their Imperial Majesties that he
could not do himself justice; and it is true that in subsequent
performances he regained so much credit that some of the nobility
and gentry now exalt him to the firmament, and even go as
far as to make heretical comparisons [i.e. with Farinelli]. There
are, however, numerous critics who, while admitting that his
voice is powerful, find it out of tune, strident, and uncontrollable;
so that he can make no effect without forcing it, when it becomes
harsh and unpleasant. They say he has no judgment, and frequently
attempts things beyond his powers, which he is forced to leave
unfinished; that he has outmoded, bad taste and reminds them
of the antique and stale *fioriture* of Nicolini and Mattucio. They
maintain that he treads the stage abominably; that in recitative
he is an old nun; and that in all he sings there is a ridiculous tone
of lamentation which can turn the most cheerful *allegro* sour. They
admit that he can sometimes please excessively but add that
such happy moments are not to be relied upon, depending
on the caprices of his voice and temper, and in themselves

insufficient to make up for the displeasure caused by his short-comings."

To be fair to Caffarelli, it must be borne in mind that Metastasio was scarcely an impartial judge; a fanatical supporter of Farinelli, he was necessarily inclined to depreciate his rival. None the less, Caffarelli does seem to have been as erratic and unpredictable in the quality of his singing as he was capricious in temperament. Zambeccari, writing from Bologna in 1733, had said of him, "Caffarelli is insufferable, as much for his forced singing and his horrible shrillness, as for his petulance and impertinence"; and one can guess that he was one of those singers who sacrifice everything to effect. Sometimes they are rewarded, and achieve results more exciting than anything that a more equable artist could produce; but often, too, they are detestable. He must by all accounts have been a dramatic rather than a lyrical singer, with the type of voice that is now called *spinto*, and have excelled in moments of vehement passion rather than in those of tenderness.

In another letter, to the Princess Belmonte, Metastasio gives an amusing account of a typical Caffarellian *fracas* that occurred while he was in Vienna. "The poet of this theatre", he begins, "is a young Milanese, born of most worthy parents, but hot-headed, a great admirer of the fair sex, despising money, and as lacking in judgment as he is rich in talent. The theatre manage-ment made this young author responsible for all stage arrange-ments: and, whether from rivalry in abilities or in personal beauty, the poet and the singer have all along been on the *qui vive*, and have treated each other with sneers and sarcasms. One day Migliavacca (the poet) gave orders for a rehearsal of the opera in preparation, and all the performers obeyed save Caffarelli, who turned up at the end of the rehearsal and asked the assembled company, in a most contemptuous voice, what use such rehearsals could possibly be. The other replied, in a voice of authority, that no one was accountable to him (Caffarelli) for what was done, that he should be glad that his failure to attend had gone unheeded, that it little imported for the success of the opera whether he was there or not, and that he might at least allow others to carry out their duties, even though he neglected his. Caffarelli, enraged, exclaimed that whoever had ordered the rehearsal was an idiot. At this, the poet's patience forsook him, and, in a towering fury, he honoured the singer with all those glorious titles he had earned in various parts of Europe, touching lightly, but in lively colours, upon some of the more memorable incidents in his career. He was far from finished when the hero of the panegyric interrupted him, and boldly called out, 'Follow me, if you dare, to some place where we are alone!' and, going towards the door, signed to him to come out. The poet hesitated for a moment and then, remarking, 'Such an opponent makes me blush; but never mind, it is a Christian act to chastise a fool or a madman', advanced to take the field. Caffarelli, who had perhaps imagined that the muses would not be so brave, or supposed that, according to the rule of criminal law, a delinquent ought to be punished in *loco patrati delicti*, changed his former intention of going elsewhere for the battle, and then and there drew his bright blade and presented its point to the enemy. Nor did the other refuse the combat. . . .

"The bystanders tremble; each calls on his tutelary saint, expecting at every moment to see poetical and vocal blood besprinkle the harpsichord and double basses. At length, however, Signora Tesi, rising from under her canopy, where hitherto she had remained a most tranquil spectator, walked with slow and stately step towards the combatants; whereupon—O sovereign power of beauty!—the frantic Caffarelli, at the fiercest of his anger yet captivated and placated by such unexpected tenderness, runs rapturously to meet her, lays his sword at her feet, begs pardon for his misdemeanour, and, sacrificing his vengeance to her, seals his protestations of obedience, respect and humility with a thousand kisses upon her hand. The nymph signifies her forgiveness with a nod; the poet sheathes his sword; the spectators begin once more to breathe; and the company breaks up amid laughter. In gathering up the wounded and the slain, none was found but the poor copyist, who in trying to separate the combatants had accidentally been kicked by the poet. Next day the battle was commemorated in an anonymous sonnet . . . today the German comedians are to represent this extraordinary event on the stage. They say that already there is not a place to be had, and it is not yet twelve o'clock." Caffarelli for once evidently forgot his habitual detestation of prima donnas; which is all the more strange in that the Tesi was at this time by no means young (in fact, she was not far off sixty), and at her best had been anything but a beauty—already in 1744 it had been said of her that "her time of making new conquests is over". Perhaps Metastasio was indulging in a little irony?

After this tempestuous visit to Vienna, Caffarelli sang at Venice, winning acclaim in Manna's 'Didone abbandonata', and at Lucca, and returned again to Naples. His success there was by now on the wane; he was on his own admission 'poco ben veduto', and the impresario was anxious to terminate his engagement (as well as that of the tenor Babbi, who had 'bored every day of the year for the last five years'). It was, however, impossible to find a replacement for Caffarelli; Carestini was in Berlin and Manzuoli in Madrid, Salimbeni had just died, whilst Monticelli "neither wants to be, nor ought to be, heard any more"—and in the end they were forced to make do with the old warhorse, declaring ungraciously that they "agreed with the public that Caffarelli ought to be changed, because he either no longer wishes to sing, or is no longer able to, being fifty years old (he was actually only about forty-two) and has become lazy; he does not bother to use expression in his recitatives, and forces composers to write conveniently for him and *largo,* avoiding fugal arias and long scenes to spare himself fatigue". Among the operas in which he sang at Naples, after his return from Vienna, were Traetta's 'Farnace', Gluck's 'La Clemenza di Tito', and Conti's 'Attalo Re di Bitinia'.

His stay at Naples was interrupted by a brief visit to Turin, during which he threw his most famous temperament. This journey was undertaken, at the express orders of the King of Naples, to sing at the wedding of the Prince of Savoy with the Infanta of Spain; but for some reason, instead of being flattered, Caffarelli was most unwilling to go—possibly because he disliked royalty in general or because the princess had been a pupil of Farinelli in her native country. On arrival, he sulked and refused to attend rehearsals, alleging that he had lost his book of closes (cadenzas) on the road. The King of Sardinia, father of the bridegroom, was placed in a difficult predicament when told about this; for Caffarelli was a Neapolitan subject over whom he had no jurisdiction, and, besides, he did not wish to offend Caffarelli's master, who had gone to the trouble of sending him.

The prince, however, tried diplomacy with happy results; for, going behind the scenes on the fateful night, he told Caffarelli that his wife, accustomed to hearing Farinelli, would not believe that another singer could ever please her. Caffarelli, much piqued, answered that he would prove himself "two Farinelli's in one", and in fact, excelled himself, earning great acclamation. On his return from this voyage, we find him playing the suppliant, petitioning the King for 1,229 ducats' back pay, plus 880 for travelling expenses "incurred in returning to Naples post haste at your Majesty's command". It does not appear, however, whether his requests were satisfied.

In 1753 Caffarelli was heard at Modena, and from there he journeyed to Paris by royal invitation, to amuse the Dauphine during her pregnancy. This lady, a Saxon princess, had been brought up in a city where the castrati were idolised, and was thus free from the French prejudice against them. Caffarelli created a sensation at court, but scarcely sang outside it, so strong was that prejudice; yet those who heard him were enraptured and he seems to have been in specially good voice while in France—unless it was only by comparison with the frightful shrieking of the native singers. Grimm, who heard him at Versailles in yet another setting of 'Didone abbandonata', this time by Hasse, writes: "It would be difficult to give any idea of the degree of perfection to which this singer has brought his art. All the charms and love that can make up the idea of an angelic voice, and which form the character of his, added to the finest execution, and to surprising facility and precision, exercise an enchantment over the senses and the heart, which even those least sensible to music would find it hard to resist."

Caffarelli, while in Paris, was so unwise as to become involved in a duel with the poet Ballot de Sauvet, apropos of a quarrel over the relative merits of French and Italian music: and he nearly killed his adversary, which was considered tactless. Soon after this occurred another famous episode, which is perhaps mythical but is by no means unlikely; Louis XV sent a courtier to Caffarelli with a gold *tabatière*, intended as a signal mark of his esteem. But the singer, far from expressing humble gratitude, disdainfully showed the emissary a collection of some thirty other snuff-boxes, each more sumptuous than the one the King had sent. The courtier, disconcerted, remarked that Louis was accustomed to present boxes identical to the latter to ambassadors, who were honoured to accept them: but Caffarelli was not impressed. "Let him, then," he replied, "ask the ambassadors to sing!" The King, according to the story, laughed when he heard of this; but he cannot have been much amused, for he had a passport delivered to the castrato, with orders to leave France within three days. The order was complied with, and Caffarelli returned to Naples, shaking the dust of France from his feet in anger.

The eccentric singer was again heard at the San Carlo, in Sabatini's 'Arsace' and other works, and soon afterwards was invited to Lisbon by King Joseph of Portugal, for the opening of the new Opera House in the spring of 1755. The opera on this occasion was Perez' 'Alessandro nell'Indie', mounted with extraordinary splendour, and sung, apart from Caffarelli, by a dazzling constellation of talent, among them Elisi, Manzuoli, Veroli, Babbi, and Raaff. He was still in Portugal at the time of the terrible earthquake of 1755, which reduced its capital city to a heap of ruins; but, being at Santarem, he escaped the consequences. However, the stricken kingdom had now no time for opera, and Caffarelli soon left, on his way back to Naples. Before returning there, however, he made a stay in Madrid, where he was amicably received by Farinelli, still absolute master of things musical in Spain, and the two virtuosi exhibited to the world a friendship which they may or may not have felt; Caffarelli was by no means incapable of generosity, as his praise of Gizziello shows, whilst Farinelli seems scarcely ever to have quarrelled with anyone. It was at Madrid that Caffarelli suddenly, for no special reason, decided that the time had come for him to retire, and enjoy his considerable fortune in peace; and on returning to Naples he purchased the Calabrian domain of San Donato and the dukedom that went along with it, and built himself a splendid house in Naples itself.[1] The rather absurd inscription that he had carved above his front door—'AMPHION THEBAS, EGO DOMUM'—is famous, and gave rise to much ribaldry at the time, particularly someone's response—'ille cum, tu sine'.

Caffarelli continued to sing on occasion, though no longer on the stage. Garrick, who heard him at Naples in 1764, writes to Burney about him: "Yesterday we attended the ceremony of making a nun; who was the daughter of a duke, and the whole was conducted with great splendour and magnificence. The church was richly ornamented, and there were two large bands of music of all kinds. The consecration was performed with great solemnity, and I was very much affected; and to crown the whole, the principal part was sung by the famous Caffarelli, who, though old, has pleased me more than all the singers I ever heard. He *touched* me; and it is the first time I have been touched since I came into Italy." The singer was then only about fifty-four; but in those days middle age had not been invented and one was either young or old. Of this or a similar occasion Kelly relates the following anecdote: "The young and beautiful daughter of the Duke de Monteleone, the richest nobleman in Naples, was destined by her family to take the veil; she consented without a murmur to quit the world, provided the ceremony of her profession was performed with splendour; and a *sine qua non* was, that Caffarelli . . . should perform at it. It was represented to her that he had retired with a fine fortune to his estate in the interior of Calabria, and had declared his determination never to sing again. Then said the reasonable young lady, '*I* declare *my*

[1] The house still exists, at No. 15, Vico Carminiello, off the Via Roma.

determination never to take the veil unless he does. He sang six years ago, when my cousin was professed, and I had rather die, than it should be said, that she had the first singer in the world to sing for *her*, and I had not!' The fair lady was firm, and her glorious obstinacy was such, that her father was obliged to take a journey into Calabria, when, with much entreaty, and many very *weighty* arguments, he prevailed on Caffarelli to return with him to Naples. He sang a *salve regina* at the ceremony; and the Signora having gained her point, cheerfully submitted to be led, like a lamb to the sacrifice, to eternal seclusion from the gay and wicked world." Even an angel's voice, however, could scarcely have atoned for the sinister and melancholy nature of such an occasion; the beautiful girl, smothered in finery and ablaze with diamonds (which, if necessary could be hired for the day), deprived of life, love, and freedom while around her her friends, some worldly and some *dévotes*, gossiped and prayed and commented. . . .

When Burney visited Naples in 1770, he met Caffarelli at the opera, and described him in flattering terms: "Caffarelli . . . looks well, and has a very lively and animated countenance; he does not seem to be above fifty years of age, though he is said to be sixty-three [he was, of course, only sixty]. He was very polite, and entered into conversation with great ease and cheerfulness." A few days later, at a private party, "the whole company had given Caffarelli over, when ʋehold! he arrived in great good humour; and, contrary to all expectations, was with little entreaty prevailed upon to sing. Many notes in his voice are now thin, but there are still traits in his performance sufficient to convince those who hear him, of his having been an amazing fine singer; he accompanies himself, and sung without any other instrument than the harpsichord; expression and grace, with great neatness in all he attempts, are his characteristics." Age had evidently dealt kindly with the virtuoso, softening his prickly and difficult spirit, but leaving him his faculties unimpaired.

In his last years, Caffarelli became ever more sweet-tempered and peaceable, spending large sums on charity and exhibiting a taste for religion, which he had formerly much neglected. He died at Naples in 1783, leaving his dukedom and the bulk of his fortune to his nephew.

MANZUOLI, Giovanni (Succianoccioli)

Of the castrati of what might be termed the mid-eighteenth-century generation, Manzuoli was perhaps the most eminent; but this was partly, perhaps, from lack of competition. In the 1750's and 1760's Farinelli and Caffarelli were already old, Pacchierotti and his contemporaries were mere children, and the art of singing passed through one of its less fortunate periods, as it did again in about 1810.

Manzuoli was born at Florence in 1725, and is first heard of at Milan in 1748, where he was engaged for the season with the *onorario* of 11,250 lire milanese. He was a particular favourite in this city, and sang there again in the years 1759, 1762, 1766, and 1769; and perhaps his greatest triumph there was in Ponzo's 'Arianna e Teseo', in which his combat with the Minotaur was much admired. In 1753, he was engaged by Farinelli for the opera at Madrid, where he earned 16,000 ducats a year.

In 1755, Manzuoli was one of the singers in the famous performances at Lisbon, and in 1763 he took part in another baptism of an illustrious theatre—that of the Communale at Bologna, when the opera given was Gluck's 'Il Trionfo di Clelia'[1]. On this occasion Manzuoli made himself unpopular with the orchestra, as related by a chronicler: "The first *musico*, who is a certain Manzoli, insists on giving the note for the instruments to be tuned; and he

[1] Gluck's music was not appreciated, and the big success of the production was the *cimieri* (plumes). Ostrich plumes played an all-important part in the theatrical costumery of the period; but they were ruinously expensive, and managements often made do with depressingly wilted and moth-eaten specimens. On this occasion, however, some ingenious person found a way of making imitation plumes, apparently out of shredded tissue-paper, which were universally agreed to be twice as large and splendid as the genuine article. Whether the idea was copied elsewhere does not appear.

legislates for the whole orchestra with a certain little bell of his. But the note he gives is always so flat, that all these players sound like our organ at Santa Lucia." Manzuoli was also heard again in Madrid, during the same year.

The following year, Manzuoli came to London and appeared in 'Ezio', a *pasticcio*. Burney writes of him: "Manzuoli's voice was the most powerful and voluminous soprano that had been heard on our stage since the time of Farinelli; and his manner of singing was grand and full of taste and dignity. In his first opera he had three songs, composed by Pescetti, entirely in different styles: 'Recagli quell' acciaro', an animated *aria parlante*; 'Caro mio bene, addio', an adagio in a grand style of cantabile; and 'Mi dona mi rende', of a graceful kind, all of which he executed admirably. The lovers of music in London were more unanimous in approving his voice and talents than those of any other singer within my memory. The applause was hearty, unequivocal, and free from all suspicion of artificial zeal; it was a universal thunder. His voice alone was commanding from native strangth and sweetness; for it seems as if subsequent singers had possessed more art and feeling; and as to execution, he had none. However, he was a good actor, though unwieldy in figure, and not well made in person; nor was he very young."

So unqualified a success was, no doubt, partly due to the fact that London had been badly off for singers for a number of years: and Horace Walpole thought him 'very disappointing'. So much, however, was Manzuoli liked that Arne decided to take advantage of him, and try his hand at an Italian opera; his English opera after the Italian style, 'Artaxerxes', having been much acclaimed. Unfortunately his 'Olimpiade' was so manifestly feeble an effort that even the public's predisposition to be pleased, and Manzuoli's fine singing as Megacle, could not save it. While in London, Manzuoli also came in contact with the eight-year-old Mozart, than an infant prodigy, and gave him some singing lessons: "The first really strong and lasting musical impression that the child received", says Dent, "was in all probability the influence of Manzuoli."

After leaving England, Manzuoli sang in Vienna and elsewhere with great success. In 1768 he was heard at Florence, and his final appearances were in Milan in 1771, in Hasse's 'Ruggiero' and Mozart's youthful *serenata,* 'Ascanio in Alba'.[1] He then retired, having purchased an estate some miles from Florence, "where", says Kelly, "I dined with him: he spoke of England with admiration, and expressed great gratitude for the attention and applause he received at the Opera House, and in concerts". Manzuoli died shortly afterwards, in about 1782, and his name was perpetuated by one of his pupils, the soprano Angelo Monanni, who took the pseudonym of Manzoletto in his honour.

MARCHESI, Luigi

If Pacchierotti was, in a certain sense, the Farinelli of the later eighteenth century, Marchesi may be called its Caffarelli; for he possessed much of that virtuoso's conceited and exacting spirit, and his lofty disregard for any other consideration but his own glory.

Marchesi was born at Milan in 1754, and first began to study at Modena; but in 1765 he became what was called an 'allievo musico soprano' at Milan Cathedral. His début was at Rome in 1774 in a female part, in a revival of Pergolesi's 'La Serva Padrona' (or possibly Paesiello's resetting of the same libretto). He must have been particularly successful at female parts, for he sang one in the following year at Florence—a city where the practice was not usual—in Bianchi's 'Castore e Polluce'. It was in Florence some years later that, as reported by Kelly, Marchesi "sang

---

[1] Mozart wrote, on November 24th of that year: "Herr Manzuoli, the *musico,* who has always been considered and esteemed as the best of his class, has in his old age given a proof of his folly and arrogance. He was engaged at the opera for the sum of 500 *gigliati* (ducats) but as no mention was made of the *Serenata* in this contract, he demanded 500 ducats more for singing in it, making 1,000. The court only sent him 700 and a gold box (quite enough too, I think) but he returned the 700 ducats and the box, and went away without anything." In general, however, Mozart seems to have liked and admired Manzuoli, apart from this particular affair.

Bianchi's 'Sembianza amabile del mio bel sole' with most ravishing taste; in one passage he ran up a voletta of semitone octaves, the last note of which he gave with such exquisite power and strength that it was ever after called 'La bomba del Marchesi'".

Nancy Storace, who was with him in the opera, was so unwise as to equal this feat; whereupon Marchesi insisted that she be dismissed from the company forthwith. Kelly also saw Marchesi at Naples in Mysliweczek's 'Olimpiade', and writes: "His expression, feeling and execution in the beautiful aria 'se Cerca, se Dice' were beyond all praise."

Marchesi had also, in 1775, been heard to advantage at Milan and Munich; and at the former city in 1780, his success in Mysliweczek's 'Armida' was so great that a silver medal was struck in his honour by the Accademia of the city. In Turin, in 1782, he triumphed in Bianchi's 'Il Trionfo della Pace', and became Court Musician to the King of Sardinia, with an annual salary of 1,500 Piemontese lire and permission to travel abroad during nine months in the year. In 1785, he ventured as far as St Petersburg, but, terrified by the climate, fled rapidly back to Vienna, where he stayed until 1788; and in that year he came to London, where his success was prodigious. He always made ravages among female hearts and much scandal was caused by Maria Cosway, wife of the miniaturist, who left husband and children for Marchesi, and followed him around Europe. She did not return until 1795.

So great, according to Lord Mount Edgcumbe, was the excitement aroused by his arrival, that on his opening night the opera could scarcely be started for the noise and confusion occasioned by the audience. The famous amateur goes on to describe the singer: "Marchesi was at this time a very well-looking young man, of good figure, and graceful deportment. His acting was spirited and expressive: his vocal powers were very great, his voice of extensive compass, but a little inclined to be thick. His execution was very considerable, and he was rather too fond of displaying it; nor was his cantibile singing equal to his bravura. In recitative, and scenes of energy and passion, he was incomparable, and had he been less lavish of ornaments, which were not always appropriate, and possessed a more pure and simple taste, his performance would have been faultless: it was always striking, animated, and effective. He chose for his début Sarti's beautiful opera of Giulio Sabino, in which all the songs of the principal character, and they are many and various, are of the very finest description. But I was a little disappointed at Marchesi's execution of them, for they were all familiar to me, as I had repeatedly heard Pacchierotti sing them in private, and I missed his tender expression, particularly in the last pathetic scene, and lamented that their simplicity should be injured, as it was, by an over-flowery style. But this flowery style was an absolute simplicity, to what we have heard in latter days. The comparison made me like Marchesi less than I had done at Mantua, or than I did in other subsequent operas here. He was received with rapturous applause." It was in London, incidentally, that Pacchierotti and Marchesi sang together, for the only time in their lives, in friendly rivalry at a private concert at Lord Buckingham's. Marchesi also, while in London, published some arias composed by himself.

Marchesi's absurd stipulations, as to the way he wished himself to be presented, are notorious (see page 76), but he evidently did not impose them when in England; perhaps it was only in later years that he did so. Towards the end of his stay in England, a newspaper reported: "Last night their Majesties and the Princesses honoured the Opera with their presence. The object of attraction was the Marchesi, and the hero, animated by the presence of the Court, exerted himself to the utmost. He has for some time past greatly corrected himself in respect of his flourishes and ornaments. He still demonstrates his wonderful endowments in the science, but not to the injury of the air, by loading it with ornament. Tune, however, is in the ear what vision is in the eye—it may be amended where it is, but cannot be conveyed where it is not. We fear it is not in Marchesi."

In any case, his popularity remained undiminished in Italy until after the beginning of the nineteenth century, and his is one of the names most frequently met with in surviving cast-lists of the period. The Italians have always been willing to forgive a great

deal for virtuosity: besides, as Vernon Lee remarks: "The frivolous part of society chatted and danced, and adored . . . the singer
Marchesi whom Alfieri called upon to buckle on his helmet, and
march out against the French, as the only remaining Italian who
had dared to resist the 'Corsican Gallic' invader, although only
in the matter of a song." This was in 1796, when he refused to
sing before Napoleon on the latter's entry into Milan. However,
in 1800, when the conqueror again captured the city after
Marengo, Marchesi was one of the first to greet him, along with
Mrs Billington and the Grassini.

He spent much time at Venice, where he became involved in
bitter rivalry with the Portuguese prima donna Luisa Todi; the
Venetian Zaguri has several references to the feud in his letters
to his friend Casanova. In 1790 he writes: "Hardly anyone talks
of the new theatre [the Fenice, then under construction], the Todi
and Marchesi[1] form the one subject of conversation for all ranks
of the city, and will do so till the end of Lent: for the marriage of
idleness and nullity becomes ever more stable and firm upon these
shores." In further letters he traces the development of hostilities
between the two singers and their respective supporters—the
victory inclining apparently towards the lady all along—until,
the following year,[2] he reports: "They have made an engraving
in the English style showing the Todi triumphant, and Marchesi
humiliated. Every verse written in favour of Marchesi is mutilated or suppressed by the magistrate of the Bestemmia [i.e. the
tribune that guarded against blasphemy]. Everything, however
inane, in favour of the Todi, is allowed, as she is under the

[1] The Todi was singing at the S. Samuele theatre and Marchesi at the S.
Benedetto. His first appearance was in Tarchi's 'L'apoteosi d'Ercole'.

[2] An English newspaper of 1791 reports that "accounts arrived yesterday
which mention the death of this great vocal performer [Marchesi] at Milan.
It is said that he fell a victim to the jealousy of an Italian Nobleman, whose
wife was suspected of too strong an attachment to the unfortunate warbler. . . .
Poison administered with the usual skill and dispatch of the Italians, is said to
have produced his unhappy exit." This must, however, have been, if not a
fabrication, a wild exaggeration, and Marchesi have been wounded or
frightened.

protection of the Damone and the Casa [noble Venetian families]."

Marchesi, however, was not to be utterly beaten, and continued to sing in Venice for a number of years. In September 1794, Zaguri writes: "The Fenice theatre is to have Marchesi this year, but it is so disapproved of for its bad construction that it will not last long. Marchesi is costing them three thousand two hundred Zecchinis." In justice to the Fenice, it must be said that Zaguri had a prejudice against it from the first, for what reason it is not clear. Still in Venice in 1798, Marchesi's name appears in one of the oddest of surviving cast-lists, that of Zingarelli's 'Carolina e Mexicow'—the latter strange piece of spelling (the name of Marchesi's role) being apparently some Italian's best effort at rendering a Scotch name such as MacKintosh. Although the city had already been assigned to the Austrians by the Treaty of Campo-Formio, the performers are still described as 'Cittadino' and 'Cittadina' so-and-so; though Marchesi himself mitigates this democratic uniformity by describing himself as 'Maestro to the King of Sardinia'.

Marchesi sang in Mayr's 'Ginevra di Scozia' for the inauguration of the Teatro Nuovo, Trieste, in 1801; and he continued to be applauded until after the 1805–6 season at Milan, during which he had sung in Mayr's 'Eraldo ed Emma' and other works, and after which he retired for good. He died at Inzago in 1829.

MARTINI, Andrea (Senesino)

This singer was particularly admired in Rome for his playing of female parts in both serious and comic operas, being handsome and elegant, and possessing an unusually sweet and flexible voice, but too little power to have suited him to a hero's role.[1]

He was born at Siena in 1761, made his début at Rome in 1780, and sang for the most part in that city, where Mount Edgcumbe

[1] For a sonnet in his honour, see page 17.

7. GIOVANNI MANZUOLI
from the portrait by Luigi Betti

6. LUIGI MARCHESI
from the portrait by Cosway

saw him some four years later, and thought him "a very promising young singer".

In 1799 he retired, and soon afterwards went to live in Florence, where he died in 1819.

MILLICO, Giuseppe

A singer who won particular approval from pundits, theoreticians, and purists, as well as from the ordinary public, Millico was born at Terlizzi near Bari in 1739. Little seems to be known about the earlier part of his career, and his first notable performance was in Vienna, in 1769, when he created the hero's role in Gluck's 'Paride ed Elena': he had attracted the composer's attention earlier in the same year, when at Parma he sang in Gluck's 'Le Feste d'Apollo', which comprised a potted version of 'Orfeo'. Millico, on first seeing the part, was aghast, and concluded that his enemies were seeking to undo him: but in fact he scored a great success, and became a staunch admirer of Gluck, and his niece's singing-master.

A few years later Millico arrived in England, together with the composer Sacchini; for some reason merciless cabals were organised against the pair of them, and the two artists had difficulty in making any headway. The hostility towards Millico seems to have been aroused to some extent by his appearance. He was exceptionally dark and swarthy, and was probably of partly Moorish or Negro extraction. Their excellence, however, eventually enforced recognition, and those who had cried the loudest that Millico could no more sing than Sacchini could compose would willingly have eaten their words. Millico was particularly identified, in England at any rate, with this composer's music, and in London appeared in his 'Il Cid', 'Tamerlano', and other works.[1] Sacchini remained some time in England to achieve a popularity unknown by any foreign composer since Handel, but Millico soon departed to take up an engagement in Berlin.

[1] "Millico", writes Mrs. Thrale, "was set to sing these English words—I come my Queen to chaste delights—He sung them thus. I comb my Queen to catch the lice."

6

In 1779 or 1780, the singer returned to Naples, and soon afterwards became *maestro da capella* to the Royal Chapel, in which capacity he gave lessons to Lady Hamilton, as did Giuseppe Aprile. He also became much admired as a composer, producing the operas 'La pietà d'amore', 'La Zelinda', and others, and received praise for these works from such captious critics as Arteaga and Mattei. He died at Naples in 1802.

MONTICELLI, Angelo Maria

Monticelli was born at Milan in 1715, and made his début at Rome in about 1730. From 1733 to 1750 he was attached to the Austrian court with an annual salary of 2,000 florins, but this did not prevent him from appearing elsewhere; notably in his native city in 1734, with Vittoria Tesi, in Sammartini's 'Ambizione superata da virtù'. He was also in the company at Florence in 1737 where an English aristocrat, Lord Middlesex, tried his hand as an impresario. The season started with great éclat, but was interrupted after a few performances by the sudden death of Gian Gastone, the last Medici Grand Duke, and the consequent closing down of the theatre.

Monticelli came to London in 1740—a difficult assignment, for he was arriving immediately after the dazzling period when Farinelli, Senesino, Gizziello, and Caffarelli had all been heard together or in quick succession—yet, though not a singer of quite their calibre, he succeeded in pleasing very greatly. What he lacked in brilliance and technique, he made up for in charm, good looks, and taste; and, says Horace Walpole, "Monticelli is infinitely admired, next to Farinelli."

"Angelo Monticelli", says Burney, "first appeared on the stage at Rome . . . and having a beautiful face and figure, began in that city by representing female characters. His voice was clear, sweet, and free from defects of any kind. He was a chaste performer, and never hazarded any difficulty which he was not certain of executing with the utmost precision. To his vocal excellence may be added the praise of a good actor; so that nothing but the recent remembrance of the gigantic talents of Farinelli, and the grand and majestic style of Senesino, could have left an English audience anything to wish."

A less flattering view of Monticelli is taken by the impresario at Naples in 1752, when he writes that "Monticelli non si vuole nè deve più sentirsi"; and since the singer would only have been thirty-seven at the time, his voice must have suffered a very premature decay for such an opinion to have been justified.

In any event, Monticelli was singing at Dresden in 1755, in the musical heyday of that city; and, after leaving Vienna for good, he took up permanent residence in the Saxon capital, where in 1758 he died.

PACCHIEROTTI, Gasparo

It is often supposed that the singers of the later eighteenth century possessed neither the renown and popularity, nor the technical proficiency, of Farinelli, Caffarelli, and their contemporaries. True, none of them rose to be virtual prime minister of Spain; yet the chorus of praise and acclaim with which Pacchierotti was everywhere greeted is fully equal to the encomiums lavished on his predecessor. As to brilliance of artistry in the age of Mozart, Burney goes so far as to remark: "Such execution as many of Farinelli's songs contain, and which excited such astonishment in 1734, would be hardly thought sufficiently brilliant in 1788 for a third-rate singer at the opera"; this is no doubt an exaggeration, but it gives some idea of the standards expected by an audience familiar with that brilliant trio of virtuosi—Rubinelli, Marchesi, and above all Pacchierotti.

This great artist was born at Fabriano near Ancona—a district peculiarly fertile in voices—in 1740; his family seem to have been what would now be called 'shabby genteel', and traced their ancestry to the painter Jacopo del Pacchia, called Pacchierotto, a native of Siena who settled in the Marches, and successfully

imitated the styles of Perugino and Raphael. He studied in Venice
with the teacher and composer Bertoni, afterwards his lifelong
friend, and according to some authorities was in the choir of St
Mark's in about 1757. He does not seem to have made his stage
début until the age of twenty-six (in Gasmann's 'Achille in
Sciro' at the Teatro S. Giovanni Grisostomo), which was perhaps
the reason why his voice retained its beauty so long. In 1769 he
succeeded Guarducci as chief singer to the church of S. Benedetto.

At the outset of his career, Pacchierotti had many difficulties to
overcome, the first of them being his appearance; for he was
painfully tall and thin, unpleasing in face and awkward in movements. Then there was the jealousy of other singers, who seem to
have realised from the start that here was a talent much above the
ordinary. He had been engaged for Naples in 1769, but the prima
donna Anna de Amicis made a scene, and threatened to walk out if
he came; the engagement was made with Guadagni instead, and
Pacchierotti had to content himself with Palermo, where he was
idolised, and remained until 1771.

It was while in Sicily that Pacchierotti first came in contact
with the famous Caterina Gabrielli, one of the greatest female
singers of the eighteenth century, and probably the most eccentric
and capricious of all prima donnas. "The first woman", says
Brydone, "is Gabrielli, who is certainly the greatest singer in the
world, and those who sing in the same theatre must be capital,
otherwise they would never be attended to. This, indeed, has
been the fate of all the performers, except Pacchierotti, and he too
gave himself up for lost on hearing her performance. It happened
to be an air of execution, exactly adapted to her voice, in which
she exerted herself in so astonishing a manner that, before it was
half done, poor Pacchierotti burst out a crying, and ran in behind
the scenes, lamenting that he had dared to appear on the same
stage with so wonderful a singer, where his small talents must not
only be lost, but where he must ever be accused of presumption,
which he hoped was foreign to his character. It was with some
difficulty they could prevail upon him to appear again; but from
an applause well merited, both from his talents and modesty, he

soon began to pluck up a little courage; and in the singing of a tender air, even she herself, as well as the audience, is said to have been moved." All his life, Pacchierotti was to remain almost unreasonably diffident for a great singer, and the most trivial mishap could put him out of his stride.

For all her vagaries, the Gabrielli had a good heart and was incapable of meanness; unfortunately, such was not the case with some of her supporters. When she and Pacchierotti sang at Naples in 1772, their rivalry was made the excuse for a great deal of energetic party warfare. "We see Pacchierotti", says a chronicler, "obtaining a greater success at the Teatro S. Carlo in Naples than the famous Gabrielli, and succeeding in creating around himself quite a party of admirers." It seems that, by now, Pacchierotti had surpassed the negligent Gabrielli in technique, and this her admirers (most of whom either were, had been, or hoped to be, her lovers) were unwilling to forgive. "One evening," continues the account, "while Pacchierotti was singing one of his favourite arias, the opposing group began with their mouths to make at him the noise called *sordino*, at which the singer, once he reached the wings, experienced such feelings of bitterness and shame that he broke into loud lamentations, and could hardly be induced to finish the opera." Eventually, one of the *Gabriellists*, a certain Ruffo, insulted Pacchierotti in the street, and the singer, an excellent swordsman, challenged him to a duel there and then, and extorted an apology.

Unfortunately, Ruffo was an officer of the Royal Guard, whose person was considered more or less sacrosanct—at least as far as civilians were concerned—and the singer found himself in prison. He was not left to languish there for long, but such occurrences made for bad blood, feelings ran increasingly high and no one in Naples would have dared not to take sides, for fear of seeming out of touch. The music, naturally, was the sufferer, and performances at the San Carlo degenerated into something resembling the chariot-races of Constantinople. The aged Caffarelli, who for some reason had taken against Pacchierotti—probably because the latter was the first castrato who looked like effacing his memory

—was inexorable against him, and maliciously blamed him for the failure of the new opera—Jommelli's 'Ifigenia'. In fact, it was the music that had displeased the Neapolitans, for it was written in the style which the composer had evolved while at Stuttgart, and seemed to them unbearably elaborate, German, and learned; it was to be one of poor Jommelli's last works, and its harsh reception is said to have hastened his death, though he had still the strength to write at least one other opera, 'Il Trionfo di Clelia'.

Kelly has the story of another quarrel in which Pacchierotti, the mildest of men, became involved while at Naples on a later occasion. His singing of the part of Aeneas in Schuster's 'Didone abbandonata', and particularly of the aria 'Io ti lascio, e questo addio', had so captivated a certain Marchesa Santa Marca, that despite his unprepossessing appearance she fell madly in love with him. This naturally displeased her *amant de titre*, who determined to have the singer assassinated, and it was only by luck that he escaped unscathed. The Irishman gives the name of this vengeful person as Cardinal Ruffo; but whether this is the man who was later to make his name odious by his cruelties, on the return of King Ferdinand from his first exile in Sicily, or whether Kelly is merely confusing his name with that of the hero of Pacchierotti's earlier affair of honour, does not appear. In another connection, Kelly mentions that the singer "was supposed to have received large sums from an English lady of high birth, who was said to be fervently attached to him".[1] If so, his voice must have possessed

---

[1] No doubt this was Lady Mary Duncan who, says Beckford, "is more preciously fond of [Pacchierotti] than a she-bear of its suckling". There is what appears to be a further allusion to this strange infatuation in the following circumstances. One Badini had sent Lady Mary tickets for his benefit, to which she replied most arrogantly: "Lady Mary Duncan is not a little surprised at the consummate impudence of *Badini*, in daring to have the insolence to send Tickets to her house, without her having sent him orders for it: had she intended going, this wo'd have prevented her; nor *dose* (sic) she see any *occasion* to employ so bad a poet as BADINI; he can be of no service, except to wife *of* (sic) the dust from the Dancers shoes, when they come off the stage."
Badini, not to be outdone, replied as follows: ". . . I thought your ladyship

an erotic quality more than sufficient to compensate for his lack of visual charms. He failed, however, to captivate the Irish adventuress Sara Goudar, with whom he fancied himself in love, but who dismissed him, remarking: "Je ne sais si c'est parce que je suis femme, mais je n'aime point les eunuques."

Meanwhile, Pacchierotti had been singing in almost all the principal cities of Italy, with unfailing brilliant success; and in 1778 he first made the voyage to England, where his début was in a *pasticcio* called 'Demofoonte'. He was received with rapturous enthusiasm; but Roncaglia had been engaged for the season of 1779–80 before his successor's qualities were known, and it was not until late in 1780 that Pacchierotti returned to England. On this visit, he stayed until 1784 and then returned to Italy before making one last appearance in London in 1790.

Lord Mount Edgcumbe has a long eulogy of Pacchierotti which is worth quoting in full: "Pacchierotti's voice was an extensive soprano, full and sweet in the highest degree: his powers of execution were great, but he had far too good taste and good sense to make a display of them where it would have been mis-applied, confining it to one *aria d'agilità* in each opera, conscious that the chief delight of singing and his own supreme excellence lay in touching expression and exquisite pathos. Yet he was so thorough a musician that nothing came amiss to him; every style was to him equally easy, and he could sing, at first sight, all songs of the most opposite characters, not merely with the facility and correctness which a complete knowledge of music must give, but entering at once into the views of the composer, and giving them all the spirit and expression he had designed. Such was his genius in his embellishments and cadences, that their variety was in-exhaustible. He could not sing a song twice in exactly the same

had only a partiality for *Cast-Rats*: but I see, that the Gentlemen of the Pump are likewise your favourites. . . . There is no accounting for the whimsies of some Beings. I remember, my Lady, I once had an old B——, that was aston-ishingly fond of vermin, and had a mortal antipathy against Nightingales and Canary-Birds." This lively exchange was reported in all the newspapers, and the noble lady made to look such a fool that she thought fit to leave London at the height of the season.

way; yet never did he introduce an ornament that was not judicious and appropriate to the composition. His shake (then considered as an indispensable requisite, without which no one could be esteemed a perfect singer) was the very best that could be heard in every form in which that grace could be executed: whether taken from above or below, between whole or semitones, fast or slow, it was always open, equal, and distinct, giving the greatest brilliancy to his cadences, and often introduced into his passages with the happiest effect. As an actor, with many disadvantages of person . . . he was nevertheless forcible and impressive; for he felt warmly, had excellent judgment, and was an enthusiast for his profession. His recitative was inimitably fine, so that even those who did not understand the language could not fail to comprehend, from his countenance, voice and action, every sentiment he expressed. As a concert singer, and particularly in private society, he shone almost more than on the stage; for he sang with greater spirit in a small circle of friends, and was more gratified with their applause than in a public concert-room or crowded theatre. I was in the habit of so hearing him most frequently, and having been intimately acquainted with him for many years, am enabled to speak thus minutely of his performance. On such occasions he would give way to his fancy, and seem almost inspired; and I have often seen his auditors, even those the least musical, moved to tears while he was singing. Possessing a very large collection of music, he could give an infinite variety of songs by every master of reputation. I have more than once heard him sing a cantata of Haydn's, called 'Arianna a Nasso', composed for a single voice, with only a pianoforte accompaniment, and that was played by Haydn himself; it is needless to say that the performance was perfect. To this detail of his merits and peculiar qualities as a singer, I must add that he was a worthy, good man, modest and diffident even to a fault; for it was to an excess that at times checked his exertions, and made him dissatisfied with himself when he had given the greatest delight to his hearers. He was unpresuming in his manners, grateful and attached to all his numerous friends and patrons."

Burney, too, thought Pacchierotti unquestionably the greatest singer he had ever heard, and devotes much space to his praises. His eulogy is too long to be quoted here, but there is one point that is worth mentioning. "The low notes of his voice were so full and flexible", says Burney, "that in private, among particular friends and admirers, I have often heard him sing Ansani's and David's *tenor* songs in their original pitch, in a most perfect and admirable manner, going down sometimes as low as B♭ or the second line in the base." Burney's daughter, Fanny, later Mme d'Arblay, was another great admirer and friend of Pacchierotti; and he seems, in fact, to have had few if any enemies or detractors. The famous eccentric Beckford was fond of him, and on several occasions had him to stay at Fonthill, together with Tenducci and Rauzzini, and the three castrati sang in several works, one of them a little opera of Beckford's own composition.

Among the operas in which Pacchierotti was admired in London, apart from the 'Demofoonte' already mentioned, were Sacchini's 'Rinaldo' and 'Idalide, o la Vergine del Sole' and Bertoni's 'Quinto Fabio', while Burney gives as his four favourite arias the following—'Misero pargoletto' and 'Non temer', the former by Monza and the latter by Bertoni, and both included in 'Demofoonte'; 'Dolce Speme' from 'Rinaldo'; and 'Ti seguirò fedele' from Paesiello's 'Olimpiade'. He sang very often with the famous German prima donna Mme Mara, and her brilliant and flexible, but rather soulless, style of singing showed off his gift for pathos to perfection; and admiration for him was general, despite the strange remarks of his compatriot Nicolò Tommaseo, who writes: "Gasparo Pacchierotti was a singer of ornate talent, and an actor who, thanks to long study, succeeded in correcting the defects of nature and changing them into added graces. But it is not much in his praise that in London he should have moved the English to tears, since the docile islanders, before putting their white handkerchiefs to their eyes, waited for a signal from the Duke of Orleans, who at that time certainly thought of nothing but the Marseillaise, and the proud equality that threatened it and so many other illustrious heads." This could only refer to Pacchierotti's last visit, but in any case is difficult to make sense of.

On his return to Italy in 1784, Pacchierotti continued his success in various cities. In Venice in 1785, he took part in the musical ceremony in honour of Galuppi's funeral, and, as he assured Burney, "I sang very devoutly indeed to obtain a quiet for his soul." It was about this time, too, in Rome, that occurred another famous incident in his life. He was singing the part of Arbace in Metastasio's 'Artaserse', set by Bertoni, and in one scene had to pronounce the words "Eppur son innocente!", which were to be followed by an instrumental *ritornello*; he did so, but was surprised to find that the orchestra remained silent. He turned to the conductor, and asked the reason. "We are all in tears," came the answer, and for some minutes the players were unable to continue, so great was their emotion. In Venice, again, he almost caused a riot when he appeared in the title-role of Bianchi's 'Disertore francese': the French uniform he wore was disapproved of, and only the interest shown by the Duchess of Courland, who happened to be visiting Venice, could reconcile the audience to it. In the end, the opera was a huge success.

Pacchierotti's last public appearance was in 1792[1], at the inauguration of the Fenice theatre, Venice, in Paesiello's 'Giochi d'Agrigento'. By this time he was over fifty, and was beginning to feel his age: "Pacchierotti with all his defects, was enchanting, whenever he happened to sing in tune, as he always addressed himself to the heart; while Marchesi, with ten times his ability and natural gifts, often disgusted, in consequence of his deviations from that nature, the want of which Pachierotti continued to supply, by a refinement of art, which no other singer, male or female, has hitherto been able to attain. His habit of singing below pitch did not arise from want of ear, or of musical science, but from excessive sensibility, whereby his metaphysical powers often got the better of his physical."[2] He now retired to Padua, where his life

1 Save or one occasion, in 1796, when he was compelled to sing for Napoleon.
2 'Venice under the Yoke of France and Austria . . . by a Lady of Quality' (the English-born Marchioness Solari).

was tranquil and uneventful, except for one occasion when a letter of his to Angelica Catalani referring to 'le splendide miserie della vittoria'[1] was intercepted by the police, and he spent a month in prison. He wrote a singing method which was not published, but on which Calegari based his 'Modi generali del Canto' (1836), and died in 1821. Stendhal, who visited him c. 1815, found that he had "all the fire of youth", and was "still sublime when he sings a recitative . . . I learnt more about music in six conversations with this great artist, than from any book; it was the soul speaking to the soul."

Today we can but guess what the great singers of the past can have sounded like; but one might hazard a guess that of all the castrati, could we hear them, Pacchierotti would please us most, and that even Farinelli, for all his brilliance and pathos, would by comparison seem stiff, old-fashioned, and peculiar.

PISTOCCHI, Francesco Antonio

Just as Porpora was a composer who is even better known as a singing master, Pistocchi's fame as a teacher far exceeded his success as a singer; he was, none the less, one of the foremost castrati of his day.

He was born at Palermo in 1659, the son of a violinist, but when he was two years old his family moved to Bologna, where his father had taken a post as one of the musicians attached to the Cathedral. Pistocchi soon developed into something of an infant prodigy, both as a singer and as a composer; at the age of five he had attracted the attention of the Grand Duke of Tuscany and the Cardinal-Legate at Bologna, and at eight he published his first composition, under the title 'Capricci Puerili'—a set of forty variations for clavier, harp, violin, and other instruments. His teacher was the distinguished composer Perti.

He was soon singing in the cathedral choir, but neither his

---

[1] Accounts vary, but the 'victory' referred to seems most probably to have been the Austrian reconquest of Italy in 1814, in which the infant Verdi so nearly lost his life.

father nor himself seem to have taken their duties very seriously, for they led a wandering life, singing and playing in theatres and the houses of wealthy amateurs wherever they could. Finally, in 1675, the long-suffering Chapter had had enough, and the two Pistocchis were given the sack. At this point we cease to hear anything of the father, who must either have died or separated from his son.

The young singer's voice had been a soprano remarkable for its beauty, and was thought unusually promising: but about this time, for some unknown reason, he suddenly lost it. The famous account quoted by Burney would have it that 'a dissolute life' was responsible for this unfortunate accident, but it may just as probably have been due to natural causes: many castrati passed through a difficult period, vocally speaking, during the years in which their voices would have broken, had they not been what they were, and some of them were never able to sing again.

In any event, Pistocchi was forced to give up singing, and lived in Venice, devoting, apparently, his time to composition. Burney's account quoted from Galliard states that he was in desperate financial straits, and was forced to earn his living as a copyist; in fact, it seems that he took up with an exact contemporary and fellow-Bolognese, the composer Domenico Gabrielli, who was also in Venice at the time, and he may well have helped to copy some of his music, though not in a professional capacity. Pistocchi's own first opera, 'Leandro', was given in 1679, at a puppet theatre with the singers behind the scenes—an eccentric manner of staging that was then enjoying a passing vogue, and which was revived, a hundred years later, by the castrato Guadagni for his own amusement. A comic opera—quite a rarity at the time—by Pistocchi, 'Girello', is said to have been composed even earlier, when he was only about ten years old, though not performed until 1682: but most authorities now doubt whether the music was really by him at all.

Not content, however, with fame as a composer—not then a very lucrative calling—Pistocchi now once more turned his thoughts to singing. He had, according to one account, attempted the stage at the age of twenty, in Perti's 'Nerone fatto Cesare',[1] but had been a failure; at all events, his first success in this capacity did not come until 1687, in Venice. By this time, by assiduous practice and perseverance, he had recovered or recreated for himself a fine voice, now a contralto, and an even finer technique; he rapidly became famous. For the next few years he visited various Italian towns—Parma, Piacenza, Modena, Bologna, and so on—being everywhere applauded under the affectionate diminutive of 'Pistocchino', until 1696, when he became *maestro da capella* to the Margrave of Anspach. Among his pupils there was the Princess Caroline, subsequently Queen of England, and he also continued his career as a composer, producing the operas 'Narciso' (1697) and 'Pazzie d'amore e dell'interesse' (1699) in which he sang himself. In the latter year he made a visit to Vienna, where in 1700 was produced his 'La risa di Democrito'. This opera must have pleased exceptionally, for it was revived at Bologna in 1708, and at Florence in 1710.

The following year, Pistocchi was reconciled with the Chapter of Bologna Cathedral, and resumed his position as singer there, relinquishing for the purpose his post at Anspach. He was still, however, free to leave Bologna for considerable periods: he had a country house near Parma where he spent much time, and he continued his theatrical career. In 1702 he sang in Milan, and then at the Tuscan court with Matteuccio, in a motet of Alessandro Scarlatti, and in 1704 he appeared in Venice in Gasparini's 'La fede tradita e vendicata'. By this time, his voice seems to have been on the decline, and a rather unflattering poem was addressed to him, which begins

> Pistocco col fa un trill' si puo eguagliare
> A quel rumor ch'è solito di fare
> Quando si scossa un gran sacco di nore.

His last stage appearance was the following year, at Genoa in Albinoni's 'Il più fedele tra Vassalli'.

---

[1] The name of the opera must at any rate be incorrect, for it was not composed until 1693. Pistocchi performed in it at Bologna in 1695.

In 1706 Pistocchi founded his celebrated school, one of the greatest in eighteenth-century Italy. Among his scholars were the castrati Bernacchi, Antonio Pasi, and G-B Minelli, the tenor Annibale Pio Fabri, and Domenico Gizzi, famous not so much for his own singing as for being the teacher of Gizziello. Bernacchi, too, was in his turn a teacher, and so the tradition was handed on till the days of Crescentini and Velluti: Pistocchi, says Galliard in a note to his translation of Tosi's treatise on singing, "refined the manner of singing in Italy, which was then a little crude. His merit in this is acknowledged by all his countrymen, and contradicted by none." He is, in fact, one of the most important figures in the whole history of singing, and just as Alessandro Scarlatti, born in the same year and place, was the founder of the Neapolitan school of opera and hence of the whole later tradition of dramatic music, Pistocchi was ultimately responsible for the voices for which that music was created.

In 1715 he entered the Order of St Philip Neri, and retired to their monastery at Forli, where he became very popular with the other monks—"he has brought joy into the cloister," they said. Though he had renounced the world, he had by no means done with music, and he employed himself in the composition of oratorios, among them 'Il Sacrificio di Gefte', 'Davide', and 'I Pastori del Presepe', until his death in 1726. The latter is supposed to have taken place in Bologna, so he must have moved in the meantime to a different house of the Oratorian Order.

Of his talents as a composer, Burney had a considerable opinion. Speaking of an oratorio of Pistocchi's called 'Maria Vergine addolorata', he writes: "There is no date to this oratorio . . . but by the elegance and simplicity of the style, it seems to have been produced about the end of the last century. Recitative now freed from formal closes and in possession of all its true forms, in this production is extremely pathetic and dramatic; and Pistocchi seems a more correct contrapuntist than the generality of opera singers whom the demon of composition seizes at a period of their lives, when it is too late to begin, and impossible to pursue such studies effectually, without injuring the chest, and neglecting the cultivation of the voice. . . . At the termination of this oratorio which is truly pathetic and solemn, all the degrees of diminution of sound are used; as *piano, più piano, pianissimo,* equivalent to the *diminuendo, calando,* and *smorzando,* of the present times."

In addition to his other gifts, Pistocchi seems to have been of an engaging and amiable disposition, and he was universally popular with his pupils and contemporaries in general. His death was much lamented.

RAUZZINI, Venanzio

No castrato had a longer or more intimate connection with Great Britain than Rauzzini; and it seems fitting to quote the account of his early life that Kelly gives: "Rauzzini was a native of Rome, and made his appearance on the stage there, at the Teatro della Valle. He was a great musician, had a fine voice, was very young, and so proverbially handsome, that he always performed the part of the Prima Donna. . . . His reception was highly flattering, and he afterwards performed in all the principal theatres of Italy. The Elector of Bavaria, who expended immense sums on his Italian opera, invited him to Munich. His success at that court was, as usual, unqualified. But alas! his beauty was his bane! an exalted personage became deeply and hopelessly enamoured of him, and, spite of his talents, it was suggested to him that a change of air would be for the benefit of his health. He took the hint, and left Munich: he then engaged himself at the Italian opera in London . . . and his acting in Pyramus, in the opera of Pyramus and Thisbe, was so fine, that Garrick has often complimented him on it." To supplement this lively narrative with a few dates; Rauzzini was born in 1746, not at Rome, but at Camerino in the Marches, and, after singing in the Papal Chapel as a boy, made his stage début in 1765. His engagement with the court of Bavaria began in 1767, and he arrived in London in 1774: in Milan he had taken part in the first performance of Mozart's youthful opera 'Lucio Silla'. Mozart's well-known 'Exsultate, jubilate' was also composed for him.

In London, Rauzzini was a great success. "His taste, fancy, and delicacy, together with his beautiful person and spirited and intelligent manner of acting . . . gained him general approbation", says Burney, and adds that his voice had a compass of more than two octaves. He was, however, a pleasing, rather than a great, singer, and his technique was limited; his acting was particularly admired in the death scene in Sacchini's 'Montezuma'. According to Goudar, however, "Rauzzini chante joliment; mais il est à craindre qu'il ne chante bientôt rondement, car il enfle de tous côtés." He is, incidentally, quite often described as a tenor, but this seems to arise from confusion with his brother Matteo (1754–91), who was a singer and composer who settled in Ireland, where he enjoyed some success.

Rauzzini was as successful as a composer as he was as a singer; the 'Piramo e Tisbe' alluded to by Kelly was of his own composition (first given in 1775), and among his other successes were 'I due amanti in inganno' (Venice 1775), 'Le ali d'amore' (London 1776), and 'La Vestale' (London 1787). Another work of his given in London, 'La Regina di Golconda', was very spectacular in staging, but less successful, whilst one of the arias from 'Piramo e Tisbe' was introduced into Sheridan's 'The Duenna' and sung to the words, 'By him we love offended'.

In this connection may be mentioned the strange quarrel between Rauzzini and the eminent composer Sacchini, whom he accused of getting him (Rauzzini) to 'ghost' his operas for him, and then refusing to acknowledge or recompense his labours. What the rights and wrongs of the matter really were has never been established. Sacchini certainly suffered from gout, and some have thought that he merely got Rauzzini to act as his amanuensis; but Rauzzini evidently believed himself to have been wronged, for he was with difficulty dissuaded from taking the matter to court.

In 1778, Rauzzini virtually gave up the stage, having earned enough money to live comfortably, and for some years led a wandering life; while in Ireland, he met the young Kelly, discovered in him the promise of talent, and was instrumental in getting his father to send him to Naples for training.

In 1787, Rauzzini settled at Bath, where he lived for the rest of his life, becoming almost as familiar a figure as Beau Nash. "He undertook", says Kelly, "to conduct the concerts, and continued to reside for many years, beloved and respected by the inhabitants and visitors of that city. He had a great deal of teaching, which, added to the profits of his performers, enabled him to entertain in the most hospitable manner he did. The expenses of those performances were to him comparatively small, as it was almost an article of faith amongst the profession to give their services gratis on such occasions. I have known Mrs Billington renounce many profitable engagements in London, when Rauzzini has required the aid of her talents."[1]

Rauzzini's house was at Perrymead, and it was there that he entertained Haydn in 1794; the great composer was struck by a memorial to the singer's dog, Turk, and composed a canon on part of the inscription, beginning with the words, "Turk was a faithful dog, and not a man." Among Rauzzini's many scholars, his favourite was the great English tenor Braham; and another occupation of his later years was the composition of chamber music, piano sonatas, and other smaller pieces. He died in 1810, and was buried in Bath Abbey, where his monument may still be seen.

RONCAGLIA, Francesco

This pupil of Lorenzo Gibelli was born at Faenza, not far from Bologna, in about 1750, and is first heard of in 1772, when he was engaged for the Elector Palatine's court opera at Mannheim. He remained there until in 1774 the Elector succeeded also to the

---

[1] Yet, according to a newspaper of the time, Rauzzini "is said to pay her [Mrs Billington] an hundred and fifty pounds, for the expedition".

crown of Bavaria, when he moved his court to Munich and the Mannheim company broke up.

Roncaglia returned to Italy and sang in various places, but particularly at Naples, until 1777, when he was engaged for London. At first he obtained a great success; he had, according to Burney, "an elegant face and figure, a sweet-toned voice, a chaste and well-disciplined style of singing; hazarded nothing, and was always in tune"; though, he adds, "of the three great requisites of a stage singer, pathos, grace, and execution, he was in perfect possession only of the second".

Lord Mount Edgcumbe was less enthusiastic, finding him "languid, feeble, and insipid, and withal extremely affected". "Yet", this critic adds, "he gave so much pleasure on his first appearance, in Sacchini's opera of Creso, that as he was under engagement to return to Italy the next year, he was hastily re-engaged for the next season but one, before it was known how his immediate successor would be liked."

Unfortunately for him, this successor was none other than Pacchierotti, the greatest singer of the age, and Roncaglia on his return visit found the public much less enthusiastic than they had been, and the effulgence of his talents much dimmed by proximity with the other's. Being of a conceited and irritable nature, he refused to admit the real reason for his decline in favour, and attributed it to the supposed intrigues of the tenor Ansani, who in any case was a better singer than himself; and the latter was so disgusted with the whole business that he eventually walked out. The season, as may be imagined, was not an unqualified success.

To be fair to Roncaglia, he was then still quite young, and seems later to have improved both in artistry and in character; and he became a very popular performer throughout Italy. He died at Bologna at the beginning of the nineteenth century.

RUBINELLI, Giovanni Maria

This contralto, with Pacchierotti and Marchesi, made up that trio of great castrati which aroused such rapture in the musical London of the 1780's, bringing a decade of operatic brilliance rivalled only by that, fifty years before, when Farinelli, Caffarelli, Carestini, Senesino, and Gizziello had all been in England within the space of ten years.

Born at Brescia in 1753, he is first heard of at Stuttgart in 1766, singing in the ducal chapel, and in 1770 he made his stage début there, in Sacchini's 'Calliroe'. He became a great favourite in Stuttgart, singing both male and female roles. In 1774 he returned to his native country, and was applauded in various cities—in Venice in Anfossi's 'Lucio Silla', in Padua in Mysliweczek's 'Atide', and at Modena in Paesiello's 'Alessandro nell'Indie'. In 1776–8 he was at Naples, where he appeared in a considerable number of works,[1] and in the latter year he went to Milan for the inauguration of the Scala Theatre, for which the operas were Salieri's 'Europa riconosciuta' and Mortellari's 'Troia distrutta'. Pacchierotti, too, sang in the latter work. The following year, again in Milan, Rubinelli had to undergo quite an ordeal. Singing with him in Alessandri's 'Calliroe', though among the chorus, were five castrati, one of whom—Antonio Duffo by name—"had earned the sympathetic notoriety of all Milan by his curly hair, his well-developed bosom, his plumpness and his pretty little voice". A group of young aristocrats, suddenly disgusted at the castrati, determined to drive them from the stage. They met together at Iselli's chocolate-house to lay their plans, and decided to make an all-out effort to barrack the next new opera, Anfossi's 'Cleopatra', in which Rubinelli was again to appear. In the event, however, his singing proved so magical that their wrath was appeased, and they instead fell to quarrelling over

---

[1] Among them Rutini's 'Vologeso', Paesiello's 'La Disfatta di Dario', Fischietti's 'Arianna e Teseo', Guglielmi's 'Ricimero', and Platania's 'Bellerofonte'.

a young dancer in the ballet 'Il tradimento di Sinone', "whose legs were quite good enough to make up for the fall of Troy".

Further successes followed in various places, particularly at Naples in 1784,[1] and in 1786 Rubinelli arrived in England. "His journey hither", says Burney, "from Rome, where he sung during the carnival of this year, was not very propitious; as the weather was uncommonly inclement, and he was not only overturned in his chaise at Macon, in France, but after quitting the ship, in which he sailed from Calais to Dover, the boat that was to have landed him was overset near the shore, and he remained a considerable time up to his chin in water, to the great risk of his health, his voice, and even his life. . . . The first opera in which Rubinelli appeared in England, was a *pasticcio,* called 'Virginia', May the 4th. His own part, however, was chiefly composed by Angiolo Tarchi, a young Neapolitan, who is advancing into eminence with great rapidity. Rubinelli is, in figure, tall and majestic; in countenance, mild and benign. There is dignity in his appearance on the stage; and the instant the tone of his voice is heard, there remains no doubt with the audience of his being the first singer. . . . His shake is not sufficiently open; but in other respects he is an admirable singer. His style is grand, and truly dramatic. His execution is neat and distinct. His taste and embellishments are new, select, and masterly. His articulation is so pure and well accented in his recitatives, that no one who understands the Italian language can ever want to look at the book of the words, while he is singing. His chest is so strong, and his intonation perfect, that I have very seldom heard him sing out of tune. His voice is more clear and certain in a theatre, where it has room to expand, than in a room. He had a greater variety of embellishments than any singer I had heard, except Pacchierotti, who not only surpasses him in richness of invention and fancy, but in the native pathos, and touching expression of his voice. Yet Rubinelli, from the fulness of his voice, and greater simplicty of style, pleases a more considerable number of his hearers than Pacchierotti,

[1] In Tritto's 'Artenice', Antonelli's 'Catone in Utica', and Paesiello's 'Antigone'.

though none perhaps, so exquisitely as that singer used to please his real admirers. Rubinelli finding himself censured on his first arrival in England for changing and embellishing his airs, sung 'Return, O God of Hosts' at Westminster Abbey, in so plain and unadorned a manner, that those who venerate Handel the most, thought him bald and insipid."

Once again, as with Guarducci, it seems that it was not so much Rubinelli's embellishments that displeased the English, as his want of virtuosity in performing them; Lord Mount Edgcumbe, while echoing Burney in many of his praises, remarks that Rubinelli "had little agility, nor did he attempt to do more than he could execute perfectly". Kelly, too, admired him as "an excellent actor as well as a sound musician", particularly in Bertoni's 'Orfeo ed Euridice', and recalls a duet that he sang in it with Brigida Giorgi Banti. Burney, however, found that he "discovered but little sensibility by his gestures or tone of voice", from the dramatic point of view.

Rubinelli left England in 1787, and returned to Italy, where he continued to sing with success until his retirement in 1800; particular triumphs being at Milan, 1789, in Bianchi's 'Nitteti'; Vicenza, 1791, in Nasolini's 'La Morte di Cleopatra'; and Verona, 1792, in Andreozzi's 'Agesilao'. After retiring, he lived quietly in his native town, where he died in 1829.

SALIMBENI, Felice

This famous pupil of Porpora was born at Milan in 1712, and made his début at Rome in 1731, in Hasse's 'Cajo Fabricio'. In 1733 he entered the service of the Emperor Charles VI at Vienna, remaining there until 1739, in which year he was heard in Genoa in 'Farnace' and 'Venceslao'. In 1743–50, he was at the court of Frederick the Great,[1] but in the latter year he signed a contract for the Royal Theatre at Dresden.

[1] Salimbeni, whose Berlin début was in Graun's 'Catone in Utica', was for long a great favourite, both with the public and Frederick the Great. Eventually,

His voice is said to have been powerful, clear with a wide range, and of rare beauty; and he earned particular admiration by his "rendering of adagios, with discreet but effective ornamentation, and for his amazing swell from *pianissimo* to an almost unbelievable degree of sonority". His handsome appearance was another advantage: "The charming part of Megacles in the 'Olimpiade'," says Vernon Lee, "of whom Argene says, 'avea bionde le chiome, oscuro il ciglio . . . gli sguardi lenti e pietosi,' etc., was suggested by a beautiful young pupil of Porpora, with fair curls and femininely soft eyes, Felice Salimbeni."

Readers of Casanova's memoirs may remember that the famous adventurer once met, at Ancona, a young girl posing as the castrato Bellino. When he had satisfied himself that she was in reality a girl, and asked her the reason for her curious masquerade, she told the following story. She was a native of Bologna, and Salimbeni (Casanova spells it Salimberi) had lodged there in her mother's house. He had fallen in love with her, and she with him, and, as she told Casanova: "No doubt men like you are much above those of his kind; but Salimberi was an exception. His beauty, his wit, his manners, his talent, and the outstanding qualities of his heart, made him seem to me preferable to all men. . . . He was modest and discreet, rich and generous."

Salimbeni had suggested that she pass herself off as a castrato, to avoid the attentions of importunate suitors, and undertook to find her employment with the Elector of Saxony, his master, saying, "When in a year or two your breasts are fully formed, it will seem a defect which you share with many of us", and assuring her that no one would discover the imposture. However, before he could carry out his intentions, Salimbeni died, and she was left disconsolate; but had determined to maintain her pretence, to be able to sing within the Papal States.

The strange thing about this incident is that Casanova places it in 1744, and a mass of circumstantial details show that he was right in doing so; yet every authority is in agreement that

however, he somehow incurred the latter's displeasure, and was blamed for the failure of 'Coriolano', for which Frederick had sketched the libretto.

Salimbeni did not die until 1751, at Ljubljana in what is now Yugoslavia, while on his way from Dresden to Naples on leave of absence, to take a holiday and recover from a recent illness. The problem seems insoluble, unless of course Casanova gave Salimbeni's name in error for some quite other singer; could it, perhaps have been Giuseppe Appiani, born in the same year and place as Salimbeni, and who *did* die at Bologna (or, according to some, Cesena) in 1742?

Casanova met the girl again in Florence in 1761, at which time, according to him, she was a famous and successful singer under the name of Teresa Lanti Palesi; but I have not been able to find this name in any extant cast-list. There was, incidentally, another Bolognese singer named Teresa Lanti, born in 1746, who may have been her namesake's daughter (by Casanova?), and whose portrait may be seen in the theatrical museum attached to the Scala Theatre, Milan.

SASSANI, Matteo (Matteuccio)

Matteuccio is commonly said to have been born at Naples in 1649. Another authority, however, gives the place of his birth as S. Severo near Foggia, and the date as 1667; and the latter year certainly seems the more probable one, considering that he was still alive in 1735. On the other hand, he was universally supposed to have attained a very great age by the time of his death.

The first time that we hear of Matteuccio is in 1693, when he was engaged as first soprano at the Naples opera and had a sensational success. In 1695 he was invited to Vienna to sing in the Empress's chapel at a salary of 3,000 scudi, but, says a chronicler, "he could not bear to stay long away from this city (i.e. Naples), where he was beloved by all, and particularly by the ladies". He not only sang so beautifully that "cantare come Matteuccio" became a proverbial phrase, but was dashing and handsome and a great womaniser.

On his return from Vienna, his popularity became greater than ever, and soon went completely to his head. He became impossibly full of himself, insulted some dukes, treated the Viceroy's servants with contempt, and refused to comply with his orders. The Viceroy, enraged, determined to send Matteuccio to the galleys, but was dissuaded by his wife who had a weakness for the singer; and he could not well disregard her wishes, for, as everyone knew, he himself was in love with the prima donna, and looked on her quite equal *incartades* with a lenient eye.

Matteuccio got off with a severe warning, and was then restored to the viceregal favour; so much so that, in November 1698, he was sent to Madrid to entertain the Viceroy's master, the half-imbecile King Charles II. He was apparently a great success there; so much so that, according to an English observer, "Matteuccio of Naples was chief Favourite to Charles II, late King of Spain, insomuch that all Favours pass'd through his Hands."

After his return from Spain, Matteuccio continued to appear on the stage until the year 1708, when he sang in Lotti's 'Il Vincitor generoso', and at Bologna in 'Il Fratricida innocente': after that, his name appears no more in cast-lists, and he seems to have devoted himself to the Royal Chapel in Naples, where he directed the singing and sang himself. "He was in the habit," says Mancini, "out of pure devotion, of singing in the church every Saturday; and though he was more than eighty years old, his voice was so fresh and clear, and he sang with so much flexibility and lightness, that those who heard him without seeing him believed him a young man in the prime of life."

He was still alive in 1735, when Caffarelli applied for, and got, his position; Matteuccio by this time being considered too old to be of use. He was no doubt retired on a pension, but we hear no more of him, and the date of his death is unknown.

SCALZI, Carlo

Never what could be called a top-ranking star, Scalzi was evidently one of those good, safe singers that never let a performance down; and he was constantly in work in the leading theatres of Italy and elsewhere.

Scalzi was born at Voghera, almost exactly half-way between Milan and Genoa, in about 1695, and his first known appearance was at Venice in 1719, in A. Pollarolo's 'Leucippo e Tenoe'. During the succeeding decade he sang in various places, and particularly at Naples, where in 1730 he created the title role in Metastasio's famous drama of 'Ezio', set on this occasion by Vinci. The poet saw him in the following year at Rome, in Vinci's 'Artaserse', and writes of the "incomparibili Scalzi e Farfallino" (Farinelli).

Scalzi was engaged by Handel at the same time as Carestini, to compete with the 'Opera of Nobility', and his success in London was considerable, if not exactly brilliant. Not long afterwards, he retired to Genoa and disappeared from view, or at least from history. The date of his death is unknown.

TENDUCCI, Giusto Ferdinando (Senesino)

Never, perhaps, a singer of the foremost rank, Tenducci none the less enjoyed a career that was in some ways absolutely unique, and is altogether a picturesque and characteristic figure of his time.

He was born at Siena in about 1736 (hence his pseudonym, little used), and is first heard of in Venice, 1753, in Bertoni's 'Ginevra'. In 1756 he was at Naples, singing in 'Farnace', set by Piccinni and Perez, in which he seems to have made a considerable success, and in 1758 he arrived in London, as 'second man' for the serious opera. However, he attracted so much attention in the first opera, Cocchi's 'Ciro riconosciuto', that he quite eclipsed the nominally principal singer, Potenza; and his fame reached its apogee some time later when he appeared in Arne's English opera after the Italian style, 'Artaxerxes' (1762). His performance in this work, says Burney, "had a rapid effect upon the public taste, and stimulated to imitation all that were possessed of good ears and flexible voices". In 1764 the Mozart family arrived in

London, and soon became intimate with Tenducci, who gave the eight-year-old genius some singing lessons, repaid by the composition of an aria specially for him.

Tenducci had already, in 1761, made a journey to Scotland, and in 1765 he further extended his knowledge of the British Isles by a trip to Ireland, where he introduced 'Artaxerxes' to the inhabitants of Dublin, causing a sensation with his singing of the aria 'Water parted from the sea'.

An even greater sensation was caused, however, the following year, when Tenducci eloped with a young girl of good family, Miss Dora Maunsell of Limerick, and married her at Cork by a Protestant ceremony. He had met her some time before while staying with some friends of her family: the horror and rage of the latter on hearing of the runaway match were almost past description.

The couple now had to endure the most grievous hardships and presecutions at the hands of the infuriated parents and various cousins, which are described in detail by the young bride herself in an account published in 1768 as 'A True and Genuine Narrative of Mr. & Mrs. Tenducci'. The whole affair is reminiscent of Richardson's 'Pamela', with its traduced heroine, its poor but honest hero, its arrogant gentry and their lofty disregard of the law; for some time the pair dodged about the country and eluded their pursuers, but eventually, once more in Cork, Tenducci was thrown into jail, and his wife kidnapped and held by her inexorable relations. The singer's main preoccupation, oddly enough, seems to have been anxiety lest people believe, as his wife's family would have it, that he had seduced her while giving her lessons; and we find him writing from prison to the editor of the local newspaper:

> "North Goal [*sic*]
> September 2nd, 1766.

"Sir,

I beg you will do me the justice, in your next paper, to contradict a circumstance inserted in your last, that I was married to a young lady who had been my pupil: Now, Sir, this is entirely

void of foundation. I never was entertained as a singing or music
master by an person, or persons, since I had the honour to perform
in this kingdom; never taught the act of singing, and consequently
never had a pupil; nor was I ever received by the friends of that
young lady (whom I cannot mention but with the utmost respect)
on any such footing, as a teacher of music, or singing, in any
degree whatsoever.

I am, Sir, your humble Servant,

F. TENDUCCI."

To continue the narrative in Dora Tenducci's own words:
"Some gentlemen, pitying his distressed situation . . . became bail
for him, and he was once more delivered from that noisome gaol.
My cousin W. desired Mr T. B. not to advertise Tenducci's name
in the bills for the theatre, assuring him, if he did, his house should
be torn to pieces. Mr B. apprehensive of danger, advertised the
Merchant of Venice, instead of an opera, for Tenducci's benefit.
Mr W. not content with the scheme he had already practised,
persuaded the commanding officer in Cork to withhold the usual
guard from attending the play house that night, in hopes that the
audience and particular friends of Tenducci might be exposed to
the insults of his party; and the more effectually to answer this
purpose, and to prevent company from going to his benefit play,
a report was industriously spread that there would be a riot at the
house that evening. However, this cruel scheme to hurt him
proved abortive, for the house was filled with the best company
in the city. At the end of the first act Tenducci was called on for
a song; this my cousin W.'s party endeavoured to oppose but
were obliged to acquiesce. When the play was over, and one
given out for the next night, the audience insisted on it's being
an opera: Which accordingly was performed with universal applause." The next day after that, however, Tenducci was again
warned to flee, for the cousins were again on the war-path. He
did so, but after many more alarms and excursions was once more
thrown into prison, where he was much maltreated and nearly
died of fever. Eventually, however, the bride's father relented,

and all ended happily for the time being. Tenducci and his wife remained in Ireland until 1768, when they returned to London.

Tenducci's marriage has another reason for celebrity, alluded to by Casanova: ". . . at Covent Garden . . . the castrato Tenducci surprised me greatly by presenting me to his legitimate wife, by whom he had two children. He laughed at those who argued that, as he was a castrato, he could not reproduce his kind. Nature had made him a monster to keep him a man: he was a *Triorchis*, and as in the operation only two of his seminal glands had been removed, that which remained was sufficient to prove his vitality." This story cannot be true as it stands, for Casanova was in London in 1763-4, and Tenducci was not even married till 1766: though Casanova might well have met him elsewhere at a later date, and misremembered the year and the place.

The matter is, however, altogether a strange one. The story that this castrato had become a father seems to have been widely known at the time, yet Tenducci's marriage was, in 1775, declared null and void through the influence of his wife's relatives. It seems almost impossible to know what the real truth was.

Tenducci now settled in London, where he remained, for the most part, until 1791. In 1776 he was forced to leave England temporarily to escape imprisonment for debt, for he lived on a scale out of all proportion with his means; but a satisfactory settlement must have been reached, for he returned the next year. He was evidently still considered as a fairly respectable and trustworthy person, for he was director of the famous Handel festivals in Westminster Abbey from 1784 till his final departure from England. He also, meanwhile, made further visits to Scotland, Ireland, and other parts of the British Isles, and became known as a teacher—though earlier he had seemed to find the occupation so degrading—publishing, in about 1785, his 'Instructions of Mr Tenducci to his Scholars'.

It was in the latter year, too, that Tenducci made his last appearance on the stage, in a revival of Gluck's 'Orfeo', after the youthful Crescentini had proved a failure and left in the middle of the season. Tenducci was no more of a success, according to

Lord Mount Edgcumbe: "The performance of an old man, who had never been very capital, and could now have scarcely any voice left, and that too in a part in which many still remembered Guadagni, was not likely to prove very attractive." This account was from heresay, as the writer was in Italy at the time, but he adds: "I had heard Tenducci in concerts before I left England but his voice was then cracked, and I did not like him." The singer was then scarcely fifty, and should still have been able to sing reasonably well: but evidently, with his insouciant and erratic character, he did not bother to look after his voice.

After Tenducci's final departure from England, following his wife's death, nothing more is recorded about him, save that he was still alive in about 1800. Neither the place nor the date of his death seem to be known.

Besides his other talents, Tenducci made his name as a composer, producing the Italian operas 'Farnace, o la vendetta di Atride' (Dublin 1765, also given at Edinburgh in 1769) and 'Il castello d'Andalusia' (Dublin 1783), and the English opera 'The Campaign' (1784). He also wrote a number of separate songs, some of them published, which were sung by him at Ranelagh and elsewhere, and a set of six sonatas for harpsichord.

VELLUTI, Giovanni Battista

A melancholy interest surrounds Velluti, the last of the castrati (as far as the stage was concerned) and for many years almost the only survivor of his glorious though unfortunate race. His solitary position had its compensation, for he was, in the best years of his career, virtually without competition; yet he must sometimes have felt a little like a freak in a travelling circus.

He was born at a place near Ancona then called Montolmo, but today known as Pausula, in 1781.[1] His parents apparently

[1] His date of birth is generally given as January 28th, 1780; but the Italians at that period were in the habit of beginning the year on April 1st, so that what we should call January 1781 was to them January 1780.

intended him, at first, to be a soldier, for soon after his birth his mother writes to a friend: "You ask whether I would have been happier at the birth of a girl baby? Oh! But in that case, how could my husband have made of her the valiant captain of whom he dreams? Just think that, the other day while admiring him, he exclaimed, 'This will be the first iron velvet!'"[1]

Given these ambitions, it is difficult to understand what could have induced the parents to allow their child to be castrated; and there is a story that the whole thing was a mistake. According to this theory, the child, suffering from some disease or other, was entrusted to a doctor, who, deliberately or otherwise, misunderstood the parents' instructions, and castrated it before anyone could stop him.

Be that as it may, the deed was done, and Velluti destined perforce for the career of a singer, or for none at all; and his first public appearance was at a tender age, when he sang in a cantata in honour of Cardinal Chiaramonti (subsequently Pope Pius VII) when the latter visited Ancona. Soon after this, the boy was sent away to study with Padre Mattei at Bologna, who took a great fancy to him, "but was obliged by the political vicissitudes of the time to entrust him to various other *maestri*", among whom was the Abate Calpi at Ravenna. The French were invading Italy, revolutions were fermenting everywhere, crowned heads and oligarchies were toppling, and the peace-loving art of singing was in a bad way; Velluti was lucky in having the chance to finish his studies undisturbed, and sensible in taking it, while his contemporaries were busy with politics and other such heady but dangerous sports.

His début was at Forli, in 1800, and we find him at Naples in 1803, in Andreozzi's 'Piramo e Tisbe'; his name rapidly became well known. At Rome he was a particular success, singing in 1805, 1806, 1807, and 1808 at a salary of 600 zecchini, in various operas including Niccolini's 'La Selvaggia nel Messico' and 'Trajano in Dacia', Tritto's 'Andromaca e Pirro', and a revival of Cimarosa's 'Orazii'; after which he appeared at Milan, to

---

[1] 'Velluto' is, of course, the Italian for velvet.

rapturous applause, in 'Coriolano', another opera of Niccolini, with Cesarini and Isabella Colbran. This composer became one of his favourites, together with Morlacchi, and in his later years he could rarely be induced to perform in the operas of other masters, considering that they showed his voice off to far less advantage. In 1809 his operas were Federici's 'Ifigenia in Aulide' and Lavigna's 'Orcamo' and in 1810 Mayr's 'Raoul de Créquy' and Pavesi's 'Arminio'.

Napoleon heard Velluti sing when visiting Venice in 1810, and remarked, "Pareils sons je ne crois pas possibles, qu'à ce qui n'est pas homme"—a dubious compliment not appreciated by the singer, who on hearing of it replied, "Non uomo, ma nemmeno quel bestione che di lui il suono della sua canone rivela!"

Not that Velluti disapproved of Napoleon on 'right-wing' grounds; he cared nothing for hereditary royalties either, as shown in the following account, taken from a contemporary chronicler: "Once at Sinigaglia, on the occasion of the famous fair of 1814, Velluti was engaged by the impresario Osca to sing in the 'Carlo Magno' of Niccolini. For thirty-two years, since the time when another famous *musico*—Marchesini [Luigi Marchesi] —had sung there, Sinigaglia had not heard any eunuch's voice in its theatre. . . . His singing was far from possessing the pathetic accents of Pacchierotti or the sober and correct elegance of Crescentini. . . . The Princess of Wales was present at two of the performances, and at her express request the opera was to be begun at the second act. The first evening, when Velluti was told of the desire of Her Highness (and being already irritated by the increase in the lighting which he said produced too much smoke and heat and made his breathing difficult) he lost patience and rebelled against this regal caprice. 'My throat is worth quite as much as a queen', he cried, and got his way."

It was in the same year, 1814, that Velluti had his first encounter with Rossini, when he went to Milan to sing in the latter's 'Aureliano in Palmira'. The brilliant young composer was enraged by the singer's lavish embroideries of his music, which he said quite obscured the melody; and he tried to insist that Velluti sing the arias exactly as written, which in turn enraged the *musico*. Velluti vowed never to sing Rossini's music again; in fact he occasionally did so, and the two eventually became great friends, but for the time being they refused to hear a good word about one another. In the same season he made a great success in Nicolini's 'Quinto Fabio', and "by his personal triumph prevented the catastrophe of 'Attila', by the maestro Farinelli". The latter was Velluti's last appearance at the Scala, and he was forced to leave the town as the result of an affair with a young girl of good family referred to by history as the Marchesa Clelia G. . . .

It was about this time that the Emperor Francis issued his ban against castrati throughout his Italian domains; but it was ambiguously worded, and soon lapsed. Meanwhile, however, Velluti was engaged for the court theatre at Modena, where the Duke had recently returned to power and, being an out-and-out reactionary, wished to have everything as if the French Revolution had never occurred. Velluti seems to have spent much of his time while there in amorous intrigue, for he fancied himself as a lady-killer; and he took up with one Giannina, a singer at the same theatre, and mistress of a certain Furio Girelli, who had made a great deal of money by dubious methods under the French occupation, and now wished to obliterate the past by playing the local Maecenas. Giannina was not indisposed to deceive him, and, as an observer remarked, she "cercava la dimestichezza d'un evirato, perchè la stimava senza pericolo".

All went well until Giannina became enamoured of the handsome tenor of the company, named Corbelli; and Velluti, perhaps sated with her charms, made the path of true love easy for the couple, and helped them to keep Girelli in the dark. In the end, they eloped together, leaving Velluti to face Girelli's wrath; he did so with a quite untranslatable wisecrack: "Ma di che cosa mai vi lamentate, signor mio? Voi affermaste di non voler *corbelli*, ma non parlaste punto di corbellature!"

Soon after this, Velluti made a voyage to Germany, which he had already visited with éclat, and been named *cantante di camera* to the King of Bavaria. In Vienna, the singer was acclaimed with

8. ANGELO MARIA MONTICELLI
from the portrait by Casali

ecstasy, and for a season every new fashion was 'à la Velluti';
continuing his wanderings, he came to St Petersburg, where the
same reception awaited him. A certain Grand Duchess became
enamoured of him, and took him off to her palace in the Crimea;
yet even the satisfaction of having the Tsar's close relative for a
mistress could not compensate for the lady's incessant tantrums
and jealousies, and Velluti soon broke with her. While the affair
is still in progress, he writes to a friend:

> "uomo a donna soli soli
> è la via d'aver figlioli

says the proverb: but it needs correction. We were so much alone
there [in the Crimea] that eventually we left our clothes off
altogether; but, whether because some utensils were missing from
my knapsack, or because she suffers from *excess* in one direction,
i.e. in having some thirty years more of age than she should have,
I am led to believe that the only way to have children *at Court* is
by using a great deal of patience."

Soon after these ludicrous amours, Velluti returned to Italy,
without losing any of his evident flair for odd adventures. Having
been much acclaimed at Bergamo, in 1821, in Niccolini's 'Ilda
d'Avenello',[1] he instantly went to Milan, hoping to arrange for a
repeat performance at the Scala; on arrival, however, some *sbirri*
climbed into his carriage, and brought him before the police.
History does not specify what exactly his offence was supposed
to be; but he had probably neglected to provide himself with a
passport, then necessary to travel from one town to another—
for red tape luxuriated in Austrian Italy of the early nineteenth
century with a profusion rarely equalled, and never surpassed.

Velluti, confronted with the Chief of Police, did not deign to

[1] The authorities unanimously agree in dating the première of this work in
1828; however, Velluti himself confirms that this contretemps occurred in
1821. He may possibly, of course, have meant a quite different opera. There was
another work of the same name, by Morlacchi, but this did not come out until
1824; and it seems not unlikely that the work in question was another opera of
Niccolini, 'L'Eroe di Lancastro', in which Velluti had earned great applause.

ask the reason for his arrest, but immediately burst into song, choosing an aria with these remarkably apposite words:

> Farmi cattivo è facile[1]
> ma non sapreste poi
> con tutto questo rendermi
> cattivo al par di voi.

At this, the policeman, who was also a music-lover, did not know which way to turn; finally, pretending to have mistaken the singer for a notorious *carbonaro* who was said to have arrived in Milan, he let him go free.

Venice was now the scene of further triumphs for Velluti, and of further burlesque incidents—including the misunderstanding caused by the wife of the chief Governor of the Fenice. This lady, to whom her husband was absolutely subservient, left a note for her dressmaker, before leaving for the country, saying that on a certain outfit she "did not want velvet" ("non voglio velluto"). The husband, finding this and jumping to the wrong conclusion, immediately dismissed the singer on some pretext; then the wife returned. Being an ardent fan of Velluti's, she made her long-suffering husband rush off in person to catch the singer up, and bring him back on whatever conditions he might stipulate. So Velluti was persuaded to return, and to create the role of the Christian knight Armando in Meyerbeer's 'Crociato in Egitto' —a role specially composed for him, and in which he scored a notable success. Later in the same year (November 16th, to be precise) in Florence, he took part in a most singular première— that of the opera 'Fedra' composed by the English minister plenipotentiary Lord Burghersh, and given in his private palace. The performance lasted four hours, and must have cost the noble amateur a small fortune.

The following year, 1825, Velluti came to England, and Lord Mount Edgcumbe has a famous account of the excitement he aroused. "I have now", he says, "to record an event which

---

[1] "To make me a prisoner is easy, but for all that you could not make me as unpleasant as you"—a play on the double meaning of the word 'cattivo'.

excited great curiosity in the musical world, and for a time was of considerable advantage to the theatre, closing the season with great éclat. This was the arrival of a male soprano singer, the only one left on the Italian stage, who has for many years, perhaps only from having no rival in his line, been looked upon as the best singer of his country. He came to this country with strong and numerous recommendations, but under no engagement for the opera, and he had been here for some time before the manager dared to produce so novel and extraordinary a performer. No singer of this description had appeared here for a quarter of a century,[1] so that the greater part of those who formerly were delighted with Pacchierotti, Marchesi, etc., were now no more, and a generation had sprung up who had never heard a voice of this sort, and were strongly prejudiced against it. His first reception at concerts was far from favourable; the scurrilous abuse lavished on him before he was heard, cruel and illiberal; and it was not until after long deliberation, much persuasion, and assurance of support, that the manager ventured to engage him for the remainder of the season. Even then, such was the popular prejudice and general cry raised against him, that unusual precautions were deemed necessary to secure a somewhat partial audience, and prevent his being driven from the stage on his first entry upon it, which seemed to be a predetermined measure. At length the first appearance of Signor Velluti was announced to take place, on an unusual night, for his own benefit, granted him, it was said, on account of the great trouble he had taken (to use a theatrical phrase) in getting up the new opera; which indeed was true, for as he had a perfect knowledge of the stage, he entirely directed all the performances in which he took a part. . . . At the moment when he was expected to appear, the

[1] Two decidedly second-rate castrati, Neri and Roselli, had been in London up till the year 1800. At that time Roselli, who had a "feeble and very limited voice, but . . . some taste, and with more power would have been a good singer", was destined by Mount Edgcumbe for the principal role in his opera 'Zenobia'; but proving during rehearsals unequal to it, he was replaced by the tenor Viganoni, for whom the music was transposed. Roselli at once left England.

most profound silence reigned in one of the most crowded audiences I ever saw, broken on his entering by loud applauses of encouragement. The first note he uttered gave a shock of surprise, almost of disgust, to inexperienced ears; but his performance was listened to with attention and great applause throughout, with but few audible expressions of disapprobation speedily suppressed." The opera in which he appeared was again Meyerbeer's 'Il Crociato in Egitto', and among the other singers were Mme. Caradori (a German, despite her name) and Maria Malibran, then very young and still known as Mlle Garcia. Velluti, incidentally, foretold her future greatness, and encouraged her to study.

Mount Edgcumbe was by no means overwhelmed by Velluti's artistry. "To speak more minutely of Velluti," he writes, "this singer is no longer young, and his voice is in decay. It seems to have had considerable compass, but has failed (which is extraordinary) in its middle tones, many of which are harsh and grating to the ear. Some of his notes are still exquisitely sweet, and he frequently dwells on, swells, and diminishes them with delightful effect. His lower notes, too, are full and mellow, and he displays considerable art in descending from the one to the other by passages ingeniously contrived to avoid those which he knows to be defective. His manner is florid without extravagance, his embellishments (many of which were new to us) tasteful and neatly executed. His general style is the *grazioso*, with infinite delicacy and a great deal of expression, but never rising to the grand, simple, and dignified *cantabile* of the old school, still less to the least approach towards the *bravura*. He evidently has no other, therefore there is a great want of variety in his performance, as well as a total deficiency of force and spirit. Of the great singers mentioned before, he most resembles Pacchierotti in one only, and that the lowest of his styles, but cannot be compared with him in excellence. He is also somewhat like him in figure, but far better looking; in his youth he was reckoned remarkably handsome. On the whole, there is much to approve and admire in his performance, and I can readily believe that in his prime he was not unworthy of the reputation he has attained in Italy. Even here, under so many disadvantages, he produced considerable effect, and overcame much of the prejudice raised against him. To the old he brought back some pleasing recollections; others, to whom his voice was new, became reconciled to it, and sensible of his merits, while many declared that to the last his tones gave them more pain than pleasure. However, either from curiosity or real admiration, he drew crowded audiences, and no opera but the 'Crociato' was performed to the end of the season."

So much, in fact, was Velluti admired, that he was entrusted with the management of the opera-house for the season of 1826; for a singer of that day, he was extraordinarily knowledgeable, and as a producer he was one of the first to bother about such details as historical authenticity in the costumes. Yet familiarity bred contempt, and he began to lose his popularity. "Velluti's favour", says Mount Edgcumbe, "sensibly declined, and in his second opera, called 'Tebaldo ed Isoline', by Morlacchi, which he considers as his chef-d'œuvre,[1] he was much less admired than in the 'Crociato'." He also occasionally sang the role of Arbace in Rossini's 'Semiramide'—composed, oddly enough, for the female contralto Pisaroni, who was so ugly that she preferred to sing masculine parts—but he was as a rule unwilling to appear with Pasta, fearing the competition of her exquisite art and superb acting.

Velluti's popularity in England was finally destroyed as the result of a financial squabble which does not show him in a very admirable light. He refused to pay the female chorus-singers in a certain production; and when they took him to court, he claimed that he was under no obligation to do so. He produced a notice he had posted, beginning with words, 'Signori Coristi' —which of course would apply only to the men—and claimed that *he* had never intended there to be any women in the chorus, but that someone else had introduced them against his wishes

---

[1] Despite the fact that he incurred much ridicule when he first sang the part of Tebaldo. He had to sing an aubade, in which occurred the words "il nostro casto amor", and someone in the gallery shouted, "What else could it be?"—or words to that effect. This simple pleasantry brought the house down and only with difficulty could the opera be proceeded with at all.

and express orders. He was not believed, and lost the case, the magistrate remarking that he had offered 'a trumpery defence'; the rest of the season was ill-attended, and Velluti soon departed in rage, never again setting foot in England (1829). What exactly the rights and wrongs of the business were, it is difficult to discover, as it usually is in theatrical squabbles; and there was probably both right and wrong on either side.

After this time, Velluti seems to have sung little in public; Stendhal heard him at a concert in Venice in 1831—"J'ai entendu Velluti, c'était dans un salon de la place Saint-Marc, au midi par un beau soleil. Jamais Velluti n'a mieux chanté. Il a l'air d'un jeune homme de trente-six à trente-huit ans, qui a souffert, et il en a cinquante-deux; jamais il n'a été mieux ... il y avait vingt-quatre femmes, mais pas un chapeau de bon goût"—but by then he had abandoned the stage, and was about to embark on quite a new career—that of a gentleman farmer. He bought an estate, and interested himself in all the latest agricultural methods, at a time when most Italians were hopelessly conservative about such matters. He also, however, retained his interest in music, and, among other activities, helped the younger Garcia to write his famous manual of singing.

In 1845 he made a visit to Paris, largely to buy agricultural equipment, and renewed acquaintance with his old enemy Rossini. The two now got on admirably well, and saw much of one another; and together they poked gentle fun at Berlioz. One day, Velluti had been speaking of a new agricultural instrument, but the Frenchman misunderstood him, and imagined the instrument to be an orchestral one. "Naturally," replied Rossini, "that instrument is Velluti, the *musico*"; and the singer added, laughing, "You who write about music, call me a 'canoro elefante',[1] don't you? Well, the elephant has a trunk, and I think a place ought to be made for it in the Wagnerian orchestra, with all those other trumpets."

Velluti's estate, comprising a luxurious villa, was at a place

[1] A reference to the famous lines of Parini against the castrati, referring to their often monstrous and ungainly bulk.

called Bruson on the river Brenta, between Venice and Padua; and as the years passed he became more and more of a recluse, though he kept up a lively correspondence with his surviving friends, among them Rossini. In 1849, while the Austrians were besieging Venice, the singer had accidentally wandered into their camp while going to see his doctor, and was arrested and taken to the nearest officer, who as luck would have it was a doctor himself. Velluti explained his symptoms, adding that he had once been a singer, and the officer answered that the best cure would be to sing. He promptly did so, choosing an aria from Traetta's 'Ifigenia in Tauride'.[1] "I remember," said the officer, "my father telling me about the time when he heard that music sung. It was Velluti who sang it, and my father always said it was the most wonderful thing he had ever heard." "I *am* Velluti," answered the singer, and the two of them talked so long that the officer got into trouble for neglecting his military duties.

Velluti eventually died in 1861, at eighty years of age; and the newspapers of the day are full of paragraphs expressing amazement that he should have been alive so recently. He was thought of as a legend, dimly remembered from the distant past; and there he had been, alive and active, among them all the time. . . .

His character, as will have been gathered, was erratic and unpredictable. An unusually intelligent man for a singer, he could be kind, witty, and perspicacious; but he also on occasion showed himself conceited and demanding, and even, apparently, downright dishonest. But then it must have been nerve-wracking to feel oneself so much an object of curiosity.

[1] That Velluti should have sung the music of Traetta—a composer long out of fashion in his time—is evidence of his interest in older music, then most unusual in a singer.

VI

THE STORY OF ONE
CASTRATO

MUCH has been written about the castrati and their careers; but, so far as can be ascertained, only one of them ever wrote an autobiography—Filippo Balatri, who entitled it 'Frutti del Mondo, esperimentati da Filippo Balatri nativo dell' Alfea in Toscana'.[1] This singular work, of considerable length and in verse composed of rhyming four-line stanzas, is for the most part very lively and readable: the author's career—though hardly typical of a castrato's life—is full of interest in its own right, and well worth recounting, and, despite the self-imposed limitations of the form he chose, he achieves much of the picaresque humour and actuality of Casanova.

Unlike so many modern writers, Balatri is laconic in the extreme about his early youth; from his known age at death he must have been born in 1676, and Alfea, his birthplace, is not far from Pisa. He baldly begins:

> Nacqui. Fin all'età di cognizzione
> ah, mi lasciasti star in aspra quiete;
> ma appena ebbi tre Lustri, con la Rete
> venisti a far di me la pescagione,

[1] Extensive extracts are reproduced in Volume 25 of the 'Collezione settecentesca', edited by Salvatore di Giacomo, together with the other documents quoted in this chapter.

Col far ch'il mio Sovrano naturale
mi chiedesse (e per grazzia) al Genitore
per mandarmi in Moscovia, et in poc' ore
sbalzato son fin nel Settentrionale.

(I was born. Until the age of knowledge,
ah, you left me in bitter quiet;
But hardly had I fifteen years, than with your net
you came and fished me forth.

It was that my natural Sovereign
asked for me—fortunately—of my father
to send me to Moscow, and in a few hours
I am cast away into the North.)

Thus we know nothing of his training or of how he came to be operated; the background and condition of his parents are alluded to at a later point in his story, while from his will (also extant) can be deduced the name of the doctor responsible—one Accoramboni of Lucca (any relation to the White Devil, Vittoria Accoramboni?). The character to whom these stanzas are addressed is 'il Mondo'—the world—which Balatri habitually personifies as a creature whose malevolence is matched only by its lack of rational principles; the 'natural sovereign' was of course Cosimo III de' Medici, Grand Duke of Tuscany, while the mission to Moscow is explained in the stanza that follows:

Pietro Gran Zar, che Regna sullo *Scita*
la Moscovia s'invoglia fecondare
di Scienze e di bell' Arti, e fa cercare
Gente ch'in quelle bene sii instruita.

(Peter, the great Czar, who reigns over Scythia,
is determined to fertilise Muscovy
with science and fine arts, and has sought out
people who in such things are well instructed.)

Balatri goes on to describe how the Czar sent envoys to every European country, to enquire into their arts, manners, usages, etc., and to report back faithfully on all that they had learnt: if Balatri's date of birth is correct, this must have been in about 1691—some years before Peter's famous journey to the West. It is interesting that the Czar should already have been showing such interest in foreign things, at a time when he is usually supposed not yet to have acquired it at all. To Italy he sent a Prince Galitzin,[1] whose especial assignment was to engage Italian singers for the court in Moscow; he was not to reappear in Russia until he had secured some. The task, however, proved unexpectedly difficult, no singers being willing to undertake so arduous a journey, to what was then looked on as almost the end of the world. In desperation, Galitzin went to Cosimo for advice, and that ruler suggested the young Balatri, who, he added, was "reso di già del gener misto, id est soprano".

The Prince and the young singer set out forthwith (it does not appear whether Galitzin had found any other artists), and, after a voyage over whose discomforts Balatri waxes eloquent, arrived safely in Moscow. The *musico* was kindly received by the Czar:

> Quel monarca dimostrasi Grazzioso
> e si umilia fin a dirmi Figlio.

> (This monarch showed himself gracious,
> and humbled himself to the point of calling me his son.)

—but such favour in high places had its disadvantages, and

> . . . mille altri perciò con torvo ciglio
> mi riguardon qual can che sia tignoso.

> (. . . a thousand others looked at me for it with stern brows
> as if I were a dog with the mange.)

Balatri, in fact, did not have an easy time of it. He was looked on askance, particularly by the lower orders of the Russian population, for not being of the Orthodox persuasion, and was on

[1] Probably Prince Peter Galitzin; but the family was a very numerous one, and it is impossible to be certain.

bad terms with the *spalniks*, who were the guards of the Imperial bedchamber:

> Questi sin Giovinotti, che in la Corte
> servon di Paggi, *Spalnicchi* nomati,
> e son si insolenti e indemoniati
> che fannomi irritare fin a morte.

> Dicemmi *Cane*, perchè son cristiano
> *Mussulmano*, perchè son buon Cattolico,
> *Pagano*, perchè son vero Cattolico,
> *Dannato*, perchè ho un Capo ch'è Romano.

> (These are youths, who in the Court
> serve as pages, and are called *Spalniks*.
> They are so insolent and bedevilled
> that they irritate me to death.

> They called me a *Dog*, because I am a Christian;
> *Mussulman*, because I am a good Catholic;
> *Pagan* because I am a true Catholic;
> *Damned*, because my Chief is a Roman.)

Eventually, however, he learnt to speak Russian well enough to answer them back, and this led, often, to physical warfare which even the Czar was powerless to control. Despairing of peace in his household, the monarch decided to send Balatri away for a time, on the advice of Prince Galitzin. The latter, knowing the Tuscan ruler's taste for exotic 'local colour', suggested that Balatri might accompany his (Galitzin's) brother Boris on an embassy to the Grand Cham of Tartary[1]; the quick-witted boy would remember everything of note, and later describe it for his master's benefit:

> Nella mente del Zar nascere festi
> di farmi far un picciolo viaggetto,
> credendo ch'al Granduca di diletto
> potesse riuscire, e l'ottenesti.

---

[1] No mention of this embassy has been found in Russian history.

Sa il Prencipo Galitzin che qual Duca
dilettasi d'aver piena la corte
di Mori, di Kalmucchi et d'ogni sorte
di musi piatti, ovver di crespa nuca.

. . . . . .

Sa che, quando mi tolse da Fiorenza,
ebbe piacer il detto mio Sovrano,
ch'io n'andassi in Moscovia, e che mia mano
ordinonne scrivesse la sequenza

Di tutto il viaggio, fin al mio ritorno,
e di quanto che io avea veduto;
onde sa ancor, che più gli avria piaciuto
quanto più d'Instruzzion io fossi adorno;

Che perciò svela al Zar suo pensiero,
ed Egli il trova bene concepito.
Così fuori dal Cielo moscovito
son spinto e batto il Tartaro Sentiero.

(Prince Galitzin knows that this Duke
takes pleasure in having his court full
of Moors, Kalmuks, and every kind
of flat snout and woolly nape.

. . . . . .

He knows that, when he took me away from Florence,
my said Sovereign's pleasure was
that I should go to Muscovy, and that my hand
should write an account

Of all the journey, right up till my return,
and of whatever I had seen;
he knows too, that he will be the more pleased
the more instruction I will have acquired;

So he reveals his thoughts to the Czar,
and the latter finds them well conceived.
And thus out of the Muscovite sky
am I pushed, and travel the path to Tartary.)

They set off, and Balatri was soon disliking the rigours and
dangers of the journey:

> A cavallo, al seren, al sol cocento,
> sempre in deserte e vaste praterie,
> senza chiesa nè casa nè osterie:
> biscotto, birra, e carne puzzolento.
>
> . . . . . .
>
> Ma come c'entro io in quest' istoria,
> che non ho volontà d'esser soldato?
> Son giovin, Italiano, e son cast . . .
> nè cerco che dal canto la mia gloria.
>
> Tant'è, così l'ambasciador l'intende,
> nè pensa che sia musica o cast . . . ti
> se più sian gl'Italiani delicati
> dei Moscoviti; ma al suo intento tende,
>
> Che è di conservar tutt' il rigore
> del militar in quel si lungo viaggio . . .

(On horseback, in the evening damp, in the cooking sun,
always among deserts, and vast prairies
without a church, a house, or a hostelry:
biscuit, beer, and stinking meat.

. . . . . .

But how do I come into this story,
who have no wish to be a soldier?
I am young, Italian, and a cast . . .
nor seek I my glory in anything but song.

It is as the ambassador intends,
nor does he think that there are such things as music and
nor whether the Italians are more delicate   [cast . . . ti,
than the Muscovites; but holds fast to his intent.

Which is to conserve all the rigour
of the military [life] in this voyage, which is so long.)

Eventually, however, they arrived at a great river (the Volga?) beyond which they espied the Tartar encampment:

> Veggio da noi non lunge una cittade,
> composta tutta di bei padiglioni
> odo sull'altra riva canti e suoni,
> ma da muover più ad ira ch'a pietade.

> (I see not far from us a city
> composed entirely of beautiful pavilions
> I hear on the other bank singing and sounds
> apt rather to move to anger than to pity.)

Everyone was filthy from the journey, and they joyfully tore off their clothes and bathed. After that, they assembled collapsible boats and rafts of wood and leather which they had brought with them, and crossed the river with all their horses and baggage. The ambassador was to wait on the Grand Cham almost at once, and told Balatri to accompany him; the appearance of this eastern potentate much intrigued the singer:

> Giunti dentro la tenda maestosa
> del Tartaro Signor, si vede in faccia
> starsi sedendo a terra; si s'accovaccia
> su due guanciali e qual Reliquia posa.

> Non si sa, se abbia gambe, perche ascose
> e rannichiate stan sotto la vesta.
> Due siedon dietro a Lui, a cui la testa
> grattando vanno, al sen di cui la pose.

> (Arriving within the majestic tent
> of the Tartar lord, he is seen face to face
> sitting on the ground, nestling
> on two pillows, and posing like an idol.

> One cannot tell whether he has legs, for [they are]
> and cowering under his robe.   [concealed
> Two [men] sit behind him, and are busy
> scratching his head, which he places on their chest.)

The head-scratching, Balatri notes, was a signal mark of honour reserved for the Cham; "quella grattata (li) serve di baldacchino". The ambassador at once presented his credentials, which were read out by an interpreter, and the Europeans then retired.

Two days later, the Cham gave a great banquet in honour of his guests, and treated them to an entertainment decidedly less luxurious than that of 'Prince Igor':

> Cantino o pianghin, par a me tutt' uno,
> e se ballano il fan di mala grazia,
> quel loro suono a tutti il cuore strazia,
> et esser sordo e cieco par fortuna.

> Nudo il capo ed il petto, gambo e braccia,
> coperto è il resto da un' incolta pelle,
> (parlo del popolaccio) e sfido Apelle
> a poter ben ritrarre la lor faccia.

> (Their singing and wailing seem exactly the same to me,
> and if they dance they do it with ill grace;
> their sounds lacerate the hearts of all,
> and to be deaf and blind appears fortunate.

> Their head, chest, legs and arms are bare,
> and the rest covered with unworked skins,
> (I speak of the common people), and I defy Apelles
> properly to depict their faces.)

Balatri has a long digression at this point on the nomads' way of life, and in particular remarks on the paucity and monotony of their diet:

> Non sanno cosa sian i pasticci,
> li ragù, la sfogliate et altri intrichi;
> li montoni, per lor son beccaficchi,
> e il medico e il special non gli fa i ricci.

(They do not know what pies are,
nor ragouts, nor puff-pastry and other such intricacies;
mutton, for them, takes the place of *beccaficchi*,
and doctors and apothecaries will not get rich from them.)

Meanwhile, the feast was not being precisely a riotous success, since the two parties did not understand a word of each other's language; and the ambassador, in despair, asked Balatri to sing:

. . . sciolgo passaggi e trilli a cento a cento
e comincio il monarca a risvegliare.

. . . . . .

Grattan i grattatori a tutta possa,
perchè il mio canto crescegli la forza
a tal che, s'in dolcezza men vo a orza,
lenta è lor man, se strillo, gratta all'ossa.

(. . . I scatter passages and trills by the hundred,
and the monarch begins to wake up.

. . . . . .

The scratchers scratch with all their might,
for my singing increases their strength,
so that when I case up in gentleness
their hand is slow, and when I shrill, they scratch right
to the bone.)

After this, the food was brought in—whole sheep with rice and other concomitants. Balatri was ravenous, but did not get a chance to eat, for the Cham insisted that he go on singing; then, thinking the boy might be hungry, he took a half-chewed hunk of mutton from his own mouth and offered it to him. Balatri was horrified but did not know how to refuse, until by a happy thought he found an excuse, alleging that meat was bad for the vocal chords. This was not the end of his perplexities, either, for after he had sung again the Cham was so enraptured that he decided he absolutely must have him in his service; and accordingly he offered to barter him with Prince Galitzin for six of his famous Tartar horses, of a race reserved for the rulers of the nation.

Balatri knew that Galitzin was a passionate lover of horses, and

could see temptation in the ambassador's face; great was his
relief when

> Grazie al ciel, ei risponde da signore
> con dir che fra Christiani non permesso
> è un tal baratto, nè che a lui concesso
> è il disporre di me . . .

> (Thanks be to Heaven, he replies as a gentleman
> that between Christians such barter is not allowed,
> nor has he been made responsible for the disposing of me.)

The Tartar took the rebuff in good part, and even presented
Balatri with one of the horses, much to the envy of all the
Russians. He also plied him with questions, through the inter-
preter, as to his country and art:

> Incomincia dal farmi domandare
> se maschio son o femmina e da dove,
> se nasce tale gente (ovvero piove)
> con voce e abilitude per cantare, etc.
>
> . . . . . .
>
> . . . rispondo che son maschio, Toscano, e che si trova
> galli nelle mie parti che fanno uova,
> dalle quali i soprani son al mondo;
>
> Che li galli si nomano Norcini[1]
> ch'a noi le fan covar per molti giorni
> e che, fatto il cappon, son gli uovi adorni
> da lusinghe, carezze e da quattrini.

> (He begins to have me asked
> whether I am male or female, and where
> such people are born (or else rain down)
> with [such a] voice and ability to sing.
>
> . . . . . .
>
> . . . I reply that I am male, a Tuscan, and that there are
> roosters in my part of the world that lay eggs,
> from which soprani are born.

[1] A reference to the town of Norcia, famous for castration (see page 43).

That these roosters are called *Norcini*
and make us incubate [the eggs] for many days,
and when the capon is born, the eggs are showered
with flattery, caresses and money.)

The Cham appears to have been satisfied with this little fable, and the banquet ended amongst conviviality and cordiality. After a further day or two Galitzin's business, whatever it was, was satisfactorily concluded, and the whole caravan set out once more for Moscow. The return journey was, if possible, even more uncomfortable than the other, and, by the time they reached their destination, Balatri was in such a state as to be almost unrecognisable; before going to see the Czar, he had to be sent to a Turkish bath and otherwise set in order.

The fights with the *spalniks* and others continued, even more virulently than before, to the point where Balatri was forbidden admission to the Palace except when he was to sing; he rails particularly against the *Baarinas*, (Boyarinas), spinsterish and spiteful court ladies of a certain age who were inexorable against him. He was still living with the Prince Galitzin who had originally brought him from Italy, but spent more and more of his time in the suburb where the foreign merchants lived; he had fallen in love with the daughter of an Englishman, but she, apparently, was a sad flirt and nothing much came of the affair. After some further misadventures, he was forbidden to leave the Galitzin palace after nightfall, and life became somewhat monotonous, but he relieved the tedium by making serious efforts to convert the Prince and Princess, for whom he had come to feel the deepest affection, to the Catholic faith, being persuaded that, failing success on his part, they must inevitably burn in hell-fire. The Galitzins, however, do not seem to have taken his efforts at all seriously.

Soon after this, the Prince Boris Galitzin was appointed Russian ambassador to Vienna, and it was decided, for some reason, that Balatri should accompany him; and it was there that he perfected his art, being taught by the eminent male contralto Gaetano Orsini:

Ei canta d'un tal metodo che mai
s'è inteso per ancora esercitare.
Mi riesce il poterlo un po' imitare.
La voce ho alta, chiara, e senza guai.

In due anni riesco un buon soprano,
e a Cesare davante so azzardarmi.
Canto alla Mensa. Ognun si da a lodarmi,
e comincia Superbia a darmi mano.

(He sings by a method such as
had never hitherto been conceived.
He succeeds in making me imitate him a little.
My voice is high, clear, and without fault.

In two years I become a good soprano,
and I even hazard myself in the presence of Caesar
[i.e. the Emperor]
I sing at Mass. Everyone begins to praise me,
and pride begins to give me its hand.)

So promising a career was interrupted by a sudden summons
from Balatri's father; and the singer was forced to return to his
native Tuscany. Arrived in Florence, he was received with such
honour by the Grand Duke that the courtiers were resentful; but
he did not stay long enough for any sinister consequences to
ensue, and hurried on to Pisa, where his parents were now living.
The town made a disagreeable impression on him, after all that
he had seen:

Esco di Mosca si ripien di gente,
et entro in Pisa quasi spopolata!
Mi sembra che la peste vi sia stata,
e fa che ipocondria si risente.

(I leave Moscow so full of people,
and arrive at Pisa, that is so deserted!
It seems as if the plague had been there,
and my hypochondria resents it.)

He arrives at his parents' house, and a touching scene follows:

> Corre la madre, e mi s'attacca al collo
> gridando: "Ah, figlio, pur t'ho racquistato."
> Corre la serva, e puzza di stufato,
> poi corre il servitor, di vin satollo.

> (My mother runs up, and flings herself at my neck
> crying: "Ah, my son, I've got you back."
> The servant-girl runs up, and stinks of stew,
> then the manservant arrives, full of wine)

—followed by Balatri's father and elder brother Ferrante. Two women friends are invited in to supper, and bore Balatri to death:

> Ponghiamoci a cenare, e si comincia
> a dar nelle dimande a tutt' andare.
> Io, che muoio di fame e vuo' mangiare,
> rispondi breve tira al piatto e trincia.

> Quelle due donne none han mai viaggiato,
> ne mai ai loro giorni un libro letto,
> onde il lor picciol debole intelletto
> gli fa aver il discorso assai scompiuto.

> Mi ricercan: se è bella la Zaressa,
> e se Moscovia è forse la sua Pisa,
> come ella viva e s'è vestita in guisa
> com'è la nostra Tosca Principessa, etc., etc.

> (We sit down to supper, and there begins
> a barrage of questions.
> I, who am dying of hunger and want to eat,
> reply briefly, take my plate and guzzle.

> These two women have never travelled,
> nor ever read a book in their lives,
> so that their weak little intellect
> makes their conversation rather limited.

They ask me: whether the Czarina is beautiful,
and whether Moscow is perhaps her Pisa,
how she lives and whether she is dressed
like our Tuscan Princess.)

Life in Pisa proves more and more tedious and bourgeois. The first time the family are going to church, Balatri puts on a very elegant coat, and is reproved for it by his father:

Di me dirassi [says the father] e diran molte bene,
che son un pazzo col lasciarti fare,
Tu, *il Sior Marchese*, ti farai nomare,
ti rideranno dietro e faran scene.

(Of me they would say, and with reason,
that I am mad to let you act like that.
You would be called the *Lord Marquis*,
and they would laugh at you behind your back and
make scenes.)

So Balatri calls in a tailor, and has a less smart suit run up; in despair he asks his brother how they usually pass the time at Pisa, and Ferrante replies:

L'ozio divora e strugge quanti siamo.
La città, senza corte, e spopolata,
non fa che la sua gente sii impiegata
così, che far del tempo non sappiamo.

(Idleness devours and destroys all of us.
The town, without a court, is deserted.
It gives its people no employment,
and we do not know what to do with our time.)

The women of Pisa, too, strike Balatri as impossible:

Le donne non son use a far l'amore,
nè san comprender cose misteriose.
Le trovo così insipide e citrose,
ch'ai gomiti mi fan venir sudore.

(The women are not accustomed to make love,
nor can they understand mysterious things.
I find them so insipid and lemonish
that they make me sweat at the elbows [*sic*].)

Balatri was, however, soon rescued from this vacuum by a
summons from the Grand Duke, and joined him at his summer
residence outside Florence, the Villa Ambrogiana. Next, he was
ordered to Florence, to serve as interpreter for the new Russian
ambassador; he fervently hoped it might prove to be his beloved
Galitzin, but it was, instead, a nobleman named Naryshkin.
Interpreting was hard work, but at least Naryshkin was a con-
genial person; after his business was terminated, he asked Balatri
to accompany him on a tour of Tuscany, and, when passing
through Pisa, insisted on putting up at his parents' house, despite
Balatri's remonstrances.

The house was fortunately not too bad a one, having been
given to Balatri senior by the Duke, for reasons that the singer
now explains:

Tale grazia fu fatta al mio buon padre,
prima, per esser pover cittadino
d'un' antica famiglia, Fiorentino;
poi per aver sposato la mia madre,

Quale fu Donna della Granduchessa
e da lei parzialmente riguardata.
Così, per non scemarsi lui l'entrata
con la pigion, tal casa fu concessa.

(So much grace was shown to my good father,
firstly, for being a poor citizen
of an old family, and Florentine;
and also for having married my mother,

Who was lady-in-waiting to the Grand Duchess,
and favourably looked upon by her.
So, in order that his income might not be diminished
by paying rent, this house was granted him.)

Returning to Florence, Balatri was given a strange new assignment—the education of a couple of Kalmucks, presents from Peter the Great to the Grand Duke; they were apparently stupid children, and Balatri had particular trouble in expounding to them the mystery of the Trinity. Soon, however, both the singer's parents suddenly died, and he had to return to Pisa and settle the family's affairs. Some years must now have elapsed, in which nothing occurred that Balatri considers worth recording.

From the strange uses to which he put Balatri, it would seem that Cosimo cared little for music; evidently Balatri was tired of wasting his vocal attainments, and conceived the idea of trying his fortune in England, then in the first flush of its enthusiasm for Italian opera. He applied to the Duke for leave of absence, but the latter—a notorious bigot—was unwilling to grant it, fearing for the singer's morals in so depraved and heretical a country:

> La libertà [he replied], li pravi sentimenti
> contro la religion potrian guastarti;
> così che trovo di dover niegarti
> la tua richiesta. Parlami altrimenti.

> (Freedom, and wicked sentiments
> against religion might corrupt you;
> so I feel myself obliged to deny you
> your request. Let us speak of other things.)

To which Balatri replied by pointing out that in Russia—an equally non-Catholic part of the world—his conduct had been exemplary, from a religious point of view at any rate. The Grand Duke relented to the extent of consulting his confessor, who urged that Balatri should be allowed to go—his singing might even make converts to the true faith. Cosimo finally agreed, though very much *contre cœur,* and Balatri set off, in company with an English envoy, who was returning home. They went as far as Genoa by road, and there took ship for Marseilles; they were overtaken by a terrible storm and wrecked on one of the Iles d'Hyères, had to hire a rowing-boat to take them to Toulon, and from there drove directly to Lyons, where they stopped to rest.

It was at Lyons that Balatri first came into contact with French music, and with the French prejudice against Italian singers. Flirting with a young woman he had met, he discovered she had musical tastes; she invited him to a musical soirée with some of her family, at which he should be "Orfeo to her Euridice". The family turned out to be very numerous, Balatri was received with much honour, and immediately asked to sing: but hardly had he commenced his aria when the room was filled, not with the applause he confidently expected, but with laughter. Furious, he stopped, and was preparing to walk out, when one of the company who spoke Italian detained him, and tried to pacify him with explanations. He pointed out:

> . . . ch'io debba scusare
> il non esser là avvezzi a un simil canto
> nè aver ancor inteso un altrettanto,
> e che in lor stil l'*ahah* non puo' passare
>
> Che i gran passaggi son per li violini
> e per le voci sono le parole;
> ch'un passagio di otto note sole
> bastar deve a un cantor delli più fini, etc, etc.
>
> (. . . that I must excuse
> their not being accustomed to such singing,
> since they had never conceived of anything like it,
> and that in their style the *ahah* could not pass;
>
> That elaborate passages were for violins,
> while for voices there were words;
> that a passage of only eight notes
> must suffice for the finest of singers. . . .)

The 'ahah' at which the French took exception was merely the wordless *vocalise* with which the aria had begun; Balatri accepted the explanation, and asked to hear a specimen of French singing. A young lady went to the harpsichord and began to perform:

> Dopp' aver per mezz' ora smorfieggiato,
> comincia a dir *Iris*, e spinge tanto
> su quel *ris* la sua voce, e dura tanto
> che da Lione a Londra saria andato.

> Cospetto di Baccone, Bacconaccio,
> che quel strido mi trapana 'l cervello,
> riprende un tuon più alto, lascia quelle,
> e c'è un *Iriiiiiiis* fa de mio cuore un straccio, etc.

> (After grimacing for half an hour,
> she begins to say *Iris*, and on the *ris*
> forces her voice so much, and dwells so long
> that it must have been heard from Lyons to London.

> I swear by Bacchus
> that this shriek bores into my brain.
> She takes up a higher note, and then a higher,
> and her *Iriiiiiiis* tears my heart to tatters.)

Several other performers follow, each more strident and disagreeable than the other, and eventually Balatri can bear it no longer. He offers to sing in the French style himself, and does so, deliberately exaggerating all the characteristics of the screechings he has just heard: but, far from being taken as a joke, his performance is actually admired. He is told that, if only he would go and study for some time in Paris, he could become a really good singer. . . .

On reaching Paris, the singer determined to go at once to visit Versailles, and dressed himself for the occasion in a coat made from material presented him by the Grand Cham. This garment was noticed and admired by one and all, including Louis XIV himself, and the monarch was graciously pleased to converse with Balatri for some little time. Fearing a recurrence of his Lyons experiences, the singer did not reveal his occupation, and pretended to be a gentleman of leisure; that evening, however, being invited to dinner by one of the courtiers, he did admit his calling, and was prevailed upon to sing. Here, he was a success, Versailles being obviously more cosmopolitan and cultivated in its taste than a provincial town like Lyons.

Returning to Paris, his coat again caused quite a sensation:

> Vado al caffé, e, appena colà entrato,
> m'assedia ognun che v'è esaminando
> l'abito mio Kamesco, onde animando
> vanno 'l mio fasto a rendermi confiato.

> (I go to the café, and hardly have I entered
> when everyone besieges me to examine
> my Chamesque coat. They encourage
> my splendour and make me puffed up with pride.)

However, it was time to press on towards London, and, still in company with the English envoy, Balatri made a pleasant journey. On arrival, the envoy invited him to stay in his house, and Balatri accepted; his visit was altogether auspicious:

> La musica è sì amata in Inghilterra,
> a tant' è ricercato quei che canta,
> se sovra tutto voce ed arte vanta,
> che ad ogni altr' arte, si può dir, fa guerra.

> (Music is so much loved in England,
> and those who sing are so much sought out,
> the vocal art is extolled so much above all else,
> that it may be said to fight against every other art.)

The envoy arranges for Balatri to be heard by Queen Anne, but first advises him as to how best to please the royal music-lover:

> M'istruisce ch'un detto Nicolino
> da lei fu ben stimato e d'or munito;
> e ch'essendo il mio canto più finito,
> a più piacerle ancor sarò vicino.

Mi dice ch'il patetico gli piace
più che l'allegro, e piacegli la voce
spinta fuor dolcente e che non nuoce
con i strilli all'orecchia nè dispiace.

(He tells me that a certain Nicolino,
was much prized by her and provided with gold;
and that since my singing is more finished,
I will be likely to please her even more.

He tells me that she prefers the pathetic
to the gay, and likes a voice
that is gently brought forth, and does not hurt the ear,
nor displeases by its shrillness.)

The deliberately casual reference to the famous Nicolino is amusing, and must arise from jealousy: Balatri could not possibly not have heard of him. Balatri goes one day to Kensington to wait on the Queen, but she is too busy to hear him; and, before he has another chance to approach her, she suddenly dies. Meanwhile, however, Balatri had been having much success with the English aristocracy, who seem to have thought him more of a gentleman than other singers, as he had never, at that time, sung on the stage. His brother had come over to be with him, and they spent some happy and prosperous months together. After the Queen's death, however, political troubles forced music into a back place:

Del regno i differenti due partiti
di Wigs e Toris vansi risvegliando.
A tutt' altro ch'a musica pensando
son vanno i gran signori, gia investi.

(The two different parties in the kingdom,
the Whigs and Tories, are rousing themselves.
The great lords, already in power,
think of anything rather than of music.)

Balatri would soon have been in sore financial straits, but happily fortune (as usual with him) intervened: he received an

order from the Grand Duke to leave for Düsseldorf, the residence
of his daughter Anna Maria Ludovica de' Medici, Electress Palatine. He set off happily with his brother, but the journey was an
unfortunate one: first they were becalmed, with no food aboard,
in the Straits of Dover and nearly died of hunger; arriving finally
at Calais, Balatri made the mistake of overeating, and fell gravely
ill; and it was only after many delays, and still not at all well,
that they finally reached the Electress's palace. She wanted
Balatri to sing at the gala in honour of her name-day, but he
could not, owing to his infirmities, and decided that he must
return to Italy for his health's sake.

The road to Frankfurt lay through a dark and sinister forest
notorious for highwaymen, and the singer nearly died of fright;
but they got safely past it, and continued their journey via Augs-
burg to Munich. Here, Balatri fell in with the composer Torri,
who presented him to the Elector, Maximilian II; Balatri changed
his mind about going home, and accepted the offer of a post in
the electoral chapel, at 1,000 florins a year. The contract was
dated October 1st, 1715. Soon afterwards, however, his stomach
trouble returned—it never seems to have left him for the rest of
his life—and he did, after all, revisit Tuscany. The Grand Duke
made, apparently, no objections to his protégé's having taken
employment elsewhere, though he did remark that, according to
information received, Balatri was shamefully neglecting his religious duties in Bavaria. The singer comments:

> Un' è la verità, bisogna dire,
> che Cosmo terzo vive da cristiano.
> Con chi ha virtù si mostr' affatto umano,
> ma chi è viziate, ohimè, non può soffrire.

> (The truth is, and it must be admitted,
> that Cosimo the third lives like a Christian.
> To those that are virtuous he shows himself most humane,
> but those that are not—by Heaven, he cannot stand them.)

Before long he was back in Bavaria, but his health was little
better:

Ma non vi son tre mesi ancor restato
che vado ricadendo in malattia,
La *birra* ch'amo quasi a idolatria,
che ne sii la cagion bien giudicato.

(But I have not been there three months,
When once more I fall ill.
The beer which I love to idolatry
is undoubtedly the cause.)

His remedy on this occasion was to go to Eichstätt, to venerate
the bones of St Walburga, considered efficacious in such cases;
they seem to have done some good, and he went on to visit a
famous music-lover of the day—Johann Philip von Schönborn,
Prince-Bishop of Würzburg. After singing for this potentate, he
returned to Munich, and at last—in 1724, at the age of about
forty-eight—made his stage début; in what opera does not appear.
He must have pleased, for he was now invited by the Emperor
Charles VI to appear in Vienna, with Faustina; and Balatri gives
a most modest account of the occasion (whose date was August
28th, 1724):

Dall'Italia Faustina fa chiamare
Cesare e vuol che ambe abbiam l'onore
di servirlo. Ma sento in me timore
di dovermi con essa ritrovare.

Ella canta 'n tal forma che apparire
mal può mia arte a fronte della sua.
Appetto a un canarin che può una grua?
Ma, pazienza, m'è forza l'obbedire.

Mi tiro fuor d'affare come posso.
Non dispiace la voce, et anch' il gesto,
Ma Faustina canta. Or dì tu il resto,
Mondo, ch'a me ta desti a roder l'osso. . . .

(From Italy Caesar has Faustina summoned,
and wishes that we two should have the honour

of serving him. But I feel frightened
at having to be once more with her.

She sings in such a way that my art
can scarcely appear in the presence of hers.
What can a crane do next to a canary?
But patience, I must perforce obey.

I do as well as I can,
My voice does not displease, nor does my acting.
Then Faustina sings. You tell the rest,
world, who told me to gnaw my knuckles. . . .)

In any event, he was paid 4,000 florins for his season at Vienna.
After this, he made a further journey to Italy, wandering between
Padua, Venice, and Verona: he did not visit his native country,
perhaps because Cosimo III had died in 1723. His son and successor, the merry but eccentric Gian Gastone, had disliked his father
greatly, and doubtless had little use for any of his entourage.
Maximilian II of Bavaria also died about this time, and when
Balatri eventually returned to Germany, he took service with the
new Elector's brother, Johann Theodor, Bishop of Ratisbon—
at this time a young man of only twenty-four. His life was henceforth quiet and uneventful, and his autobiography soon comes
to an end.

The next information we have of Balatri comes from the
records of the monastery of Furstenfeld: "On July 16th, 1739,
the ninth Sunday after Whitsunday, was the inauguration festival
for the new church of the monastery, and for the altar of St
Sebastian. His Highness Johann Theodor, Bishop of Freising and
Ratisbon, wished to take charge of the solemn function himself,
actuated, as it appears, by the following motives. This day of consecration was also set for the first mass of our monk Theodore
Balatri, formerly Signor Dionisio[1] Balatri, who as a castrato was
admired and honoured in all the courts of Europe for the rare

[1] Presumably an error for Filippo.

quality of his voice. Eventually he came to the court of this Prince Bishop, whose esteem he won, and who in his turn entered into Balatri's confidence. One day, he confessed to the Prince Bishop his inner desire to renounce the world and to serve God alone, as a member of a religious order. The Prince Bishop, having well examined his zeal and found it constant, easily obtained the necessary dispensation for him to enter this cloister. In memory and gratitude to this encouragement of his vocation, he accepted at his solemn profession the name of Theodore. Now, having attained the priestly dignity, he was consecrated parson at Ismaning,[2] the summer residence of the Prince Bishop, by the latter on July 13th, i.e. three days before the inauguration of our church."

Balatri remained at the monastery until his death on September 10th, 1756, and a certain Abbé Gerhard writes of him in his last years: "When I was a boy, I used to sing in our seminary. There I got to know the great Filippo Balatri, who still at this time directed the sacred music. Despite his advanced age—he was then seventy-six—one could still hear the ruins of a voice which once had been the admiration of all."

However, in spite of his sacred leanings, Balatri by no means renounced his lively and mocking fancy, to judge from his will, dated November 27th, 1737. Opening with an address to some unspecified friend, he writes: "You have found the buffoon in all my writings; but you know that the reason was because I could not do otherwise. So, if you find the same in this, you will be all the more certain it is mine. He who was born a fool will never be cured, says the proverb." Passing to the substance of the will, he produces a splendid parody of legal jargon, which must be reproduced in the original Italian: "Essendo io N.N. ignaro dell' usata formula in distendere i validi testamenti per renderli sicuri da dispute, litigi, cabale, male interpretazioni (et reliqua), nè volendo informarmene, per non farmi tirar per il naso in qua e in là col farmi lasciare le mie sostanze a fantasia di altri, si come per non farmi rompere di capo da mille intrighi, impicci, intrecci,

___

[1] A place six or seven miles north-east of Munich.

impacci et imbrogli di chi volesse persuadermi, avvertirmi, ricordarmi, suggerirmi, ammonirmi e consigliarmi per proprio ed altrui interesse, suggestione, avidità, brama e desiderio, intendo e pretendo che questi tocchi di carte sian validi in presento mano (qual è la mia man dritta, nè se ne deve dubitare) voglio, dissi, che tutto sia valido come se fosse quella di pubblico notaro; acciò il tutto sia eseguito senza replica, eccezione, male interpretazione, virgole e punti cancellate o aggiunti, et infine senz' appello o difficoltà di sorte alcune."

"I," he continues, "by the grace of God, by my industry and thanks to the surgeon Accoramboni of Lucca, never took a wife, who after loving me for a little would have started screaming at me"; and in a digression he imagines his deathbed scene, supposing he had been married. All he wants is peace to die, but his dear wife can think of nothing but the will and keeps pestering him to know where it is. . . .

He will not allow his corpse to submit to the custom of the country, and be washed by "certain women . . . not only for the indecency I see in it, but because I do not want them to amuse themselves by examining me, to see how sopranos are made". He then indulges in a long diatribe against the 'Selnunn' (Seel-Nonne) whose task was to watch over the body, and who was usually one of the women who had done the washing. He imagines the harpy telling her friends that "so-and-so had had false teeth, and no one had ever suspected it, while someone else had a wooden leg, a wart on her thigh", etc., etc. He makes various satirical legacies—"to the courtiers Psalm 36", etc.—and ends by referring, with a mixture of nostalgia and macabre humour, to the picture of a musical party at Ismaning in which he appears seated at the harpsichord (and which now hangs in the National Museum at Munich). He imagines that "at this moment the courtiers perhaps are saying: 'Look at that ——ed eunuch, how he used to be idolised!'" But then, he reflects, "One by one, the courtiers that knew me will die, and people will begin to ask 'Who is he?'"—and eventually no one will remember at all, and the picture itself will be relegated to the scrapheap. . . .

9. A MUSICAL PARTY AT ISMANING
(Balatri at the harpsichord)

10. FILIPPO BALATRI
An enlargement from plate 9

Appendix

A CASTRATO VOICE ON THE GRAMOPHONE

By Desmond Shawe-Taylor

IT will perhaps come as a surprise to most readers to learn that gramophone records have been made by a professional castrato singer. The singer in question, Professor Alessandro Moreschi (1858–1922), made in 1902–3 about ten 'G. & T.' records, on the labels of which he is described as 'Soprano della Cappella Sistina'; he also conducts the Sistine Choir in some purely choral recordings made at the same period. I am not sure how much the Vatican is prepared to concede about Professor Moreschi, but it seems to be agreed that he was a genuine castrato and not merely a falsettist with an unusually high range. The part of the Seraph in Beethoven's 'Christus am Ölberge', in which Mr Heriot tells us that Moreschi was famous, would take him up to the C above the stave, with an alternative E two notes higher still. I have heard five of his records, and none of them goes so high as that. With recordings of this period there is always an element of uncertainty about the proper speed, and therefore also about the pitch; but it seems almost certain that Moreschi's recording of the Bach-Gounod 'Ave Maria' was made in the usual soprano key of G; if this is correct, he rises at the climax to a strong, clear B natural, which is about a fifth higher than the top notes of a modern counter-tenor such as Alfred Deller.

Professor Moreschi's records are all devoted to sugary nineteenth-century religious music of the type attacked in Pius X's famous 'Motu proprio' of 1903. Another year or two, therefore, and we could hardly have had such recordings as these from the

Pope's own director of music. But they remained in the catalogue for several years, and seem to have been quite popular, since they are by no means the rarest records of their date. For us today the great question is: how far do Moreschi's records allow us to form any notion of the characteristics of castrato singing in the great periods? To that question there can be no certain answer, but I fancy that the resemblance must be slight. To begin with, Moreschi's technique, far from being impeccable, often sounds shaky; in some passages he fumbles for his notes and wavers almost as comically as Florence Foster Jenkins herself. He is at his vaguest in the 'Crucifixus' from Rossini's *Messe Solennelle*, but this record (54764) was apparently his first venture in the recording studio, and he was probably very nervous. Evidently he was ashamed of the result, for soon afterwards he re-recorded the aria; unfortunately I have never heard his second attempt (54773). The other recordings which I know are a good deal more confident, though none are flawless. Their vocal shortcomings can hardly be ascribed to the singer's advanced age, for in his mid-forties he ought to have been not far past his prime, and he was evidently still a popular favourite, having been chosen to sing at the funeral of Umberto I as recently as 1900. Sometimes he surprises us by soaring easily and gracefully through high-lying passages of considerable difficulty. Like most singers of the past, he uses a great deal of *portamento* by modern notions, and he has a peculiar habit of 'taking off' for some of his higher notes with a barely audible grace note an octave or so lower—as though throwing his voice up with the help of a miniature yodel.

Ancient though the records are, they are reasonably well recorded and probably give a fairly accurate impression of Moreschi's tonal quality, if not of his volume. The voice, unquestionably a soprano, resembles that of neither boy nor woman, being stronger than the one and less suave than the other. Chest notes are freely used, with considerable effect in the octave drops of the 'Ave Maria'. Most people find the timbre, with its occasional suggestion of a whine, displeasing; but one musical acquaintance of mine not only likes it but declares that he finds it preferable to that of Deller. For myself, I cannot say that I count Alessandro Moreschi among my favourite singers, but I find something distinctly fascinating about the unabashed, yet curiously disembodied, passion and intensity of his singing. With a more secure technique and a style less vitiated by the sentimental taste of his day, he might well please—on all but humanitarian grounds—a modern audience. But I am sure that he is a long, long way from Farinelli. He is surprising, but never exquisite.

BIBLIOGRAPHY

ADEMOLLO, Alessandro: *I teatri di Roma nel secolo decimosettimo*. Rome, 1888

ALGAROTTI, Francesco: *Saggio sopra l'opera in musica*. Livorno, 1763

ANCILLON, Charles d' (pseud. OLLINCAN): *Traité des Eunuques*. 1707

ARCHENHOLZ, Johann Wilhelm von: *A Picture of Italy*. Translated . . . by Joseph Trapp. London, 1791

ARTEAGA, Stefano: *Le rivoluzioni del teatro musicale italiano, dalla sua origine fino al presente*. Venice, 1785

BALATRI, Filippo: *Frutti del Mondo* (Collezione settecentesca, Vol. XXV)

BECKFORD, William: *Italy; with sketches of Spain & Portugal*. London, 1834

—— *The Journal of William Beckford in Portugal and Spain, 1787–8*. London, 1954

BELLONI, Antonio: *Il Seicento* (Storia letteraria d'Italia). Milan, 1900

BEYLE, Henri (STENDHAL): *Vie de Rossini*. Paris, 1922

—— *Rome, Naples et Florence*. Paris, 1854

—— *Promenades dans Rome*. Paris, 1829

—— *Correspondance*. Paris, 1908

BIGNAMI, Luigi: *Cronologia di tutti gli spettacoli rappresentati nel Gran Teatro Communale di Bologna*. 1880

BROSSES, Charles de: *Lettres familières sur l'Italie*. Paris, 1931

BURNEY, Charles: *General History of Music*. London, 1776

—— *Memoirs of the Life and Writings of the Abate Metastasio*. London, 1796

—— *The Present State of Music in France and Italy*. London, 1771

—— *The Present State of Music in Germany, the Netherlands, and United Provinces*. London, 1773

BURNEY, Fanny (Mme D'ARBLAY): *Memoirs of Doctor Burney*. London, 1832

CAMETTI, Alberto: *Christina di Svezia, l'arte musicale e gli spettacoli teatrali in Roma*. Rome, 1931

—— Critiche e satire teatrali romane nel 1700 (*Riv. Mus. Ital.*, IX, p. 1)

CAMETTI, Alberto: *Un poeta melodrammatico romano . . . Jacopo Ferretti.* Milan, 1898

—— *Il teatro di Tordinona, poi di Apollo.* Tivoli, 1939

CASANOVA, Giacomo: *Memoirs*

CELANI, Enrico: Musica e musicisti in Roma (*Riv. Mus. Ital.*, XVIII, p. 1; XX, p. 33; XXII, pp. 1, 357)

—— I Cantori della Cappella pontificia (*Riv. Mus. Ital.*, XIV, pp. 83, 752; XVI, p. 55)

COMANDINI, Alfredo: *L'Italia nei cento anni del secolo XIX.* Milan, 1900–42

CROCE, Benedetto: *I Teatri di Napoli. Secolo XV–XVIII* (Società di Storia Patria, Archivio Storico, 1876–)

D'ANGELI, Andrea: *Benedetto Marcello, vita e opere.* Milan, 1940

DA PONTE, Lorenzo: *Memoirs*

DENT, Charles: *Mozart's Operas; a Critical Study.* London, 1913

—— *Opera.* London, 1940

DI GIACOMO, Salvatore: *I quattro antichi conservatorii di Napoli MDXLIII–MDCCC* (Collezione settecentesca, Palermo, 1925–8)

—— (ed.) Collezione settecentesca, *passim*

DIO CASSIUS: *Dio's Roman History*, with an English translation by Earnest Cary. London, 1914

DONATI, Paolo: *Descrizione del gran teatro Farnesiano di Parma e notizie storiche sul medesimo.* Parma, 1817

DORAN, John: '*Mann*' *and Manners at the Court of Florence, 1740–1786.* London, 1876

EVELYN, John: *Diary*

FANTONI, Gabriele: *Storia universale del canto.* Milan, 1873

FASSINI, Sesto: *Il melodramma italiano a Londra nella prima metà del settecento.* Turin, 1914

FAUSTINI-FASSINI, Eugenio: Gli astri maggiori del bel canto napoletano (*Note d'Archivio*, Nov.–Dec. 1935; May–June, July–Oct., Nov.–Dec. 1938)

FLORIMO, Francesco: *La scuola musicale di Napoli e i suoi conservatorii* Naples, 1880–4

FRATI, Lodovico: Antonio Bernacchi e la sua scuola di canto (*Riv. Mus. Ital.*, XXIX, p. 443)

—— Un impresario teatrale del settecento e la sua biblioteca (*Riv. Mus. Ital.*, XVIII, p. 64)

—— Metastasio e Farinelli (*Riv. Mus. Ital.*, XX, p. 1)

FRATI, Lodovico: Musicisti e cantanti bolognesi del settecento (*Riv. Mus. Ital.*, XXI, p. 189)

GANDINI, Alessandro: *Cronistoria dei teatri di Modena dal 1529 al 1871.* Modena, 1873

GIARELLI, F.: Giambattista Velluti (*Gazzetta Musicale*, Milan, 1886)

GOETHE, Johann Wolfgang von: *Travels in Italy.* London, 1883

GOLDONI, Carlo: *Memoirs*

GOUDAR, Ange: *Le Brigandage de la musique italienne.* 1777

GRIMM, Friedrich: *Correspondance littéraire, philosophique et critique.* Paris, 1877–82

HABÖCK, Franz: *Die Gesangskunst der Kastraten.* Vienna, 1923

—— *Die Kastraten und ihre Gesangskunst.* Stuttgart, 1927

HAWKINS, John: *A General History of the Science and Practice of Music.* London, 1776

HOGARTH, George: *Memoirs of the Musical Drama.* London, 1838

KELLY, Michael: *Reminiscences of the King's Theatre.* London, 1826

KOTZEBUE, August Friedrich von: *Travels through Italy in 1804 and 1805.* London, 1807

LABANCHI, A. G.: Gli Eunuchi e la scuola di canto nel secolo XVIII (*Riv. Mus. Ital.*)

LA LANDE, Joseph Jérôme de: *Voyage d'un François en Italie, fait dans les années 1765 & 1766.* Geneva, 1790

LEE, Vernon: *Studies of the Eighteenth Century in Italy.* London, 1880

MACHADO, Cyrillo: *Collecção de memorias . . . etc.* Lisbon, 1823

MANCINI, Giovanni Battista: *Pensieri e riflessioni pratiche sopra il canto figurato.* Vienna, 1774

MARCELLO, Benedetto: *Il teatro alla moda.* Venice, 1887

METASTASIO: *Lettere.* Florence, 1787–9

MOLMENTI, Pompeo Gherardo: *La storia di Venezia nella vita privata.* Bergamo, 1905–8

MONALDI, Gino: *Cantanti evirati celebri del teatro italiano.* Rome, 1920

—— *I teatri di Roma negli ultimi tre secoli.* Naples, 1928

MORGAN, Lady: *Italy.* Paris, 1821

Musicista, Il (Rome): Qual'è la patria del Farinelli? (Mar.–Apr. 1937)

MUTINELLI, Fabio: *Storia arcana ed aneddotica d'Italia.* Venice, 1855–8

NAPOLI-SIGNORELLI, Pietro: *Storia critica dei teatri antichi e moderni.* Naples, 1787–90

PAROLARI, Cornelio: Giambattista Velluti (*Riv. Mus. Ital.*, XXXIX p. 263)

PECORONE, Bonifacio: *Memorie dell'abate D. Bonifacio Pecorone della città di Saponara, musico della Real Cappella di Napoli*. Naples, 1729

PROTA-GIURLEO, Ulisse: *Musicanti napoletani alla corte di Portogallo nel 700*. Naples, 1925

QUADRIO, Francesco Saverio: *Della storia e della ragione d'ogni poesia*. Bologna, 1739–49

Raccolta di melodrammi giocosi scritti nel secolo XVIII. Milan, 1822

RAGUENET, François: *A Comparison between the French and Italian Musick and Opera's . . . etc*. London, 1709

RICCI, Corrado: *Burney, Casanova e Farinelli in Bologna*. Milan, 1890
—— *Figure e figuri del mondo teatrale*. Milan, 1920

RICCOBONI, Luigi: *Reflexions historiques et critiques sur les différens théâtres de l'Europe*. Paris, 1738

ROBERTI, Giuseppe: La musica in Italia nel secolo XVIII secondo le impressioni di viaggiatori stranieri (*Riv. Mus. Ital.*, VII, p. 698; VIII, p. 519)

ROLLAND, Romain: *Musiciens d'autrefois*. Paris, 1924

ROSA, Salvator: *Satire di S. Rosa, dedicate a Settano*. 1664

SACCHI, Giovenale: *Vita del cavaliere Don Carlo Broschi*. Venice, 1784

SALVIOLI, Giovanni: *I teatri musicale di Venezia nel secolo XVII*. Milan, 1879

SCHMIDL, Carlo: *Dizionario Universale dei Musicisti* (and Supplement)

SOLARI, Marchioness: *Venice under the Yoke of France and Austria . . . by a Lady of Quality*

STREATFIELD, Richard: Handel, Rolli, and Italian Opera in London in the Eighteenth Century (*Mus. Quarterly*, III, p. 428)

TIBALDI CHIESA, Maria: *Cimarosa e il suo tempo*. Milan, 1939

TOMMASEO, Niccolò: *Dizionario estetico*. Milan, 1852

TOSI, Pietro Francesco: *Observations on the Florid Song*. London, 1742

TOYE, Francis: *Italian Opera*. London, 1952

VALDRIGHI, Luigi Francesco: *Cappelle, Concerti e Musiche di Casa d'Este*, 1844.
——*Musurgiana*, 1894–

WALKER, Frank: *A Chronology of the Life and Times of Nicola Porpora*

WALPOLE, Horace: *Letters*

WIEL, Taddeo: *I teatri musicale di Venezia nel settecento*. Venice, 1888

ZAGURI, Pietro: *Lettere del patrizio Zaguri a Giacomo Casanova* (Carteggi Casanoviani, Vol. 2 in Collezione Settecentesca)
—— *Lettere inedite del patrizio Pietro Zaguri*

INDEX

Abell, John, 44
Accademia Filarmonica (Bologna), 90, 105
Accoramboni, Doctor, 201, 224
Achille in Sciro (Gasmann), 164
—— (Jommelli?), 116n
—— (Sarro), 34
Acquini, Guiseppe, 17n
Acton, Harold, 114
Addison, Joseph, 126-7
Adriano in Siria (Metastasio), 78
Agesilao (Andreozzi), 181
Agujari, Lucrezia (La Bastardina), 50
Aida (Verdi), 34
Alcina (Handel), 111
Alessandro nell'Indie (Paesiello), 179
—— (Perez), 135, 157
—— (Sarro), 112, 145
—— (Sarti), 87
Alfieri, Vittorio, 159
Algarotti, Count Francesco, 124
Ali d'Amore, Le (Rauzzini), 176
Aliberti, Teatro (Rome), 96
Allgemeine Musikalische Zeitung, 119
Almahide (Buononcini?), 126
Almansor in Alimena (Pollarolo), 133
Alonso e Cora (Mayr), 119
Althann, d', Cardinal, 89
Amadigi di Gaule (Handel), 128
Ambizione superata da Virtù, L' (Sammartini), 162
Ambleto (Gasparini), 127
Amicis, de, Anna, 164
Amorevoli, Angiolo, 67, 68, 112, 136n, 142
Ancillon, d', 44n
Andromaca e Pirro (Tritto), 190
Andromeda (Manelli), 28

Angelica e Medora (Porpora), 96
Anne, Queen of England, 218-9
Annibali, Domenico, 84-5
Annibalino (Domenico Annibali), 84-5
Annibalino (Annibale Pio Fabri), 31, 84, 128, 174
Ansani, Giovanni, 178
Anspach, Margrave of, 173
Antigone (Paesiello), 180n
Antioco (Gasparini), 124
Apoteosi d'Ercole, L' (Tarchi), 159n
Appiani, Guiseppe, 68, 85-6, 183
Aprile, Guiseppe, 86-7, 162
Apulia, connection with castration, 41, 42-3
Arato in Sparta (Ruggeri), 88
Archenholz, Johann Wilhelm von, 27, 46-7, 53, 65, 70
Arianna (Handel), 111n
—— (Orlandini), 94
Arianna a Nasso (Haydn), 168
Arianna e Teseo (Abos), 146
—— (Fischietti), 179
—— (Leo), 128
—— (Ponzo), 154
Ariodante (Handel), 111, 116
Armida (Mysliweczek), 157
—— (Rossini), 36
Arminio (Handel), 84
—— (Pavesi), 36, 191
—— (Pollarolo), 128
Arne, T. A., 15, 155
Arsace (Gasparini), 85, 128
—— (Orlandini), 94
—— (Sabatini), 151
—— (Sarro), 128
Artaserse (Bertoni), 170
—— (Cherubini), 118n

8*

Artaterse (Hasse), 90, 100
—— (Metastasio), 104
—— (*pasticcio*), 98–9
—— (Vinci), 115, 185
Artaxerxes (Arne), 155, 185, 186
Arteaga, Stefano, 78, 162
Artemisia (Cimarosa), 20n
Artenice (Tritto), 180n
Ascanio in Alba (Mozart), 156
Astarto (Terradellas), 84
Astianatte (Buononcini), 92n, 128
Astrua, Giovanna, 145–6
Atide (Mysliweczek), 179
Atilla (Farinelli), 192
Attalo Re di Bitinia (Conti), 149
Aureliano in Palmira (Rossini), 20, 191

Babbi, Gregorio, 116n, 136n, 149, 151
Bach, J. C., 15
Bagnolese, 80
Balani, 47
Balatri, Filippo, 200–24
Balfe, William, 110
Ballad opera, 18
Ballets in Italy, 72–3
Ballot de Sauvet, 151
Balsamone, Theodore, 10
Balzac, Honoré de, 27
Banti, Brigida, 181
Barbara of Portugal, Queen of Spain, 101, 102, 106
Barbaruccia, (Barbara Voglia?), 56, 113, 115
Barilli, Antonio, 104
Baritone voice, emergence of, 36
Baroni, Leonora, 24n
Bass voice, use of, 32, 36
Bassiano, o il maggior impossibile (Pallavicino), 130
Bastardina, La (Lucrezia Agujari), 50
Bavaria, Electors of, 60, 121, 175, 178, 220, 222
——, King of, 192
Beckford, William, 28, 166n, 169
Bellerofonte (Platania), 179
Belmonte, Princess, 147
Benti-Bulgarelli, Marianna, 128

Berenice (Handel), 84
Berenstadt, Gaetano, 44, 92
Berezovsky, Maxim, 15
Berlin, opera at, 25n, 30n, 60, 61
Berlioz, Hector, 198
Bernacchi, Antonio, 39, 87–91, 93n, 97, 174
Bernardi, Francesco (Senesino), 67, 91–5, 98–9, 179
Bertoni, Ferdinando, 164
Bianchi, Giuseppe, 59
Bibiena family, 15, 80
Billington, Mrs, 20n, 159, 177n
Bologna, as mart for singers, 53, 65; opera at, 25n, 36, 88–9, 154; residence of Farinelli, 104–10; singing-schools at, 39, 174
Bolognese surgeons, 44
'Bomba del Marchesi', La, 157
Bonaparte, Joseph, 40n
Bonaparte, Napoleon, 26n, 35, 110, 119–20, 159, 191
Bonetto, Luigi, 68
Bordoni Hasse, Faustina, 29, 60n, 66n, 92n, 93n, 221–2
Borghese, Cardinal, 54
Bortnyansky, Dmitri, 15
Braham, John, 20n, 177
Broschi, Carlo (Farinelli), 13, 49, 52n, 66n, 68, 74, 88–9, 90, 92, 93, 95–110, 111, 115, 116, 134n, 141, 142, 143, 146, 147, 150, 151
Broschi, Riccardo, 95, 98–9
Brosses, Charles de, 14, 27, 68, 71, 75n, 94n
Brydone, Patrick, 164
Buona Figliuola, La (Piccinni), 18
Buononcini, G.-B., 92
Burney, Charles, 9, 14, 17n, 42–3, 44, 45, 60n, 87, 97, 99, 105–6, 110, 111, 116, 136–7, 139–40, 152, 153, 155, 162–3, 169, 174, 178, 180–1, 185
Byzantine music, 10

Caduta de' Decemviri, La (Ballarotti), 114
—— (A. Scarlatti), 124

Cafaro, Pasquale, 141
Caffarelli (Gaetano Majorano), 48–9,
    56, 67, 68, 103, 112, 115–6, 141–54,
    156, 165, 184
Cajo Fabricio (Caldara), 145
—— (Hasse), 142, 181
Calegari, 171
Calliroe (Alessandri), 179
—— (Sacchini), 179
Calvé, Emma, 22n
Calzabigi, Ranieri, 82
Campaign, The (Tenducci), 189
Camporese, Luigi, 36
Canne de Jonc, La (Alfred de Vigny),
    119
Cantante e l'Impresario, La (Mestas-
    tasio), 82
Capuleti ed i Montecchi, I (Bellini), 20n
Carasale, Angelo, 89, 112
Carattaco (J. C. Bach), 140
Carestini, Giovanni, 67, 68, 85, 89,
    92, 98, 111–2, 149, 179, 185
Carlo Magno (Niccolini), 191
Carlo Re d'Alemania (Gasparini and
    Orlandini), 88
Caro, Giulia di, 28–9
Carolina e Mexicow (Zingarelli), 160
Cartella, used in teaching, 48, 49
Casanova, Giacomo, 27, 54, 75, 106–7,
    108, 159, 182–3, 188
Castello d'Andalusia, Il (Tenducci),
    189
Castore e Polluce (Bianchi), 157
Castration, measures against, 35, 42;
    operation of, 44n; place where
    performed, 42–4
Catalani, Angelica, 80, 171
Catone in Utica (Antonelli), 180n
—— (Graun), 181n
—— (Vinci), 33
Cavaletto, punishment of, 74
Cecchi, Domenico (Cortona), 56, 59,
    113–5, 134n
Cecchina, o la Buona Figliuola (Piccinni),
    18
Cecconi, Alessandro, 59
Cerè, Maria, 34n

Cesare in Egitto (Giacomelli), 85
Charles II, King of England, 44
Charles II, King of Spain, 184
Charles III, King of Spain (previously
    K. of Naples), 50, 100, 103, 143,
    144, 145
Charles VI, Emperor, 97, 111, 181,
    221
Chiaramonti, Cardinal, 190
Christina, Queen, 25, 29, 58–9, 113,
    122, 130
Christus am Ölberge (Beethoven), 22
Church, attitude of towards castra-
    tion, 24–5; castrati in, 9–11, 21–2,
    23, 47
Ciccolino, Antonio Rivani, 59
Cicognara, Cardinal, 27
Cid, Il (Sacchini), 161
Cimarosa, Domenico, 19
Ciro riconosciuto (Cocchi), 185
—— (Leo), 145
Cisalpine republic, ban on castrati,
    26n
Clearco (pasticcio), 128
Clement VIII, Pope, 12
Clement XIV, Pope, 25
Clemenza di Tito, La (Gluck), 149
—— (Mozart), 36
Cleopatra (Anfossi), 179
Cneo Marzio Coriolano, 131
Colbran, Isabella, 191
Communale, Teatro (Bologna), 154
Conquista del Messico, La (Vento), 140
Conquista del Vello d'Oro, La (Pescetti),
    143n
Conservatorios, 19, 35, 39–42, 45–51
Consolino, 27
Constantine Porphyrogenitus, 10
Constantinople, eunuchs at, 10
Contadina in Corte, La (Sacchini), 17n
Conti, Gioacchino (Gizziello), 115–7,
    135n, 136, 145, 174, 179
Convenienze teatrali, Le (Sografi), 81
Coriolano (Graun), 182
—— (Niccolini), 191
Cortona (Domenico Cecchi), 56, 59,
    113–5, 134

Cosimo III de' Medici, Grand Duke of Tuscany, 114, 201, 202, 211, 214–5, 220, 222
Costa, Luigi, 50n
Costanza e Fortezza (Fux), 111
Cosway, Maria, 157
Council of Ten, 69n
Covent Garden, 73, 188
Crescentini, Girolamo, 35n, 36, 117–21, 174, 188, 191
Crescenzi, Cardinal, 122
Creso (Sacchini), 178
Crociato in Egitto, Il (Meyerbeer), 21, 194, 196–7
Cryptorchidism, 22, 47
Curriculum for singers' training, 48
Cusanino, see Carestini
Cuzzoni, Francesca, 29, 66n, 92n, 93

Dal Prato, Vincenzo, 121–2
David, Giacomo, 117, 160, 169
de Amicis, Anna, 164
de Brosses, Charles, 14, 27, 68, 71, 75n, 94n
Deidamia (Handel), 34n
del Po, Andrea, 66n
Della Valle, *Discourse*, 11, 53
de' Medici, Anna Maria Ludovica, Electress Palatine, 220
——, Cosimo III, Gd. Duke of Tuscany, 114, 201, 202, 211, 214–5, 220, 222
——, Ferdinando, 113–4
——, Gian Gastone, Gd. Duke of Tuscany, 113, 162, 222
Demetrio (Hasse), 52n, 85, 90
Demofoonte, staging of, 76–7
—— (Jommelli), 87
—— (*pasticci*), 145, 167
Dent, Professor, 155
di Caro, Giulia, 28–9
Didone abbandonata, first production of, 71
—— (Albinoni), 97
   (Hasse), 150
—— (Manna), 149
—— (Perez), 117

Didone abbandonata, (Piccinni), 140
—— (Sarro), 128, 142
—— (Sarti), 118n
—— (Schuster), 166
Di Giacomo, Salvatore, 200n
Dio Cassius, 9
Dirindina, La (Girolamo Gigli), 82
Disertore francese, Il (Bianchi), 18, 170
Disfatta di Dario, La (Paesiello), 179n
Donati, Saverio, 145
Donizetti, Gaetano, 20
Dragon of Wantley, The (Carey), 126
Dresden, opera at, 60, 61, 76–7, 91–2
Dreyer, Antonio, 44
Due amanti in inganno, I (Rauzzini), 176
Due Baroni di Rocca Azzurra (Cimarosa), 17n
Duenna, The (Sheridan), 176
Duffo, Antonio, 179
Duncan, Lady Mary, 166n
Durante, Francesco, 19

Egiziello, see Gizziello
Electors Palatine, 17n, 60, 88, 177
Eliogabalo (Cavalli), 33
Elisabetta Regina d'Inghilterra (Rossini), 36
Elisi, Filippo, 136, 151
Elizabeth Farnese, Queen of Spain, 100, 134n
Enea e Lavinia (Guglielmi), 117
England, opera in, 61, 68, 73, 124–5, 132, 218–9
Epaminonda (Giacomelli), 85
Eraldo ed Emma (Mayr), 160
Eroe di Lancastro, L' (Niccolini), 193
Eumene (Albinoni), 128
—— (*pasticcio*), 85
—— (Porpora), 96
Europa riconosciuta (Salieri), 179
Evelyn, John, 44, 132n
Ezio (Lampugnani), 85, 142
—— (*pasticcio*), 155
—— (Vinci), 185

Fabbris, Luca, 47
Fabri, Annibale Pio, 31, 83, 128, 174
Facchinelli, Lucia, 33
Fago, Nicola, 124, 129
Fairies, The (Christopher Smith), 135
Falsettists, 9, 10–12, 45
Falsetto, used by castrati, 49
Faramondo (Handel), 143n
Farinelli (Carlo Broschi), 13, 49, 52n, 66n, 68, 74, 88–9, 90, 92, 93, 95–110, 111, 115, 116, 134n, 141, 142, 143, 146, 147, 150, 151, 154, 179, 185
Farinelli (Barnett), 110
Farnace (Leo), 112
—— (Piccinni and Perez), 185
—— (Porta), 89
—— (Traetta), 149
Farnace, o la vendetta di Atride (Tenducci), 189
Faustina (Bordoni Hasse), 29, 60n, 66n, 92n, 93n, 221–2
Favore degli Dei (Sabadini), 133
Fede ne' tradimenti, La (Sarro), 128
Fede tradita e vendicata, La (Gasparini), 173
Fedeltà coronata, La (Orlandini), 88, 97
Fedra (Lord Burghersh), 194
Fenice, Teatro la (Venice), 118, 159, 160, 194
Ferdinand IV, King of Naples, 26, 46, 51, 75, 166
Ferdinand VI, King of Spain, 100–2
Ferrara, opera at, 25n
Ferretti, Jacopo, 81
Ferri, Baldassare, 122–3, 124
Feste d'Apollo, Le (Gluck), 161
Fétis, F. J., 119
Finazzi, Filippo, 57
Flagello dei Musici, Il (Marcello), 57–8
Flavio Anicio Olibrio (Gasparini), 115
—— (Porpora), 97
Floralia, festival of, 23n
Florence, opera at, 70; as place of castration, 43
Florimo, Francesco, 40
Folignato, Pietro Paolo, 12

Fonthill, opera at, 169
Formagliari, Teatro de' (Bologna), 68
Foscolo, Ugo, 53
Foster Jenkins, Mrs, 74n
Fra i due Litiganti il terzo godo (Sarti), 19
France, music in, 13–14, 216–7
Fratricida innocente, Il, 184
Frederick the Great, 25n, 30n, 60, 112, 181n

Gabrielli, Caterina, 56, 74n, 80, 164–5
Gabrielli, Domenico, 172
Galitzin, Princes, 202–3, 208–10, 214
Galuppi, Baldassare, 170
Gare generose, Le (Albinoni), 127
Garibaldi, Giuseppe, 21
Garrick, David, 135, 152, 175
German singers, 44, 59
'Germania', 22
Germanico (Porpora), 142
Germany, opera in, 60–1
Gian Gastone, Gd. Duke of Tuscany, 113, 162, 222
Gibelli, Lorenzo, 121
Ginevra (Bertoni), 185
Ginevra di Scozia (Mayr), 160
Giochi d'Agrigento, I (Paesiello), 170
Giorgi Banti, Brigida, 181
Giorgina, La (Angela Voglia), 29, 115, 184
Girardi, Lorenzo, 51n
Girello (Pistocchi?), 172
Giulietta e Romeo (Zingarelli), 20, 118, 119, 121
Giulio Sabino (Sarti), 19, 78n, 158
Gizzi, Domenico, 115, 174
Gizziello (Gioacchino Conti), 115–7, 135n, 136, 145, 169, 174
Gluck, Christoph Willibald von, 15, 16, 34, 154, 161
Goethe, Johann Wolfgang von, 26, 55
Goldoni, Carlo, 17, 82
Gorani, *Mémoires secrètes*, 84
Goudar, Ange, 138, 140, 176
Goudar, Sara, 167
Grassetto, Il, 43, 142

Grassini, Giuseppa, 118, 159
Graun, Karl Heinrich, 15, 60
Greco in Troja, Il, 133
Grimaldi, Nicolò (Nicolino), 91, 123–9, 131, 146, 219
Grimm, Friedrich, 150–1
Griselda (Buononcini), 111
Grossatesta, 50n
Grossi, Francesco (Siface), 59, 124n, 129–35
Guadagni, Gaetano, 16, 17, 46n, 80, 135–9, 164, 189
Guarducci, Tommaso, 50n, 90, 139–40, 181
Guglielmi, Pietro, 48

Hamburg, opera at, 61
Hamilton, Lady, 46, 87n, 162
Hamlet (Shakespeare), 83
Handel, Georg Friedrich, 32, 44, 90, 92, 98, 111, 127, 135, 181, 188
Hasse, Johann Adolf, 15, 29, 34, 60, 84
Hawkins, Sir John, 98, 99
Heidegger, Johann Jakob, 93
Hogarth, George, 126
Hogarth, William, 99
Homosexuality and Castrati, 54–5

Idalide, o la Vergine del Sole (Sacchini), 169
Idaspe fedele (Mancini), 126–7, 128
Idomeneo (Mozart), 31n, 32, 121
Ifigenia (Jommelli), 166
Ifigenia in Aulide (Federici), 119, 191
—— (Graun), 25n
Ifigenia in Tauride (Traetta), 199
Ilda d'Avenello (Morlacchi), 193n
—— (Niccolini), 193
Impresario di Smirna, L' (Goldoni), 82
Inconvenienze teatrali, Le (Sografi), 81–2
Incoronazione di Poppea, L' (Monteverdi), 33
Ines de Castro (Guglielmi), 20n
Infedeltà fedele, L' (Cimarosa), 18
Innocent XI, Pope, 25, 59, 113
Innocent XII, Pope, 25

Iron Cross of Lombardy, awarded to Crescentini, 119
Issipile (Hasse), 145

John Casimir, King of Poland, 122
Jommelli, Nicola, 16, 60, 86
Joseph, King of Portugal, 151

Kelly, Michael, 50, 87, 138, 152, 156, 166, 175, 177, 181
Kotzebue, August von, 20n, 65, 71

Ladislas VII, King of Poland, 122
La Lande, Joseph Jérome de, 14, 43
Lanti Palesi, Teresa, 27, 182–3
Lassus, Orlandus, 11
Leandro (Pistocchi), 172
Lecce, as place of castration, 42
Lee, Vernon, 111, 159, 182
Leo, Lionardo, 19, 73
Leo XII, Pope, 26n
Leopold I, Emperor, 122n
Leucippo e Tenoe (A. Pollarolo), 185
Lewis, 'Monk', 18
Linley, Miss, 140
Lisbon, earthquake at, 116, 151; opera at, 116, 135, 151
Litiganti (Sarti), 19
Locandiera, La (Auletta), 17n
London, opera at, 62, 79, 92–3, 98, 99, 218–9
Louis XIV, 132, 217
Louis XV, 151
Lucio Silla (Anfossi), 179
—— (Mozart), 176
Ludwigsburg, opera at, 44

Madrid, opera at, 62, 101–2
Majorano, Gaetano, (Caffarelli), 48–9, 56, 67, 68, 103, 112, 115–6, 141–54, 156, 165, 184
Malibran, Maria
Mancini, Giovanni-Battista, 184
Mann, Sir Horace, 14, 80, 116n, 117, 145
Mannheim, opera at, 24

Mantua, Duke of, 113; opera at, 24

Manzoletto (Angelo Monanni), 18n, 43, 156

Manzuoli, Giovanni, 67, 136n, 139, 149, 151, 154–6

Mara, Mme, 169

Marcello, Benedetto, 31, 38n, 39n, 56n, 57–8, 72, 78, 79

Marchesi, Luigi, 19, 36, 56, 76, 117, 156–60, 163, 170, 179, 191, 195

Marchesini, see above

Marchesini, La, 29n

Maria vergine addolorata (Pistocchi), 174

Marianino, 27

Marriage of castrati, 22, 56–7

Marsigli family, 133–4

Martinez, Signora, 110

Martini, Andrea, 17, 160–1

Martini, Padre, 90, 104, 105, 106

Mary of Modena, Queen of England, 131, 132–3

Massiminiano (Orlandini), 128

Matrimonio Segreto, Il (Cimarosa), 11, 19

Mattei, Padre, 19, 162, 190

Matteuccio (Matteo Sassani), 55, 67, 128, 142, 146, 173, 183–4

Maunsell, Dora, 186–8

Maurizio (Gabrielli), 133

Mayr, Simon, 20

Medea (Cherubini), 18

Medinaceli, Dukes of, 29, 103, 114–5, 184

Medo, Il (Vinci), 89

Mengs, Raphael, 85

Merighi, Anna, 89, 90

Merope (Giacomelli), 142

Messiah, The (Handel), 135

Metastasian opera, 12, 13, 15, 19, 32, 66

Metastasio, 17, 32, 76–8, 82, 90, 96, 101, 102–4, 110, 111, 146–9

Meyerbeer, Giacomo, 21

Milan, attacked by Foscolo, 53–4; opera at, 72, 179, 183, 192

Millico, Giuseppe, 16, 87n, 161–2

Milton, John, 24n

Minga, Papa, 25, 59, 113

Mingotti, Caterina, 102

Missa Solennis (Beethoven), 122

Mitridate (Porpora), 142

Modena, Dukes of, 56–7, 59, 129–31, 133–4

Modena, Mary of, Queen of England, 131, 132–3

Monanni, Angelo (Manzoletto), 18n, 43, 156

Monteleone, Dukes of, 42, 152

Monticelli, Angelo Maria, 60n, 149, 162–3

Moreschi, Alessandro, 22, 225

Morgan, Lady, 72, 73

Morlacchi, Francesco, 191

Morte di Cleopatra, La (Nasolini), 181

Morte di Semiramide, La (Borghi), 118

Mount Edgcumbe, Lord, 18n, 73, 80, 117, 138, 157, 167–8, 178–81, 194–7

Mozart, Wolfgang Amadeus, 31n, 121, 155–6, 163, 175–6, 185

Musico, meaning of, 25n

Mustafà, Domenico, 21–2

Muzio Scevola (A. Scarlatti), 124

Mysliweczek, Josef, 15

Naples, conservatorios at, 19, 35, 39–42, 45–51; opera at, 17, 27n, 36, 50, 65, 75, 89–90

Napoleon, 26n, 35, 110, 119–20, 159, 191

Napoleonic period, 20, 35

Narciso (Pistocchi), 173

Naryshkin, Prince, 214

Naumann, Johann Amadeus, 15

Neri, 195n

Nerina (A. Pollarolo), 142

Nerone fatto Cesare (Perti), 125n, 173

Niccolini, Giuseppe, 129, 191

Nicolino (Nicolò Grimaldi), 91, 123–9, 131, 146, 219

Nina (Paesiello), 18

Ninfa ed Apollo, La (Galuppi), 85

Nitteti, La (Bianchi), 181

—— (Metastasio), 96

Norcia, castration performed at, 43, 141, 209–10
Norma (Bellini), 19
Nozze d'Ercole e d'Ebe, Le (Gluck), 33
Nuovo, Teatro (Trieste), 160

Obizzi, Marquis, 145
'Observations on the Florid Song' (Tosi), 30, 39, 43n, 49, 79, 194
Old Pretender, 88
Olimpia nell'Isola d'Ebuda (Latilla), 144
Olimpiade, L' (Arne), 155
—— (Metastasio), 182
—— (Mysliweczek), 157
—— (Paesiello), 169
Opera buffa, 16–19
Opéra comique, 18
'Opera of the Nobility', 93–4, 98, 111, 143n, 185
Opera semi-seria, 18
Opera seria, 14–16, 19
Opera seria, L' (Calzabigi), 82
Operation of castration, 44n
Orazii ed i Curiazii, Gli (Cimarosa), 19, 81n, 118, 120, 190
Orcamo (Lavigna), 191
Orfeo (Graun), 112
—— (Luigi Rossi), 55n
Orfeo ed Euridice (Bertoni), 181
—— (Gluck), 136, 161, 188–9
Orleans, Duke of, 169–70
Orsini, Gaetano, 210–1
Ottone Re di Germania (Handel), 111

Pacchierotti, Gasparo, 18, 79, 117, 154, 156, 158, 163–71, 178, 179, 180–1, 191, 195
Pace, Teatro della, 17n
Padua, singers at, 46n, 137–8, 171
Paer, Ferdinando, 20
Paesiello, Giovanni, 19, 46
Paita, Giovanni, 78n
Palazzo del Segreto, Il, 17n
Palermo, opera at, 164
Panati, Giacomo, 78n
Panciroli, Ercole, 129–31

Panzacchi, Enrico, 36–7
Papal States, opera in, 25n, 62
Paride ed Elena (Gluck), 161
Parini, Giuseppe, 52n, 198n
Parma, Dukes of, 59, 75, 104
Parrucchierina, La (Anna Peruzzi), 34n, 68, 142
Parsons, William, 106
Part du diable, La (Auber), 110
Partenio (Veracini), 143n
Partenope, La (Handel), 90
—— (Sarro), 94n
Pasquini, Giovanni Claudio, 76–7
Pasta, Giuditta, 197
Pastor fido, Il (Handel), 111
Patti, Adelina, 37
Paul et Virginie (Saint-Pierre), 18
Pazzie d'Amore e dell'Interesse (Pistocchi), 173
Perez, Davide, 15
Pergetti, Paolo, 21
Pergolesi, G.-B., 73
Perosi, Lorenzo, 22
Perseo (pasticcio), 134
Peruzzi, Anna (La Parrucchierina), 34n, 68, 142
Peter the Great, 201–3
Philip, Duke of Parma, 75, 104, 144
Philip V, King of Spain, 99–100, 110
Pietà d'amore, La (Millico), 162
Pietà dei Turchini, conservatorio, 35, 40, 50, 86
Piramo e Tisbe (Andreozzi), 190
—— (Rauzzini), 175, 176
Pirro e Demetrio (A. Scarlatti), 125
Pisani, Matteo, 108–9
Pisaroni, Benedetta, 34n, 197
Pistocchi, Francesco Antonio, 39, 125n, 171–5, 134n
Più fedele tra Vassalli, Il (Albinoni), 173
Pius VII, Pope, 190
Pöllnitz, Carl Ludwig von, 27
Pompadour, Mme de, 103
Pompeo (A. Scarlatti), 33, 131
Popes, attitude of, towards castrati, 12, 24–5

Poro Re dell'Indie (Handel), 84

Porpora, Nicola, 39, 41, 48–9, 74, 85, 93, 95–6, 141, 142, 171, 181, 182

Porporino (Antonio Hubert), 27, 44

Portugal, actresses banned in, 28; opera in, 116, 135, 151

Potenza, Pasquale, 185

Poveri di Gesù Cristo, conservatorio, 40, 41

Pozzi, Anna, 78n

Prigioniero fortunato, Il (A. Scarlatti), 124

Prima la musica e poi le parole (Casti), 78n, 82

Provenzale, Francesco, 124

Psyche (Locke and Draghi), 123

Quadrio, Francesco, 17n, 86, 125n

Quantz, Johann, 49, 60, 94

Quinto Fabio (Bertoni), 169

—— (Niccolini), 192

Raaff, Anton, 31, 136n, 151

Raffaelli, Raffaelle, 12

Rake's Progress, The (Hogarth), 99

Range of singers' voices, 49–50

Raoul di Crequy (Mayr), 191

Ratisbon, Prince-Bishop of, 222–3

Ratto delle Sabine, Il (Augustini), 129

Ratto di Proserpina, Il (Winter), 118n

Rauzzini, Matteo, 176

Rauzzini, Venanzio, 169, 175–7

Redi, Tommaso, 129

Regina di Golconda, La (Rauzzini), 176

Reginella, Nicola, 42, 144

Ricci, Corrado, 107

Riccoboni, Luigi, 66n

Richardson, Samuel, 15, 18

Ricimero (Guglielmi), 179n

Rinaldo (Handel), 127

—— (Sacchini), 169

Risa di Democrito, La (Pistocchi), 173

Ritorno di Bacco dall'Indie, Il (Tarchi), 118n

Rolli, Paolo, 92n, 93n, 98

Roman Republic, ban on castrati, 26

Rome, opera at, 17, 20n, 25–8, 54–5, 68, 71, 73–4, 80–1

Romolo ed Ersilia, staging of, 81–2

Roncaglia, Francesco, 167, 177–8

Rosa, Salvator, 43n, 53

Roselli, 195n

Rossini, Gioacchino, 20, 34n, 36, 191–2, 198

Rossini, Girolamo, 12

Rubinelli, Giovanni Maria, 80, 163, 179–81

Ruffo, Captain, 165

Ruffo, Cardinal, 166

Ruggero (Hasse), 156

Russia, opera in, 61, 68

Sacchi, Giovenale, 102, 103

Sacchini, Antonio, 161, 176

St Augustine, 23n

St Joseph's staff, obtained by Nicolino, 127–8, 129

St Paul, 9

Salaries of singers, 66–8

Salimbeni, Felice, 181–3

Salustia, La (Pergolesi), 128

Sampson (Handel), 135

San Angelo, Teatro (Naples), 112

San Angelo, Teatro (Venice), 69n

San Bartolommeo, Teatro (Naples), 114

San Benedetto, Teatro (Venice), 69n, 159n

San Carlo, Teatro (Naples), 17n, 47, 50, 65–6, 75, 114, 145, 149, 151, 165

San Cassiano, Teatro (Venice), 51n

San Donato, Dukedom of, 152

San Moisè, Teatro (Venice), 69n

San Pietro a Majella, Royal College of (Naples), 40n, 121

Sanctos, Giovanni de, 12

Santa Marca, Marchesa, 166

Santa Maria di Loreto, conservatorio, 40, 45n

Sant' Onofrio, conservatorio, 40, 41–2, 45, 50n

Sarassin, 27

Sardou, Victorien, 26

Sarti, Giuseppe, 19, 76
Sassani, Matteo (Matteuccio), 55, 67,
    128, 142, 146, 173, 183–4
Savoy, Duchess of, 58; Prince of, 150
Saxony, Electors of, 44, 60–1, 85, 182;
    Maria Antonia, Electress of, 107–8,
    137; Xavier Augustus, Prince of,
    107–8
Scala, Teatro alla, 72, 179, 183, 192
Scalzi, Carlo, 184–5
Scarlatti, Alessandro, 16, 32, 34, 174
Schönborn, Johann Philip von, 221
Schopenhauer, Arthur, 119
Schubart, Christian Friedrich, 86
Scipione Africano (Cavalli), 129
Scipione il giovane (Predieri), 85
Scipione in Cartagine (Giacomelli), 89
Scribe, Eugène, 110
Sebastian, King of Portugal, 11
Secret Marriage, The (Cimarosa), 19
Selvaggia nel Messico, La (Niccolini),
    26n, 190
Semiramide (C. Pollarolo), 78n, 91
—— (Rossini), 34n, 36, 197
Semiramide riconosciuta (Perez), 146
Senesino (Francesco Bernardi), 67,
    91–5, 98–9, 179
—— (Andrea Martini), 17, 160–1
—— (G. F. Tenducci), 117, 169,
    185–9
Septimius Severus, 9
Serse (Handel), 143n
Serva Padrona, La (Paesiello), 156
—— (Pergolesi), 18, 156
Sgatelli, Domenico, 20n
Shakespeare, William, 20n, 32, 34
Siface (Francesco Grossi), 59, 124n,
    129–35
Siface (Leo), 68
—— (Porpora), 142
Sigismund III, King of Poland, 122
Singing-masters, 39
Singing schools, 39, 174
Singspiel, 18
Sinigaglia, fair of, 191
Siroe Re di Persia (Hasse), 68, 142
—— (Vinci), 128

Sografi, Simone, 81–2
Solari, Marchioness, 46, 170–1
Sorlisi, Bartolomeo de', 57
Soto, Padre, 11
Spanish falsettists, 10–12, 45
Spohr, Ludwig, 121
Staging of opera, 75–83
Steele, Richard, 125
Stellidaura (Provenzale), 124, 131
Stendhal, 35, 64, 73, 171, 198
Storace, Nancy, 157
Strauss, Johann, 88
Stuttgart, opera at, 60, 86
Succianoccioli, see Manzuoli
Sweden, opera in, 61

Tamerlano (Sacchini), 161
Tancredi (Rossini), 20
Tarchi, Angiolo, 180
Tartary, Grand Cham of, 203, 206–10
Teatrini, 17
Teatro alla Moda, Il (Marcello), 31,
    38n, 72, 78, 79
Tebaldo ed Isoline (Morlacchi), 197
Tenducci, Giusto Ferdinando, 117,
    169, 185–9
Tenors, use of, in opera, 31–2, 34, 36
Terradellas, Domingo, 15
Tertullian, 23n
Tesi, Vittoria, 29, 34, 67, 68, 128, 142,
    148–9, 162
Thrale, Mrs, 161n
Tito Manlio, 85
—— (C. Pollarolo), 124
Todi, Luisa, 159–60
Tommaseo, Niccolò, 169
Tor di Nona, Teatro (Rome), 25, 129
Torcchino, 61
Torri, Pietro, 220
Tosca, La, 26
Tosi, Pietro Francesco, 30, 39, 43n,
    49, 79, 174
Traetta, Tommaso, 16, 199
Training of castrati, 38–42, 45–6,
    48–51
Traité des Eunuques (d'Ancillon), 44n,
    113

Trajano in Dacia (Niccolini), 190
Trionfo dell'Onore, Il (A. Scarlatti), 16
Trionfo della Pace, Il (Bianchi), 157
Trionfo di Clelia, Il (Gluck), 154
—— (Jommelli), 166
Tristan und Isolde (Wagner), 34
Troja distrutta (Mortellari), 179
Trovatore, Il (Verdi), 50, 70n
Turin, opera at, 73

Umberto I of Italy, 22
Urbani, Valentino, 125n, 134n

Valdemaro, Il (Sarro), 142
Valerius Maximus, 23n
Vatican singers, 11–12, 21–2, 36–7
Velluti, Giovanni-Battista, 20–1, 35, 36, 129, 174, 189–99
Venice, opera at, 28, 52n, 65, 66n, 69, 159–60; singing-schools at, 40
Verdi, Giuseppe, 20, 21, 50
Verità nell' inganni, La (Gasparini), 127
Veroli, Giacomo, 136, 151
Vespasiano (Pallavicino), 88
Vestale, La (Rauzzini), 176
Victor Emmanuel II, King ot Italy, 22
Vienna, opera at, 25n
Viganò, Salvatore, 72
Viganoni, 195n
Vigny, Alfred de, 119
Vincitor generoso, Il (Lotti), 184
Violante, Beatrice, of Bavaria, Princess of Tuscany, 113
Virginia (Francesco Federici), 26n

Virginia (pasticcio), 180
Vittori, Loreto, 11, 39n
Voglia, Angela (la Giorgina), 29, 115, 184
Voglia, Barbara (Barbaruccia?), 56, 113, 115
Vologeso (Rutini), 179n

Wagner, Richard, 21, 70n, 198
Wales, Princess of, 191
Walker, Frank, 49
Walpole, Horace, 155, 162
Werther (Goethe), 81n
Winckelmann, Johann Joachim, 15
Wolf-Ferrari, Ermanno, 17n
Women, debarred from church singing, 9, 23; debarred from stage, 23–8
Wortley, Montagu, Lady Mary, 126
Württemberg, Duke of, 44, 60, 87

Young England, 74n

Zaguri, Pietro, 159–60
Zaïre (Voltaire), 28
Zambeccari, Count Francesco, 52n, 66n, 89, 91, 147
Zambinella, 27
Zarzuela, 18
Zelinda, La (Millico), 162
Zémire et Azor (Grétry), 18
Zenobia (Lord Mount Edgcumbe), 195n
Zingarelli, Nicola, 20